I0304767

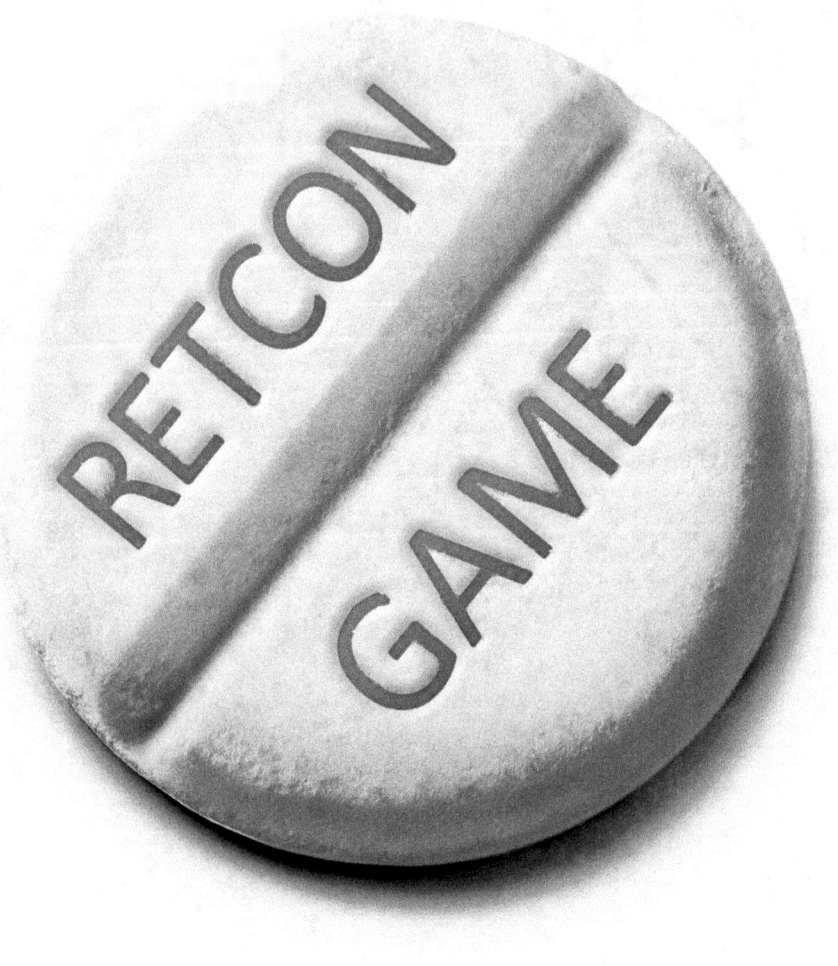

Retroactive Continuity and the Hyperlinking of America

ANDREW J. FRIEDENTHAL

University Press of Mississippi | Jackson

www.upress.state.ms.us

The University Press of Mississippi is a member of the Association of American University Presses.

Copyright © 2017 by University Press of Mississippi
All rights reserved

First printing 2017

∞

Library of Congress Cataloging-in-Publication Data

Names: Friedenthal, Andrew J., author.
Title: Retcon game : retroactive continuity and the hyperlinking of America / Andrew J. Friedenthal.
Description: Jackson : University Press of Mississippi, 2017. | Includes bibliographical references and index.
Identifiers: LCCN 2016027224 (print) | LCCN 2016042246 (ebook) | ISBN 9781496811325 (cloth : alk. paper) | ISBN 9781496811332 (epub single) | ISBN 9781496811349 (epub institutional) | ISBN 9781496811356 (pdf single) | ISBN 9781496811363 (pdf institutional)
Subjects: LCSH: Narration (Rhetoric) | Mass media. | Storytelling in mass media. | Discourse analysis, Narrative. | Historiography—Philosophy.
Classification: LCC P96.N35 F75 2017 (print) | LCC P96.N35 (ebook) | DDC 302.23—dc23
LC record available at https://lccn.loc.gov/2016027224

British Library Cataloging-in-Publication Data available

To Dad, Mom, & Kaley, the immutables

of my past, present, and future

Contents

Acknowledgments |	ix
Introduction | A HYPERLINKED PAST Theorizing Retroactive Continuity	3
1 | A BRIEF PREHISTORY OF RETROACTIVE CONTINUITY	15
2 | HIGH SOCIETY Historical Revisionism in Justice Society Comics	33
3 | CRISIS CONTROL *Crisis on Infinite Earths* and the Creation of a Unified Comic Book Universe	71

4 | MOVING IMAGES, MOVING HISTORY   107
Retroactive Continuity in Television and Film

5 | PUTTING IT ALL TOGETHER   127
Retroactive Parody and Play

6 | CITATION NEEDED   145
Wikipedia and the Mutability of the Past

Conclusion | **PLAYING THE RETCON GAME**   159

Notes | 163

Works Cited | 169

Index | 177

ACKNOWLEDGMENTS

In the years this book has taken to write, and in the years of academic training that led to this book, I have built up an enormous amount of intellectual and emotional debt. Though I know that a simple "thank you" will never pay back what I owe to the following people, I hope that this is a start.

First and foremost, I need to thank those members of the Department of American Studies at the University of Texas at Austin whose comments on this work strengthened me as a scholar and enlightened the project as a whole. Janet Davis's patience, insight, and good humor helped me to push beyond my own boundaries and follow the intellectual thread that engaged me and enlivened my argument. Similar thanks go to Brian Bremen, Michael Kackman, Randy Lewis, and Julia Mickenberg, who encouraged me to make my ideas both larger and more focused at the same time. My other cohorts and writing group colleagues in the department (particularly Tracy Wuster, whose one-sentence suggestion completely changed the direction of my research) are similarly owed a tremendous debt of gratitude.

The process of writing was made extremely easy thanks to the shepherding of my editor, Vijay Shah, who asked all the right questions to help me fine-tune my thinking about the larger ideas in this book. The same is true of the two anonymous reviewers, who provided excellent critiques that forced me to specify certain crucial definitions and more fully realize some of my examples. The review process can often be harrowing, but their feedback was entirely constructive and helpful, which I greatly appreciate. Lisa McMurtray and Kristi Ezernack, at the University Press of Mississippi, and Debbie Upton have also been crucial to negotiating the minefield of the final stages of producing a manuscript.

Parts of chapter 3 were previously published, in slightly different form, as "Monitoring the Past: DC Comics' *Crisis on Infinite Earths* and the Narrativization of Comic Book History," in the journal *ImageTexT: Interdisciplinary Comics Studies* (6, no. 2, Spring 2012).

Various other chapters in this book have been presented—in different forms—as papers at several academic conferences, but the most important of these has been the Comic Arts Conference, run every summer as a part of San Diego Comic-Con International. I would like to thank Peter Coogan, Randy Duncan, and Kathleen McClancy, the CAC's tireless organizers, for having me present at the conference multiple times, and thus allowing me to finally live out the fannish dream of being on a panel at Comic-Con. The Comics and Comic Art Area of the Pop Culture Association / American Culture Association, helmed by Terrence Wandtke, also provided me with the opportunity to speak on several panels and engage in vital conversations that allowed my thinking on this subject to develop and evolve. William Proctor, an expert in the narrative technique of the reboot, provided similarly important conversations via e-mail. Randy Scott and the rest of the staff at the Michigan State University Comic Art Collection, an invaluable archive for any researcher of mainstream American comics, were enormously helpful with the initial research for this project. Other intellectual help came from Jamie Tyler and Charles Hames, who helped me grapple with the difference between the New and Old Testaments; Alan Valdmets-Harris, who lent me material, and provided me with knowledge, about J. R. R. Tolkien; and my father, Martin Friedenthal, who helped me with important information relating to Sherlock Holmes and Sir Arthur Conan Doyle.

Without the people listed above I would never have been a strong enough scholar to finish this project; without the people that follow, I would never have been a strong enough person. The many friends and colleagues in the Departments of American Studies, English, and Radio, Television, and Film at the University of Texas commiserated with me on the many challenges of being in academia. The friends I have made in Austin, Texas, particularly the National Karaoke League and Random Geeky folks—especially the littlest one, who came *this close* to sharing a birthday with me— have reminded me of the importance of having fun and being a happy person, despite those challenges. My brothers, David and Brian, sister-in-law, Stephanie, and my extended family (especially Perin, Harriet, Jay, Gail, and Lena) have been unwavering in their vocal support and pride over the years, which has helped keep me going. Although I will keep her name private for professional reasons, my excellent therapist, who was recommended to me my first year of graduate school by a fellow student and whom I have recommended to other colleagues in turn, has literally kept me sane throughout this entire process. Lyla, Iko, and Binx provided much-needed snuggles at all hours of the day and night and frequently made my own whining seem minor in comparison to their always-urgent needs.

I owe my biggest debt of gratitude to the many excellent teachers I have had over the years. From high school teachers Mary Skinner and Bill Esner to college professors Annabelle Winograd, Dan Kotlowitz, and Kathleen Cunneen and graduate school professors Barbara Kirshenblatt-Gimblett and Janet Davis, my formal education has been filled with some of the wisest, kindest, and most caring people I will ever have the pleasure of meeting. Before encountering any of those people, though, I had the fortune to be taught about life, love, and humanity by several important figures: my grandparents Adelaide (whom I never knew, but who has informed my life down to my very name), Irving, Lou, and Vicky, all of whom I miss very much; my unofficial grandparents, Uncle Bernie and Aunt Marylin; and, most importantly, my parents, who may not have taught me everything I know, but who taught me everything *important* that I know. I love and thank them all.

When this project began, I had never met Kaley Horton. As I finish it, we are busy with wedding plans. Though this book has been in my life for longer than she has, I look forward to her being a part of that life for all the years to come. Her love, support, and unflagging cheerleading have kept me going through many periods of doubt and despair. Though this book may have been possible without her, the life surrounding it would not, and that is more important by far. She is a true golden girl.

INTRODUCTION:
A HYPERLINKED PAST
Theorizing Retroactive Continuity

The narrative technique known as retroactive continuity, often overlooked by literary scholars and media historians alike, has become a naturalized and ubiquitous part of popular culture. A careful look at the history of retroactive continuity—or retconning—will reveal how its growing acceptance as a part of popular narratives has led to a complex, complicated understanding of the ways in which history and story can interact, ultimately creating a cultural atmosphere that is increasingly accepting of revisionist historical narratives. I posit that retconning, on the whole, has a positive impact on society, fostering a sense of history itself as a constructed narrative and thus engendering an acceptance of how historical narratives can and should be recast to allow for a broader field of stories to be told in the present. However, one of the most famous statements ever made vis-à-vis retconning takes a far more cynical stance than mine.

"Oceania was at war with Eurasia: therefore Oceania had always been at war with Eurasia" (Orwell 34). This line, from George Orwell's classic dystopian novel *1984*, refers to two of the story's three totalitarian nations (Oceania, Eurasia, and Eastasia) that collectively control the world. Oceania is home to the book's protagonist, Winston Smith, and through him we learn that Oceania changes its enemy seemingly at random: "Actually, as Winston well knew, it was only four years since Oceania had been at war with Eastasia and in alliance with Eurasia" (34). We are never privy to the political machinations behind these shifting alliances, but simply understand that every few years Oceania is at war with a different nation and must change its history so that this war was the same one it had forever been engaged in. In the absolutist terms of the mass-surveillance "Big Brother" government controlling Oceania, there is no gray zone between good and evil, and that stark line of contrast must be painted in the past as much as it is in the present.

In order for the government of Oceania to so blatantly alter history, they not only rely on workers at the "Ministry of Truth," who delete documents contrasting the official historical narrative, but they must also ensure that their citizens employ the technique of "doublethink":

> To know and not to know, to be conscious of complete truthfulness while telling carefully constructed lies, to hold simultaneously two opinions which cancelled out, knowing them to be contradictory and believing in both of them, to use logic against logic, to repudiate morality while laying claim to it, to believe that democracy was impossible and that the Party was the guardian of democracy, to forget whatever it was necessary to forget, then to draw it back into memory again at the moment when it was needed, and then promptly to forget it again, and above all, to apply the same process to the process itself—that was the ultimate subtlety: consciously to induce unconsciousness, and then, once again, to become unconscious of the act of hypnosis you had just performed. (34)

Doublethink is at the heart of *1984*, the keystone to Orwell's warnings to his readers against totalitarianism. In his estimation, the nature of truth itself was under assault in the industrial nations of the world after World War II, and Winston, as the protagonist, stands in for the citizens of this new world.

Winston must contend directly with the strange nature of doublespeak, particularly because he works at the Ministry of Truth and plays an active role in altering the past: "The Party said that Oceania had never been in alliance with Eurasia. He, Winston Smith, knew that Oceania had been in alliance with Eurasia as short a time as four years ago. But where did that knowledge exist? Only in his own consciousness, which in any case must be annihilated" (34). For Winston, and for Orwell, doublethink is a dangerous idea. It is the end result of gravitating away from core values of truth and reality, an extreme form of relativism that allows for political elites to brainwash the masses and control the historical/political narrative that makes up the present (and thus the future).

More than half a century after Orwell wrote *1984*, we in the United States find ourselves living in a society very familiar, in some ways, to the one he imagined. This is perhaps most visibly seen in the fluidity and malleability of information on the Internet, where the truth of that information is constantly brought into question. As the flow of information grows faster and faster, "truth" is often left by the wayside in favor of speed and sensationalism. Comedian Stephen Colbert popularly coined the term "truthiness" to describe this notion that something may feel like the truth, or become the truth we wish existed, even if it is not actually true. This ironic insight into the manipulatable nature of truth in the present day has in turn led to a societal questioning of the nature of historical truth as well. There is an ever-increasing awareness of the nature of historical consciousness and how it is constantly open to revision and reinterpretation.

In late 2014, for example, Oklahoma lawmakers attempted to defund the teaching of AP US history in their state, in part because of the Republican National Committee's assertion that the course provides "a radically revisionist view of American history that emphasizes negative aspects of our nation's history while omitting or minimizing positive aspects" (Macneal). The RNC's denouncement was only the beginning of a national conversation about historical revisionism. In a *New York Times* editorial, James R. Grossman, the executive director of the American Historical Association, responded to the RNC's claim by noting, "This essential process of reconsideration and re-evaluation takes place in all disciplines; imagine a diagnosis from a physician who does not read 'revisionist' medical research. Revisionism is necessary—and it generates controversy, especially when new scholarship finds its way into classrooms."

As this controversy shows, the concept and vocabulary of "historical revisionism" has taken on real, immediate relevance in the teaching and learning of American history. Some, like the RNC, contend that it is no more than contemporary doublespeak, mentally altering the past in order to brainwash children into being more compliant to contemporary politically correct indoctrination, at the expense of learning "true" history. Others, like Grossman and the majority of the professional historians he represents, see revision as a way of getting ever closer to the truth via an increasing understanding of the multiple layers of history. In this view, history is not a body of facts but rather the ongoing creation of a contextualized narrative. Revisionism is thus a double-edged sword, viewed as both a deliberate, malignant, political distortion and as part of a shifting understanding of how the past is constantly rewritten through new information and interpretations.

Although revisionism is an important part of today's conversations about history, it is certainly not a new concept. In the academy, historical revisionism has been a concern for decades, if not longer. However, it has also long been a large part of American popular consciousness, albeit in a very different form. In the realm of popular culture and mass entertainment, audiences have been taught to accept revisionism in the form of retroactive continuity.

⊘ ⊘ ⊘

Although the term "retroactive continuity" only dates back to the 1980s, as a practice it is as old as storytelling itself. In its most common contemporary implementation, retconning is just one of several narrative tropes of renewal utilized by authors, artists, and producers to make media franchises, as well as individual stories, more appealing and salable to mass audiences. The most direct of these techniques is the reboot, wherein an entire franchise begins anew, with no connection to past versions beyond certain textual and/or visual resonances. This was the case, for example, in director Christopher Nolan's successful revitalization of the Batman movie franchise following the critical and commercial degradation of the series in the 1990s. Other media properties, such as the James Bond film series and the Spider-Man films produced by Sony, soon followed suit.

However, sometimes the creators and/or corporate caretakers of a long-form narrative choose not to start from scratch, but rather to make explicit or subtle revisions and rewrites to past stories. They do this through retconning. Retroactive continuity involves the revisiting of past stories, told in previous installments of a long-form narrative, and adding a new piece of information to that older story, literally rewriting the past. In order for retconning to be a viable option for a story world, however, it needs to be a long-lasting world, one that has had multiple installments presented to an audience over time. The retcon revisits these past installments in order to revise and rewrite them to create new narrative potential in the present (and thus in the future). This is what differentiates a retcon from a behind-the-scenes rewrite—a retcon replaces an aspect of a story that an audience has already experienced, not just an early author's draft.

A retcon is also explicitly different from a reboot. Richard Rosenbaum, writing for the pop culture analysis website *Overthinking It*, notes how a retcon is often used "not just to tell a good story but also to fix up bad storytelling decisions in previous installments of the series without just pretending they never happened. It *narrativizes* what was basically a marketing decision and, interestingly, it mostly succeeds." William Proctor, a comics scholar who focuses on the concept of the reboot, further refines this difference: "The retcon differs from the reboot in the sense that it alters elements of a series' chronology without collapsing the narrative continuum altogether— i.e. it does not 'begin again.' . . . [T]he retcon does not begin again but, rather, alters details in the continuum for purposes of story." A retcon is different from a reboot, then, in that the changing continuity is a part of the story world, not simply an unexplained marketing decision imposed from the outside (though economic pressures do clearly exert their influence).

If a retcon is not a reboot, then what, precisely, *is* it? I define retroactive continuity as a narrative process wherein the creator(s) and/or producer(s) of a fictional narrative/world—often, but not always, the same person or people—deliberately alter the history of that narrative/world such that, going forward, future stories reflect this *new* history, completely ignoring the old as if it had never happened. This can take a variety of different, increasingly stringent, forms, all of which in some way recontextualize previous story elements: (1) A retcon may be a *reinterpretation*, changing how an earlier work is seen and interpreted, but in a less-than-definitive way, allowing for some choice on the part of audience members to determine which history is still considered canonical to the narrative. (2) A retcon may be a *reinscription*, which is a more solidified change to how an earlier work is viewed, concretely and canonically changing that work's meaning going forward. (3) At its most extreme end, a retcon may be a *revision*, wherein an older work is not only viewed differently, but even altered through republication, editing, new editions, and so forth, such that the material text itself is now different in the physical world, not just in the minds of characters and/or audience members. I will examine all three of these types of retcons—even though there are important differences among them, and stricter definitions of retconning harp on those distinctions—as part of the larger definition and phenomenon of "retroactive continuity."

The website TV Tropes, which catalogs and describes different narrative tropes and techniques utilized across a variety of different media and genres, subdivides retconning—which it broadly defines as "reframing past events to serve a current plot need"—into a variety of different categories, including Backported Development ("When someone's characterization in flashbacks is tweaked to more closely resemble their current self"), Cerebus Retcon ("Sometimes a result of Cerebus Syndrome that makes a past event more serious as a part of a shift to drama"), Orwellian Retcon ("The prior events that contradict the new continuity get rewritten"), Cosmic Retcon ("An in-story event alters reality, which results in a retcon"), and Remember the New Guy ("A new character is introduced, but is retconned to have been part of the story all along"). Included among these are two terms that I have used here: "Revision," which the site defines as "A continuity alteration that doesn't directly contradict any previous material," and "Rewrite," which is "A retcon that openly overwrites the facts of the previous continuity." Clearly, we are using these terms differently. However, as we can see from TV Tropes's somewhat unwieldy list of subdivisions, most with cumbersome, tongue-in-cheek names, one can go on trying to divide up and define different variants of retconning ad nauseam. In this book I am not concerned as much with categorizing retroactive continuity as I am with looking into its history and meanings. I have no explicit desire to contradict TV Tropes's work creating these categories, but will utilize my somewhat more simplified reinterpretations/reinscription/revision taxonomy throughout this book because, I feel, it more accurately focuses on the ways in which artistic creators/producers enact and define these changes, rather than relying on definitions that largely speak from inside of the narrative text. As such, it better fits my purpose of exploring the implications of retroactive continuity than TV Tropes's schema does.

My goal here is not to stringently parse out the differences of these subheadings of retconning, but rather to explore retroactive continuity as a narrative and world-building technique that serves as a vital and important force that has implications on how we view our history, society, and daily reality. In a culture saturated by editable media, where interest groups argue over Wikipedia pages and politicians can delete questionable tweets, the retcon serves as a perfect metaphor for the ways in which history, and our access to information in general, has become endlessly mutable.

I contend that the editable hyperlink, rather than the stable footnote, has become the de facto source of information in America today, and that the groundwork for this major cultural shift has been laid for decades via our modes of entertainment. To embrace the concept of retroactive continuity in fictional media means accepting that the past, itself, is not a stable element, but rather something that is constantly in contentious flux. Similarly, the frequent negative reactions that fans and audiences have to retcons reflect the fear engendered by the notion that history is unstable and ever on the verge of being rewritten. Thus, I find the hyperlink, with its inherent instability as to what, exactly, it links *to*, to be as apt a metaphor as the retcon for this transition between reliance on a universal, monumentalist sense of history and a more nuanced understanding of historical revisionism.

Because of the growing ubiquity of retroactive continuity within our popular media, Americans have grown more comfortable with accepting that narratives are inherently unstable and multimodal, a realization that has a vast impact upon how individuals curate and process information. As Michael Saler posits in his cultural history of early "world-building" literature, *As If: Modern Enchantment and the Literary Prehistory of Virtual Reality*, these stories have contributed to "increasing comfort with the notion that the real world is, to some degree, imaginary, relying on contingent narratives that are subject to challenge and change. Imaginary worlds, in other words, have trained their inhabitants to question essential interpretations of the world" (21).

Retconning has been made most explicit in the imaginary worlds of the superhero "universes" found in comic books published over the past seventy-five years by DC Comics and Marvel Comics. It was in the letters page of a comic book—writer/editor Roy Thomas's 1980s *All-Star Squadron* title—that the term *retroactive continuity* was first printed, and it was in the unfolding of those superhero universes that the active nature and impact of retconning was first explicitly felt. As a 2007 article in the British *Telegraph* newspaper proclaimed, "The exceptionally Baudrillardian world of comics—with its panoply of alternative dimensions and parallel time-lines, and its cast of shape-shifters, mind controllers, time-travelers, and all-but-omnipotent cosmic entities—offers endless possibilities . . . The world of mainstream superhero comics, then, is one of infinite plasticity in terms of events" (Leigh). Contemporary retconning is in part defined by this plasticity. Thus, although retconning has its roots in the earliest of mankind's oral and written narratives, it reached its present form as a result of the complicated workings of superhero comic book continuity.

The complicated, long-form storytelling worked out over decades of continuity in these superhero universes began to have a major impact on other media in the 1990s, with television shows like *Buffy, the Vampire Slayer* and *The X-Files* utilizing their episodic format to relate elaborate storylines that would intentionally unfold over the course of multiple seasons. With the massive success of the show *Lost* in the early 2000s, helmed by writers who were not only influenced by comic books but who were often comic book writers themselves, this complicated comic book-style continuity became almost ubiquitous among primetime television dramas. Many shows that have followed *Lost*, such as *Heroes, Once Upon a Time, The Walking Dead*, and *Game of Thrones*, combined the fantastic world-building of comic books with the complex, interweaving (often-confusing), social drama narratives of soap operas.

Similarly, the early 2000s saw the rise of film franchises that relied upon long-term investment from viewers who were able to follow continuity from movie to movie. The *Harry Potter*, *Lord of the Rings*, and Marvel Cinematic Universe (MCU) films have, together, earned almost twenty billion dollars in the past two decades. What these movies have in common with shows like *Buffy* and *Lost*, and with the DC and Marvel comic book universes, is that they often utilize the complexity of their fictional universes in order to refresh the narratives and maintain audience interest across multiple platforms. It's no coincidence, for example, that *Buffy* and the MCU each have spin-off comic book series that are considered canonical additions to their worlds.

Given the dominance of this type of storytelling (whether one chooses to call it "franchising," "world-building," "long-form narratives," or simply "imaginary worlds") in today's mediascape, it is more important than ever to analyze the retcon's unique attributes and potentials, both within the narratives themselves and in the greater culture that those narratives arise from. Retroactive continuity is a narrative device that exists most comfortably within these large-scale imaginary worlds, and it is a device that is important not just to fictional worlds, but to the contemporary world of readers and audiences as well. By putting the history and implementation of retconning into conversation with the growing public acceptance of historical revisionism (as seen in the ascendance of open-access information sources like Wikipedia), we can begin to understand how decades of retroactive continuity in popular media have prepared American audiences to view history as an ongoing process that relies on shifting sources and interpretations (the metaphorical "hyperlink") rather than a solid body of facts ("the footnote").

⊘ ⊘ ⊘

In simplified terms, retroactive continuity is the process whereby creators and/or producers in some way alter the events of the origin, backstory, and/or history of a particular character or story world—changing, for example, the identity of the mugger who killed Batman's parents. Retconning is most often utilized to literally rewrite some aspect of a character's past, in order to keep that character more contemporary (Batman could not have been active during World War II, or else he would now be in his eighties); to erase stories from continuity that no longer fit by today's standards (Batman either carrying a gun, in his first appearances, or serving as a goofy, well-adjusted father figure in the 1960s); or to create future story potential (adding a character into Batman's past who then becomes an important ally or enemy of the hero in the present day). Retconning is a revision of the fictional universe in order to make that universe fresh and exciting for contemporary readers, but it also involves the influence of the past, as it directly inscribes itself upon that past.

As such, retconning has a direct and important correlation to historical revisionism. Within the fictional realm, retconning establishes a past that is inherently changeable, since any creator can completely alter any aspect of established continuity, which serves as the "history" of an imaginary world. In the real world, this notion of an alterable past is often termed "revisionist history." As we have seen, this phrase is frequently used today as a pejorative, particularly by conservative stakeholders interested in a "traditional," positivist narrative of American Exceptionalism (these forces will frequently equate revisionist historians with Holocaust deniers). In actuality, though, as John Grossman points out, the vast majority of historians working today could be considered practitioners of revisionist history. The very job of a historian in the twenty-first century is to mine the past for untold narratives that reshape the way we view and understand that past. Historians do not simply reify a predetermined view of history, but rather they unearth information and craft arguments to continually shape that view. Although Orwellian fears of an altered past may apply in totalitarian states, in a society with open access to information and a panoply of voices debating about history the process of historical revision is productive rather than repressive.

This way of understanding the past as something that can constantly be revised has reached beyond the academic field of history and permeated the general American consciousness in regards to how information is received and processed via the Internet. The online texts and other sources from which many Americans today derive their notion of history, and even their contemporary news, are contingent upon a variety of unstable, mutable factors. While not arguing for an inherent instability in contemporary life, I do contend that in a society moderated more and more by digital media, Americans have become increasingly adept at using that media to view the past, present, and even future as shifting, slippery bodies, rather than as solid bedrock. We have been prepared for this awareness not simply through official forms of education and cultural uplift, but also through the long history of the retcon in the imaginary worlds in which we spend our leisure time. These worlds have a distinct and crucial relationship to the "real world," and we must continue to mine their ever-changing history for discoveries about how audiences understand themselves and their place in the world.

This book attempts to engage in that ongoing practice by looking at the history of retroactive continuity and exploring its implications for audiences, fans, and engaged, aware citizens of the digital era.

In chapter 1 I explore the "prehistory" of retroactive continuity; that is, its implementation in narratives that preexist its conceptualization as a term. This chapter will necessarily be more of an overview than an in-depth history, since such a project would be a book unto itself. However, an understanding of where retroactive continuity originates will be necessary for exploring its contemporary importance.

Chapter 2 is the first of a pair of related chapters looking at retroactive continuity in superhero comic books. The beginning of cohesive comic book universes can be traced to the first team-up between heroes, in the form of the Justice Society of America in 1940s *All-Star Comics* #3. In the course of the over seventy-five years since that first appearance of the team, the Justice Society has gone through a variety of changes and revitalizations, including a multitude of retcons. It was, in fact, in the letters page of a 1980s Justice Society-centered book, entitled *All-Star Squadron*, that the term retroactive continuity was first published and, thus, directly and publicly discussed as a narrative technique. The chapter focuses on the writer and editor of *All-Star Squadron*, Roy Thomas, and the ways in which his scripts, along with his interaction with readers through the letters columns, helped to define exactly how retroactive continuity could be utilized in long-form narratives. More importantly, Thomas's work on *All-Star Squadron* shows us most clearly the direct and potent link between retroactive continuity and historiography/historical revisionism that serves as the basis for my argument.

In chapter 3 I will begin by discussing a seminal moment in superhero comics—1985's *Crisis on Infinite Earths* crossover series from DC Comics—to show how retconning came to be a valuable asset in comic book creators' toolboxes by the 1980s. The second half of the chapter explores that process at work two decades later, in an Internet-savvy America living in the aftermath of September 11, 2001. I examine DC Comics' reactions and responses to the tragic events of 9/11 through the following decade's worth of *Crisis*-inspired line-wide crossover stories. Those stories—steeped in retroactive continuity, and demanding that audiences be versed in complex narratives—show how the preponderance of technology and new media in the twenty-first century has created a different kind of awareness of the past, one that stresses history's contingency and mutability.

Building upon the foundations of retconning established by superhero comic books, chapter 4 shifts the focus to the medium of television, and specifically the kinds of long-form, continuity-rich dramas that draw heavily upon the narrative traditions of both comic books and soap operas. It will also briefly explore how some recent film franchises have adopted the retcon technique as well.

After these first four chapters examining the development of retroactive continuity in various media, in chapter 5 I argue for a cultural awareness of retconning through an exploration of retroactive continuity in the realms of parody, satire, and play. For a piece of parody to be successful, an author requires that the audience has a knowledge of that which is being referenced. The opening of the chapter, then, explores various moments satirizing the concept and usage of retroactive continuity. In the second half of the chapter I examine several texts that, while not exactly parodying retroactive continuity, do play freely with the concept to such an extent that they place all of literature, retroactively, within the same fictional realm. These texts often engage in their own form of subtle satire, and require a vast network of paratextual knowledge (referring to ancillary works related to, but separate from, a central text) for full appreciation by readers.

In chapter 6 I explore how the concepts of historical revisionism, mutable pasts, and even retroactive continuity have increasingly become a part of life in the twenty-first century. This is seen most clearly in the rise to cultural prominence of the online, open-source encyclopedia, Wikipedia. The chapter examines the impact of Wikipedia upon contemporary thoughts about history, in particular, and how its immense popularity has resulted in a differing conception of how digital culture views and receives information about the past. The notion of an alterable and debatable past, an idea that has become a central part of Internet culture, is, at heart, reliant upon a society that has been prepared for such views by decades of retconning in the world of popular entertainment.

In my conclusion, I return to the differences between retroactive continuity and politically motivated retconning. In so doing, I discuss how retconning is most often celebratory in nature and how it represents an embracing of the past rather than an Orwellian erasing of it. I once again return to my metaphor of "hyperlinked America" in order to show how the narrative game of retroactive continuity has helped to create a more fluid, changeable, and dynamic world.

A BRIEF PREHISTORY OF RETROACTIVE CONTINUITY

The term *retroactive continuity* was first coined in the letters pages of the 1980s comic book *All-Star Squadron*,[1] but as a concept it very much predates that "secret origin." In fact, as this chapter will show, it dates back to the earliest narratives of mankind, those that precede the development of the written word. In order to understand how what I have termed a "literary technique" can actually predate literature itself, though, we must first see the difference between oral and literate cultures, a distinction drawn by ethnographers and literary theorists alike.

By their very nature these oral cultures had much in common with the "hyperlinked America" that I discuss in this book. Similar to the fluid nature of the Internet, oral narratives were constantly in flux, varying from storyteller to storyteller and even from retelling to retelling. The active nature of these stories, and the worlds created by them, have more in common with today's malleable imaginary worlds than they do with many written, canonical literary traditions. However, ancient and historical written texts were no stranger to mutability. Looking beyond oral cultures and their epic tales, toward the development of literate societies, we can see more concrete examples of retconning at work. Biblical writing, for example, is full of examples of shifting and changing histories. The New Testament, with its emphasis on a renewed relationship with a personalized God rather than fearing the wrath of a vengeful deity, was a further "retconning" of the narrative and message of the original Hebraic Bible.

More recent "classic" narratives also display instances of retroactive continuity and are directly related to the kinds of retconning we see in contemporary storytelling. Thus, this chapter will conclude with an examination of how retconning was implemented in the works of writers Sir Arthur Conan Doyle, J. R. R. Tolkien, and H. P. Lovecraft, creators of popular fictional realms who were among the first to actively engage in "world-building" in conjunction with their readers and fans. By understanding how these classic authors utilized and developed retroactive continuity we will gain the historical basis from which to analyze the process in more recent decades.

The Singers and the Songs: Retconning in Oral Societies

In his exploration of the differences between oral and literate cultures, *Orality and Literacy*, Walter Ong defines the former type of society as a culture "with no knowledge at all of writing" (1). These preliterate cultures (whether historical or, less commonly, contemporary) are thus built on verbal communication, and their stories and narratives are passed on from person to person rather than through the written word. It is hard, then, to fully analyze these narratives, since once they are written down they have, by nature, passed into the realm of the literate. However, several anthropologists have gone to great lengths to understand the transmission of these tales, and we can look to their work to provide us with insight into how the stories function and, most importantly in this context, how they change.

As Ong notes, repetition was extremely important to oral cultures[2]: "knowledge, once acquired, had to be constantly repeated or it would be lost: fixed, formulaic thought patterns were essential for wisdom and effective administration" (23). Stories needed to be told over and over again, and they had to be structured according to patterns that allowed for their memorization by future storytellers. Without the technology of writing, this was the only way for individuals—and entire cultures—to transmit important information, narratives, and morals from generation to generation. Repetition is facilitated in oral culture, according to Ong, by "the physical conditions of oral expression before a large audience, where redundancy is in fact more marked than in most face-to-face conversation," as well as by "the public speaker's need to keep going while he is running through his mind what to say next" (40). Oral societies thus focus heavily on retaining important information through transmission, and as a result they do not hold on to less important details: "By contrast with literate societies, oral societies can be characterized as homeostatic. . . . [They] live very much in a present which keeps itself in equilibrium or homeostasis by sloughing off memories which no longer have present relevance" (46).

The narratives of oral cultures, then, tend to eschew the kind of complexity and rich detail that are heralded by literary standards. They lend themselves, instead, to what Ong calls "heavy" characters, "persons whose deeds are monumental, memorable and commonly public" (69). These characters are "outsize figures, that is, heroic figures," because their stories "organize experience in some sort of permanently memorable form. Colorless personalities cannot survive oral mnemonics. To assure weight and memorability, heroic figures tend to be type figures" (69). The heroes of oral cultures were larger-than-life figures, the kinds of characters who we would today say belong to "genre fiction." This links those stories with the kinds that, in the present, lend themselves to the plot mechanics of retroactive continuity.

Retconning, of a kind, occurred most frequently in oral culture due to the nature of orating. Memorization was not rote, but formulaic; that is to say, a story would vary from teller to teller, and from telling to telling. These stories were always in flux, as Ong explains:

> Formulas are of course somewhat variable, as are themes, and a given poet's rhapsodizing or "stitching together" of narratives will differ recognizably from another's. Certain turns of phrases will be idiosyncratic. . . . Originality consists not in the introduction of new materials but in fitting the traditional materials effectively into each individual, unique situation and/or audience. (59)

Such occurrences were clearly not intentional retcons in the way we see them used today, but they *do* show how oral cultures were accepting of narrative instability. Without a written text as a solid, unchanging guide to constantly return to, both storytellers and listeners were open to the variation that was a natural part of the narrative process.

It is precisely this acceptance of variation, along with the tendency to mythologize heroic figures, that causes literary scholar Terrence Wandtke to equate oral culture with contemporary superhero comic books. Wandtke is not claiming that comic books, a clearly textual medium, are somehow orally transmitted, but rather he ties them to what Ong describes as "secondary orality." Ong differentiates the "primary orality" of oral cultures from "secondary orality" in modern culture, describing the latter as "present-day high-technology culture, in which a new orality is sustained by telephone, radio, television, and other electronic devices that depend for their existence and functioning on writing and print" (11). Wandtke takes this a step further, linking the culture of fandom that surrounds superhero comic books with the culture of oral societies:

> Despite the fact that superhero comic books are a print medium, the dynamics of their stories and their treatment of the audience resemble what takes place with epics in oral cultures. . . . I am identifying the ideals of oral culture as being enacted in certain terms within the culture of [the] superhero industry. However, I am also using orality as a metaphor to describe the dynamics of comic book narrative and illustration. (23–24)

Part of these dynamics includes drawing a direct line between narrative techniques utilized by oral cultures with those seen in comic books: "superhero comic book readers become willing to do something easily seen within oral culture but considered to be wholly unacceptable within literate culture . . . [T]hese readers will allow not only repetitions but also 'corrections' to the story already told" (40). In oral cultures, such corrections are simply a part of the refinement of the storytelling process; in comic books, the corrections are often pieces of intentional retroactive continuity. Their acceptance, however, stems from a culture surrounding those comic books that inherits from orality (rather than literacy) an acceptance of instability and change (even if that acceptance is often only partial and/or begrudging by some fans and readers). Indeed, Wandtke contends that in today's superhero comic books, as well as in the billion-dollar multimedia franchises associated with them, "we can see a radically increased number of variations that are presented simultaneously, the result of self-conscious choices made within new traditional culture. . . . The retcon is not the exception to the regular flow of superhero stories but rather the new norm" (193). This "new norm," however, is really just a resurgence of the *old* norm. It represents literate culture, after centuries of focusing on the solidified text, becoming more comfortable with the ancient notion of variation that was at home in oral culture.

Pioneering scholar of comparative literature Albert B. Lord discovered these variations among surviving oral traditions, writing extensively about the "living organism which is the oral epic" and examining "the structural heart of the formulas [in order] to discern the various patterns which merge to give them form. . . . [T]he formulas are not the ossified clichés which they have the reputation of being, but . . . they are capable of change and are indeed frequently highly productive of other and new formulas" (4). In his firsthand studies of these epics—many of which he recorded for posterity—Lord noted that their stories, formulas, and themes were not static, but rather constantly shifting and evolving over time: "If we cease to expect verbal identity between different performances of the same song, whether they be by different singers or by the same one, whether they be over a shorter or longer period of time, we are bound to notice that there are a few simple types of differences between them" (119).

Orality scholar John Miles Foley further explains, "A second and third recording [of a modern-day bard's performance] made the next day or in front of a different audience or even with the same bard in a different frame of mind will reveal inevitable disparities that quickly put the lie to the authority of any one version. The song lives outside any single performance" (21). Strangely, though, according to Lord these changes were precisely what allowed the oral epics to actually *maintain* cultural traditions:

> [T]he changes of which we have been speaking have been brought about, not by forces seeking change for its own sake, nor by pure chance, but by an insistent, conservative urge for preservation of an essential idea as expressed either in a single theme or in a group of themes. Multiformity is essentially conservative in traditional lore, all outward appearances to the contrary. (120)

These epics change from singer to singer, and even performance to performance, *because* they serve as a concerted cultural effort to maintain and transmit certain essential information. Similarly, as we shall see in the following chapters, retcons in long-standing media franchises are frequently utilized in order to return a narrative to its original core elements. The fluctuation of story, both in the oral epics and in our current mediascape, is thus a somewhat conservative effort to maintain tradition (albeit with often vastly different purposes). The most famous example of retroactive continuity in the history of the Western world involves such a direct attempt to similarly link tradition with change: the retconning of the Bible in the New Testament.

In the Beginning Was the Words: Biblical Retcons

The New Testament, the foundational text for Christianity, can in many ways be interpreted as a retcon of the Old Testament, the Bible of the Jewish people. I should note here that this interpretation relies upon reading the Bible (specifically the New Revised Standard Version) as a single literary text rather than as the collection of historically separate texts put together that it actually is. Though both Testaments of the Bible were written by multiple authors over long periods of time, for the sake of simplicity I will be looking at them here as a unified text, as well as examining their literary elements without specific regard for religious connotations. This interpretation, then, is not one that is attempting to hew to historical fidelity; instead, it examines the Bible as a literary narrative, one with two distinct parts/Testaments and featuring a crucial moment, in the second Testament, of recontextualizing much of the content of the first Testament.

The first book of the New Testament, the Gospel According to Matthew, opens with an attempt to genealogically link Jesus, the Christian Messiah, with the father of Judaism, Abraham. The very first section concludes with the summation, "So all the generations from Abraham to David are fourteen generations; and from David to the deportation to Babylon, fourteen generations; and from the deportation to Babylon to the Messiah, fourteen generations" (Matthew 1:17).[3] The very first action in the New Testament, then, is to retroactively link it to the Old. In the same chapter Matthew writes about "an angel of the Lord" who comes to Joseph (the foster father of Jesus) in a dream to speak of Jesus's mother Mary's impending virgin pregnancy, and to explain why Joseph should not divorce her: "All this took place to fulfill what had been spoken by the Lord through the prophet: 'Look, the virgin shall conceive and bear a son, and they shall name him Emmanuel'" (Matthew 1:22–23). This refers to a passage in the Old Testament, wherein the prophet Isaiah states, "Therefore the Lord himself will give you a sign. Look, the young woman is with child and shall bear a son, and shall name him Immanuel" (Isaiah 7:14).

The linking of these two passages is a huge moment. Matthew directly takes a prophecy of the Old Testament and attaches it to the story of Jesus, turning the Christian messiah into the fulfillment of the messianic promises made to the Jewish people. On a practical level, this may have been a move on the part of early Christian church founders to convince Jews to convert to their new religion. In purely literary terms, though, this moment exists to make the New Testament—which can be viewed as either a sort of "unauthorized sequel," from a Jewish perspective, or a divinely inspired reinterpretation of the original text, from a Christian perspective—a direct outgrowth of the Old. This is done even more forcefully a few chapters later in Matthew, during Jesus's famous "Sermon on the Mount." Here, Jesus proclaims, "Do not think that I have come to abolish the law or the prophets: I have come not to abolish but to fulfill. For truly I tell you, until heaven and earth pass away, not one letter, not one stroke of a letter, will pass from the law until all is accomplished" (Matthew 5:17–18).

In Jesus's own words, as recorded by Matthew, he is the fulfillment of prophecy, the promised messiah come to save his people and the world. This is not, however, a complete "reboot" of the religious traditions of the Jews; rather, it is additive, taking the entire Old Testament and recontextualizing it not as a hope for something still yet to come, but rather as the precursor for that hope's realization in the New Testament. For Christians, this fundamentally changes the nature of the Old Testament and is a massive bit of retroactive continuity that provides the entire basis for their faith. However, it should be pointed out that this form of retconning is, at best, a reinterpretation, since it relies upon a split between two groups, each providing a different interpretation of the same material text: for Jews, the traditional interpretation that the messiah was yet to come, and for Christians a newer interpretation that Jesus had fulfilled the prophecies of the Torah, thus leading to the need for a New Testament chronicling his new teachings. This is a loose interpretation of retconning, but I use it here to make the point that even the foundation of much of contemporary Western faith is not immune to retroactive continuity. The New Testament, itself, would come to be similarly retconned in the texts of religions that came later, including Islam and Mormonism, whose holy books accept both testaments of the Bible as truth but further recontextualize them as leading to future prophets and divine action/fulfillment.

However, even prior to the advent of Christianity, members of the Jewish faith were not unfamiliar with confused continuity. In fact, the first two chapters of Genesis, the opening book of the Old Testament, feature two differing accounts of the creation of the universe, Earth, and mankind. To look at just one difference, in the first version, "God created humankind in his image, in the image of God he created them; male and female he created them" (Genesis 1:27). In the second version, though, God creates woman *after* creating man, and in fact makes her out of the first man's rib (a contention that would be the source of misogyny for centuries to come): "And the rib that the lord God had taken from the man he made into a woman and brought her to the man. Then the man said, 'This at last is bone of my bones and flesh of my flesh; this one shall be called Woman, for out of Man this one was taken'" (Genesis 2:22–23).

From its very outset the Judeo-Christian Bible is awash with contradictions. It is no wonder that biblical scholars would attempt to reconcile some of these conflicting accounts and would thus engage in their own form of retroactive continuity. A. David Lewis, in his article "The Secret, Untold Relationship of Biblical Midrash and Comic Book Retcon," makes this connection explicit:

> Aggressively or innocuously, directly or indirectly, a retcon is, in essence, a rewrite by the current creative staff done to past stories where there seems "an invitation by the text itself to 'fill in the blanks' and so account for the perceived anomaly"—however, this quote was written about Hebrew mythos, not comic books . . . Specifically, it applied to the sources used by Louis Ginzberg as he elaborated on certain biblical stories. (263)

Lewis goes on to explicate Ginzberg's use of the Midrash, a body of texts created by rabbinical scholars to analyze the Hebrew Bible and help the faithful interpret the Torah.

Though the Midrash are not holy texts in and of themselves, rabbis and biblical scholars alike study them as a source of information about the Old Testament. According to the Jewish Theological Seminary of America, "The term comes from the Hebrew root . . . which means 'to explain, deduce, ferret out.' . . . The ability to do that is what made it possible for the rabbis to answer new questions as they arose" (quoted in Lewis, 264). Thus, the Midrash serve as a crucial body of text allowing for followers of the Torah to fully understand it and interpret its multiple meanings in their contemporary world:

> Instead of tearing apart the fabric of an antiquated tale, Midrash and retcon can stretch it into the present. And, in the ideal case, the new threads introduced to a tale do not clash, but tighten; they may not tangle, but mend. . . . Therefore, Midrash, instead of undermining the Bible through interpretive investigation, leaves the book open to further generations' reflections. (Lewis, 267)

As with the changes made from song to song in oral traditions, the changes and alterations proposed by Midrash don't somehow warp the original text, but rather maintain the important traditions and mores that the text was originally created to impart.[4] Therefore, Lewis explains, "*Midrash*, like retcon, serves as both the name and practice of later texts reflecting on, reinterpreting, and sometimes reshaping the old—albeit, Midrash does this specifically for biblical works" (264).

Biblical literature, from both the Old Testament and New Testament, is thus awash with early examples of retroactive continuity. Although these examples have been extremely brief—a necessity given just how much biblical exegesis one would otherwise have to work their way through—they hopefully provide a clear picture that the "holy words" of the Bible were as open to change, alteration, and interpretation as the oral epics of preliterate societies. Although the biblical text itself may have been permanent and unchanging (and even this is open to debate, given how many different versions, editions, and translations of the Bible have been created over the past two thousand years), within that book itself was a fluctuating story that related the same events differently and created multiple histories.

It continues to be important to note here that retconning relies upon a long-lasting narrative, whether that be a media franchise, an influential biblical text written over the course of centuries, or oral epics passed down from generation to generation. Lewis explains,

> The common element is Time. Among their other reasons for being, Midrash and retcon can be seen as the offspring of Time—of a text's temporal distance from its audience and the need to bridge that gulf. This distance could plague a comic book publisher with over 30 years of history. . . . The same principles apply for tailoring biblical narrative through Midrash. (269)

Retcons—from oral epics through Midrash—have a long and (literally) storied history in both oral and literate societies, dating back to the foundational texts that served to create and maintain the cultural traditions and beliefs that often hold those societies together.

The State-Sponsored Past and Other Real-Life Retcons

Though retroactive continuity is a narrative technique, one applicable to fictional realms where past events can be metaphorically and/or literally rewritten, something quite like it can take place in real life as well. Indeed, it is the thesis of this book that historical revisionism is a kind of real-world equivalent to retconning, one that—despite its name—relies upon reinterpretation and recontextualization far more than revision. However, there *are* historical examples of attempts to completely revise the past, often for explicitly political purposes. Whereas historical revisionism is generally the attempt to view history through a lens that allows for the voices of the previously disenfranchised to be heard and given weight, this kind of retconning of the past instead attempts to further marginalize the voiceless, for the sake of further entrenching those who are already in power.

The most infamous purveyor of this form of historio-political retconning was Joseph Stalin, the brutal dictator of the Soviet Union from 1922 to 1952.

Stalin was known to support the rewriting of Soviet history (and sometimes to engage in such rewriting and editing personally, as was the case with the propaganda text released by the Soviet Information Bureau, *Falsifiers of History*), in order to glorify his own regime, taking credit for the accomplishments of others and/or writing them out of Soviet history entirely, sometimes going so far as to edit individuals out of photographs after he had them executed (Roberts). A similar practice of revising national history, and claiming responsibility for others' accomplishments, has long been practiced by the Kim family of supreme leaders of the Democratic People's Republic of Korea (more commonly referred to in the West as North Korea).

However, not all real-world instances of retconning are the purview of totalitarian regimes. In classical painting, for example, the term *pentimento* refers to changes in a painting as shown by traces of the previous work, allowing insight into an artist's revision process in a way that we don't see with, for example, the printed copy of a novel (though publicly released rough drafts, or revised editions, can serve this same purpose). More pertinent to contemporary media, though, is the kind of retconning found in athletics, and the retroactive stripping of medals, honors, and titles from particular athletes, coaches, and programs when they have been found to have violated important rules. This was the case when cyclist Lance Armstrong lost multiple bicycle racing titles after having been found to have used drugs to enhance his performance (the races are now officially said to have had no winner those years). On an even larger scale, the University of Pennsylvania's football program had all of its victories between 1998 and 2011 removed from official records (though this decision was later reversed) after it became public that university officials had covered up the sexual abuse of children by a former assistant coach. These kinds of changes have a measurable impact upon the statistics and records used to organize sports leagues, and thus show how these alterations to the past—or at least to how the past is interpreted and contextualized—are important.

It is no small wonder that when retroactive continuity can be used to alter and manage interpretations of the actual past, fictional retcons play an increasingly large role in allowing creators and corporations to manage large-scale media franchises. They are, after all, drawing on tradition that dates back thousands of years. Yet this tradition also has relatively recent predecessors that more explicitly developed a retroactive method to rejuvenate popular literary/media franchises.

Sir Arthur Conan Doyle: Sherlock Holmes Lives!

The late nineteenth and early twentieth centuries saw the beginnings of the kind of character-based media franchises that would come to dominate the world of popular entertainment in the present day. Multiple writers created memorable stories and worlds that are still salable names to this day, including Edgar Rice Burroughs (creator of Tarzan and John Carter of Mars), Robert E. Howard (creator of Conan the Barbarian), and Johnston McCauley (creator of Zorro). These long-lasting characters tended to adhere to the kind of "outsize" heroics that Albert B. Lord discovered were the protagonists of oral epics, allowing for a wide variety of adventurous stories based around these character types' progression through various plot mechanics, rather than following the extended character arcs of a "literary" novel. The three masters of world-building of this era, each of whom created imaginary characters and worlds that practically live and breathe among us to this very day, were Sir Arthur Conan Doyle, J. R. R. Tolkien, and H. P. Lovecraft.[5]

Historian Michael Saler contends that Doyle was the originator of the modern mass-media franchise: "Imaginary worlds of fiction first became virtual worlds, persistently available and collectively envisaged, in late nineteenth-century Europe and America, commencing with the first 'virtual reality' character in fiction, Sherlock Holmes" (6). Holmes, the world's greatest detective, was insanely popular, inspiring dedicated followers from the time of initial publication of Doyle's stories through to the present day. An entire branch of popular culture, Sherlockiana, takes its name from the character, and new stories and films starring the hero are produced regularly. As Saler explains,

> Sherlock Holmes was the first fictional creation that adults openly embraced as real while deliberately minimizing or ignoring its creator, and the fetishization of Holmes has continued for over a century. The cult of Holmes focuses not just on a singular character, but on his entire world: fans of the "canon" obsess about every detail of the fictional universe Conan Doyle created, mentally inhabiting this geography of the imagination in a way that was never true for partisans of earlier characters. . . . Sherlockian devotion is thus a departure from preceding public infatuations with fictional characters and a template for subsequent public infatuations for imaginary worlds and their protagonists. (107)

The stories featuring Sherlock Holmes created one of the first popular culture media franchises to last long enough for retconning to come into play. It is significant, then, that Doyle engaged in one of the most forceful acts of retconning in all of literature.

By 1893, six years after Holmes's 1887 debut in the novel *A Study in Scarlet*, Conan Doyle had grown tired of writing his now-signature character, and he mercilessly killed him off at the end of the story "The Final Problem." In the story, Dr. John Watson, Holmes's partner and chronicler, opens by foreshadowing the great detective's death: "It is with a heavy heart that I take up my pen to write these the last words in which I shall ever record the singular gifts by which my friend Mr. Sherlock Holmes was distinguished" (301). The ending of the story is even more unambiguous in its relation of Holmes's 1891 death in battle with his archenemy, Professor James Moriarty, on the edge of the Reichenbach Falls:

> An examination by experts leaves little doubt that a personal contest between the two men ended, as it could hardly fail to end in such a situation, in their reeling over, locked in each other's arms. Any attempt at recovering the bodies was absolutely hopeless, and there, deep down in that dreadful cauldron of swirling water and seething foam, will lie for all time the most dangerous criminal and the foremost champion of the law of their generation. (317)

Conan Doyle wished to devote more time to his other writings, and so he deliberately ended Holmes's "final" story with the character's death. Holmes proved to be so popular, though, that the author would find himself coming back to his most famous creation.

In 1901, Conan Doyle returned to Holmes with the novel *The Hound of the Baskervilles*, but here the story is explicitly set prior to Holmes's death. Two years later, though, the detective returned yet again in "The Adventure of the Empty House," this time set in 1894, *after* his demise. Conan Doyle takes advantage of the fact that his narrator, Watson, was not there to witness Holmes's demise, and allows for the hero's reappearance to startle Watson just as much as it does the reader: "I moved my head to look at the cabinet behind me. When I turned again Sherlock Holmes was standing smiling at me across my study table. I rose to my feet, stared at him for some seconds in utter amazement, and then it appears that I must have fainted for the first and the last time in my life" (332–33). Once Watson comes to, Holmes explains to him how he survived falling into the chasm at the bottom of the Reichenbach Falls:

> I had no serious difficulty in getting out of it, for the very simple reason that I was never in it. . . . [Moriarty and I] tottered together upon the brink of the fall. I

have some knowledge, however, of baritsu, or the Japanese system of wrestling, which has more than once been very useful to me. I slipped through his grip, and he with a horrible scream kicked madly for a few seconds and clawed the air with both his hands. But for all his efforts he could not get his balance, and over he went. (333–34)

Here, Conan Doyle retcons the struggle at Reichenbach to end with Moriarty's death and Holmes's survival. This explanation hinges on Holmes's knowledge of baritsu, something that Conan Doyle and/or Watson have not yet seen fit to inform the reader of. This is a pure example of retroactive continuity in action: in order to save Holmes from certain death, Conan Doyle adds to his history a particular skill set that is his only possible saving grace in that moment. With this new piece of continuity in Holmes's life—the multiyear study of a complex martial art—the detective's survival becomes merely incredible, rather than impossible.

Conan Doyle goes further than that, though, and has Holmes explain that he saw an opportunity to fake his own death in order to escape other enemies who wanted to see him dead. He climbed the cliffs along the path where the confrontation had taken place, finding a small ledge, and, "There I was stretched when you, my dear Watson, and all your following were investigating in the most sympathetic and inefficient manner the circumstances of my death" (336). As a result, the expert examination Watson spoke of in "The Final Problem" was incorrect, because it was based on Holmes's sudden disappearance, which, it turns out, the detective had purposely engineered. This is more retroactive continuity, provided so as to explicitly contradict the assured ending of "The Final Problem." Conan Doyle needs to tidy up and alter the details of that story's ending—rather than "an examination by experts" we are now shown an "inefficient" investigation—in order to retroactively save Holmes's life for future stories (for which Conan Doyle had been offered a lucrative publishing contract).

Through retroactive continuity, Conan Doyle was able to satisfy his fans' desire on two levels—he not only brought Holmes back from the dead for more stories, but he also undid the "ending" to Holmes's story. It was entirely possible that Conan Doyle could have simply written more Holmes stories set prior to "The Final Solution," as he had done with *The Hound of the Baskervilles*, and leave the detective's death intact. By bringing the character back to life, though, Conan Doyle was able to add to Holmes's mythos indefinitely, without worrying about a predetermined ending that might box him into a narrative corner. The only way to accomplish this was with a retcon.

J. R. R. Tolkien: The Trouble with Hobbits and Rings

Another author who found himself in need of the retcon as a narrative tool was the bookish university professor J. R. R. Tolkien. In works including such tomes as *The Hobbit*, *The Lord of the Rings*, and *The Silmarillion*, Tolkien created his own mythological world, called Middle-earth, which featured dragons, wizards, elves, orcs, and half-sized human-like creatures called hobbits. Middle-earth, media scholar Mark J. P. Wolf notes, was a watershed in the history of imaginary world-building:

> While much of what Tolkien did, in terms of world-building, had already been done by others—a pantheon of gods, maps, timelines, glossaries, calendars, invented languages and alphabets—it was the *degree* to which he did them that gave his world its rich verisimilitude, and the *quality* of his work, with meaningful details integrated into an elaborate backstory, that set a new standard for world-building. (131)

This complex world of Middle-earth was one that evolved over time in Tolkien's mind and writing, and we find evidence of this in the way he changed crucial elements of the story from work to work. The first Middle-earth work, *The Hobbit*, is ostensibly a children's book, telling the fantasy story of a hobbit named Bilbo Baggins who sets out on a quest, along with several dwarves, to capture the ill-gotten treasure of a fierce and greedy dragon. *The Hobbit*, first published in 1937, is relatively simple and straightforward, relating Bilbo's adventures and ending with his return to a quiet life at home. Tolkien, however, was taken with the idea of Middle-earth, and he readily agreed when his publisher asked for a sequel. It was in the development of this sequel—the more mature epic fantasy *The Lord of the Rings*—that Tolkien began to retcon certain events from *The Hobbit*.

The Lord of the Rings, as the title suggests, centers on the One Ring, an ancient and corrupting golden band with the ability to confer power upon its wearer, enabling him or her to rule the world. This ring was first introduced in *The Hobbit*, but with a very different nature. In the first edition of the book, Bilbo encounters the ring in the possession of a disgusting, downtrodden creature named Gollum. The ring has the power to turn its wearer invisible, but no more. Bilbo wins it from Gollum in a riddle game, and Gollum willingly hands it over.[6] When the ring became central to *The Lord of the Rings* (as did Gollum's obsession with it), Tolkien needed to change the portrayal of this scene in *The Hobbit*. Instead of winning it from a willing Gollum, Bilbo uses its power to escape from the enraged creature. These changes first appeared in the second edition of *The Hobbit* (published in 1951, prior to the publication of *The Lord of the Rings*), as part of bringing Tolkien's entire imaginary world more into line with the author's thinking.

Wolf describes this process of authorial change: "Authors who change their work will undoubtedly prefer the later versions to the early ones (or else the changes would not be made). When those changes amount to retconning, the later work can be seen as preferable, because retconning usually ties earlier works more firmly into the author's world, eliminating inconsistencies" (273). Along these lines, in a preface to later editions of *The Hobbit*, Tolkien crafts a piece of retroactive continuity to explain away these real-world publishing revisions:

> [T]he true story of the ending of the Riddle Game, as it was eventually revealed (under pressure) by Bilbo . . . is now given . . . in place of the version Bilbo first gave to his friends, and actually set down in his diary. This departure from truth on the part of a most honest hobbit was a portent of great significance. It does not, however, concern the present story, and those who in this edition make their first acquaintance with hobbit-lore need not trouble about it. Its explanation lies in the history of the Ring, as it was set out in . . . *The Lord of the Rings*. (ix)

The retcon here is doubly strong. Not only does Tolkien explain how the original portrayal of Gollum losing the ring to Bilbo was inaccurate in the story world (Bilbo lied because the ring was influencing him), but he also provides a reason for *The Hobbit* to reflect the changed version (at the time of the original publication the lie was all that was known, whereas with the publication of *The Lord of the Rings* the truth has now come out).

This decision is similar to the types of games that many readers would come to play with imaginary worlds of great depth and complexity, like those created by Tolkien and Conan Doyle. Readers would discuss these works, write their own analyses and pastiches, and sometimes come to different conclusions than the authors themselves. According to Saler, "many came to appreciate the provisionality not only of fictional texts, but also of normative interpretations of reality. Public spheres of the imagination often compelled [readers] to acknowledge the constructed dimension of identities as well as the liberating capacity to juggle multiple allegiances" (19).[7] In this game, we see a melding of the real and the fictional that allows for the instability of the latter to bleed over into the former, creating a shifting understanding of the construction of reality, identity, and history.

Despite Tolkien's revisions to *The Hobbit*, he does not add in any explanation of the true nature of the ring. The ring feels cold to the touch when worn and provides the magic of invisibility, but beyond that its power goes undescribed. Toward the very end of the novel Tolkien notes that "His magic ring [Bilbo] kept a great secret, for he chiefly used it when unpleasant callers came" (302). In a letter written in 1951, Tolkien himself would note that, in *The Hobbit*, Bilbo "becomes possessed by seeming 'accident' of a 'magic ring,' the chief and only immediately obvious power of which is to make its wearer invisible" (*The Letters of J. R. R. Tolkien*, 159).

According to Tolkien scholar David Day, the author had no initial intention of this ring being anything more than a plot convenience:

> Tolkien once described how the discovery of the Ring in an Orc cavern by Bilbo Baggins was as much a surprise to the author as it was to his Hobbit hero. Tolkien knew as little of its history as Bilbo Baggins did at that time. He also explained how it grew from a simple vehicle of plot in *The Hobbit* into the central image of his epic tale *The Lord of the Rings*. (11)

Thus, in the first book of *The Lord of the Rings*, *The Fellowship of the Ring*, the wizard Gandalf, a character from *The Hobbit*, visits Bilbo's nephew Frodo, who is now in possession of the ring. Here, Gandalf warns Frodo of the ring's true danger and power, beyond mere invisibility: "It is far more powerful than I ever dared to think at first, so powerful that in the end it would utterly overcome anyone of mortal race who possessed it. It would possess him. . . . Yes, sooner or later—later, if he is strong or well-meaning to begin with, but neither strength nor good purpose will last—sooner or later the dark power will devour him" (76). This version of the ring is much different from the "magic ring" portrayed in *The Hobbit*. Here, the ring is part of an ancient struggle between good and evil, and it possesses untold amounts of power, especially for the dark lord, Sauron, who would use it to conquer Middle-earth.

Tolkien would later express that he much preferred this darker, more adult tone of *The Lord of the Rings* to the light adventure of *The Hobbit*, and would have made the latter a more mature work had he known he would expand upon it to create his signature imaginary world:

> *The Hobbit* was originally quite unconnected, though it inevitably got drawn in to the circumference of the greater construction; and in the event modified it. It was unhappily really meant, as far as I was conscious, as a "children's story," and as I had not learned sense then, and my children were not quite old enough to

correct me, it has some of the silliness of manner caught unthinkingly from the kinds of stuff I had had served to me. . . . I deeply regret them. So do intelligent children. (*The Letters of J. R. R. Tolkien*, 215).

Although Tolkien was able to retcon Gollum's attachment to the addictive ring by tweaking one chapter of *The Hobbit*, he could not alter the tone of the entire novel without completely rewriting it. The evil ring of power would be out of place in the generally lighthearted children's story, and he would have to rely on retroactive continuity, rather than rewrites, to effect the changes necessary for *The Hobbit* to serve as a prologue for the much more important (in Tolkien's mind) trilogy of *The Lord of the Rings*.

H. P. Lovecraft: Many Hands Make a Mythos

Howard Phillips Lovecraft was a writer for pulp magazines who never obtained, during his lifetime, the prestige or notoriety of Conan Doyle or Tolkien. Nevertheless, his stories and novels have inspired more pastiches than perhaps any other author's body of work this side of Shakespeare. Without intentionally setting out to create an iconic character or mythic world, Lovecraft's own interest in the dark nature of the cosmos and mankind's role in it led him to craft a series of tales focusing on ancient, frightening deities and other beings who are constantly on the verge of destroying mankind. As Saler describes, "Lovecraft created a cohesive imaginary world that became virtual during his lifetime; after his death it was dubbed the 'Cthulu Mythos'" (131). This title came from the name of one of the most popular ancient gods featured in Lovecraft's tales, and it highlights the fact that Lovecraft's imaginary world was one built on shared imagery and frightening creatures rather than on a franchise character or specific fictional realm.

Saler goes into depth explaining how Lovecraft went from writing independent stories to creating an interconnected mythos:

> Lovecraft did not plan from the outset to create a Secondary World of extraterrestrials that infest sleepy New England towns. He adopted his realist approach in the mid-1920s and found himself referring to the same set of creatures, locales and artifacts in different stories; as he became conscious of this he decided to impose some consistency on this developing "artificial mythology." He enhanced the reality effect of his imaginary world by including references to characters, places, beings, and objects from story to story, a technique he borrowed from fin-de-siècle writers of weird fiction . . . (He also included references to their fictional creations, creating a shared constellation of modern Secondary Worlds.)

> Such intertextual links among his stories gave them cohesion and, in the case of references to works by other writers, served as ironic winks to readers in the know. (144)

Lovecraft didn't just reference other writers' stories, but also, unlike Conan Doyle and Tolkien, expanded and extended his fictional world to others, opening it up for his colleagues to write about and within. Wolf explains, "Lovecraft encouraged other writers who were friends of his to use his mythos in their stories, so as to increase the verisimilitude of his creation through intertextual references, which implied that the mythos was based on something real that was being alluded to by multiple authors" (190).

Lovecraft's retroactive continuity was thus an intertextual and metatextual one, akin to that utilized by Tolkien in his preface to the revised version of *The Hobbit*. Stories that were originally intended to stand alone were now recontextualized as being part of a vast, universal mythos that connected all of Lovecraft's work, as well as the works of other authors. In fact, it was not even Lovecraft himself who developed the "Cthulu Mythos," as such, but rather the writer and publisher August Derleth, who first collected Lovecraft's pulp stories after the author's death. As horror writers/editors Stephen Jones and Kim Newman explain, Derleth expanded on Lovecraft's writing in the short novel *The Lurker at the Threshold*, a posthumous "collaboration" that is, "apart from two fragments totaling about 1200 words, wholly Derleth's work. Aside from pastiching his mentor's style . . . Derleth systematizes Lovecraft's collection of hints and references into what has become known as the Cthulu Mythos, thus opening the way for many subsequent tales by other hands" (145).

The retroactive continuity of the Cthulu Mythos, then, is the retroactive imposition *of* continuity upon Lovecraft's stories, both on the part of the author himself and by his friends and followers during and after his life. This is one of the first examples of the kind of retconning we see most often today. Rather than an individual author changing an aspect of his/her past work in order to address current concerns, most contemporary retroactive continuity takes the form of a different creator—or just as frequently, a corporate entity—altering the history of a fictional world in order to continue milking that franchise for story/monetary potential. By tying together diverse stories into a single "universe," the Cthulu Mythos presages the ways in which the major superhero comic book publishers (by far the greatest implementers of retcons big and small) would come to tie together thousands of individual stories into monolithic "universes," as we shall see in the next few chapters.

HIGH SOCIETY
Historical Revisionism in Justice Society Comics

In 1965, English teacher Roy Thomas made the leap from comic book fan to comic book professional. He worked briefly as an assistant to editor Mort Weisenger at DC Comics before moving to Marvel Comics, where he became editor-in-chief Stan Lee's confidante. However, because Lee asked Thomas not to reveal publicly any of the goings-on at Marvel, especially future plots and story concepts, he was forced to make a sudden, full-on transition between the worlds of fandom and professional comics creators.

Roy Thomas became the first of a new breed of comics creators—the fan-turned-pro, who had grown up reading comic books, had been active as a fan of them, and was now creating them for a new generation of readers. Far from being passive consumers of the "culture industry" that creates the comic books they read, these fans become an active part of their very production, effectively "writing back" to the comics that they enjoyed as readers. This was the ultimate expansion of Thomas's own belief, as summarized by scholar Peter Coogan, in "the mere proliferation of superhero titles as proof that fans were influencing the output of comics companies" (Coogan 2010, 60). Now the fans were not only influencing the comic companies, but were a part of them, and created their own work that was included in the ongoing tapestry of stories they enjoyed.

Often this wave of creators who followed in Thomas's path crafted new work that drew upon the stories they had read as fans, recasting those older works in the context of new styles of storytelling, new rules of continuity, and new estimations of cultural memory. Their stories featured tighter, more complex stories that referred back to previous tales, asking readers to not just pick up an individual issue but also to be an ongoing audience of a particular title and a particular publisher. The advent of the fan-turned-pro was crucial in the evolution of continuity (retroactive or otherwise) into a driving force behind the DC and Marvel "universes," and indeed was even behind this very conceptualization of them *as* fully realized universes. In order to create a universe out of what had originated as disparate stories, though, these new creators needed to revisit older stories and figure out how they could fit inside of the "rules" established for contemporary stories that, playing to an audience of adult fans as much as to children, called for a bit more pseudoscientific realism in their explanation of superheroic happenings. As such, new stories frequently worked to actively rewrite older ones through retconning.

This specific form of retcon is a way for fans-turned-pros to engage with history and memory, both in terms of the fictional universe/continuity within which they are writing and the real world context in which those older stories were originally created. As a result, retconning that deals with specific historical instances, such as World War II, reveals how superhero universe narratives constitute a body of historiography. The ways in which historical events are narrativized in superhero comic books alter along with the prevailing historical modes of their time; thus the patriotic narratives of American exceptionalism told during World War II slowly give way to revisionist, interrogatory stories in the 1970s and 1980s. I use the term *revisionism* here as a form of reexamining the past in light of contemporary mores, as well as the discovery of new data. As Aviezer Tucker explains,

> Historiography, our beliefs about the past, history, is in constant flux; our beliefs are constantly being revised. In that sense, all historians who conduct research are "revisionists." . . . Historiography is a progressive and innovative discipline composed of various dynamic research programs precisely because it is capable of revising itself, constantly improving itself, expanding knowledge and becoming relevant in new historical contexts. (1)

Though the chief example of historical revisionism for many people is Holocaust denial, there is an important distinction to be drawn between revision and denial. Denial does not rely upon the methods and standards of historical research, but rather explicitly rejects such processes, standing outside of actual historiography and relying instead on entrenched biases. Tucker explains, "When historians prove *using evidence and standard historiographic methods* that there was a Holocaust, the revisionists can and do fall back on disputing the epistemic standards of mainstream historiography" (3, emphasis in original). Furthermore, he points out, "A uniquely heterogeneous community of historians . . . agree that there was a Holocaust. 'Revisionist historians' who deny it compose a homogeneous community composed exclusively of Nazis or Nazi sympathizers" (5).

Historical revisionism is a cultural project and not a conspiratorial or solely political one. This chapter will show that, through superhero comic book retcons, and their reflection of the narrative construction of an ongoing "universe," we can see how historiography is not just a process that impacts textbooks and college professors, but rather an ongoing method of dealing with and reflecting upon the past, even in the most seemingly innocuous and "popular" of places. By looking at several creators' interpretations of DC Comics' World War II superteam, the Justice Society of America, I will show how the advent of the fan-turned-pro in the 1970s and 1980s, culminating in Roy Thomas's *All-Star Squadron* series, led to an interest in constantly revisiting and revising the teams' historical origins. This will not only display the literary and historiographical uses of retroactive continuity in a superhero "universe," but will also allow us to view the process of historical revisionism at work in stories that reevaluate the meanings and complexities of the Second World War. One way to begin examining the ongoing negotiation of these complexities is with the evolving answers that creators have come up with to the question, "Why couldn't Superman have won World War II single-handedly?"

Superman vs. Hitler

When the United States entered World War II in 1941, Superman was already a cultural phenomenon. *Action Comics*, the home to the character, sold 900,000 copies a month; Superman's newspaper comic strip appeared in 250 papers; and the hero himself had become "a ubiquitous comic art figure" (Gordon 132). However, most of the readers of his comic book adventures were children, who rarely questioned the logic of the stories they were being presented with. As such, it posed little or no problem to them that Superman could be on the cover of a comic book selling war bonds while, on the inside, he was featured in stories where he dealt with mad scientists or mob bosses in the United States instead of joining the armed forces in battling the Axis powers.

However, Superman's creators, Jerry Siegel and Joe Shuster, first-generation sons of Jewish immigrants, naturally wondered what it would take to stop the powerful forces of the Nazis and their Allies. In February 1940, Siegel and Shuster created a two-page strip—entitled "How Superman Would End the War"—in *Look* magazine, before America was even officially involved in the war, presenting how Superman would "solve the international situation." In this short story, Superman flies first to Germany and then to Russia, where he scoops up Adolf Hitler and Joseph Stalin, bringing them to the League of Nations, pronouncing, "Gentlemen, I've brought you the two power-mad scoundrels responsible for Europe's present ills." *Look*, normally in black and white, added an extra color, red, especially for the strip, in order to highlight the level of action being portrayed as Superman races through battlefields, engaging in such superhuman feats as twisting a cannon into a knot and tearing the tops off of concrete bunkers.

The most important aspect of this strip is the juxtaposition of Superman—a character created by two young Jewish men to stand in as the ultimate immigrant, having traveled to Earth from the distant planet Krypton—against Hitler and Stalin. The two powerful dictators are like ragdolls in the superhero's hands, with Hitler screaming, "Put me down! You're hurting me!" Superman is dismissive of them, infantilizing them by cheekily calling them by their first names and telling Hitler, while dealing with his guards, "I'll get around to you in a few seconds." Most importantly, though, Siegel and Shuster have Superman highlight the fact that he is standing in for what they wish *they* could do to Hitler, by having the hero proclaim, "I'd like to land a strictly non-Aryan sock on your jaw."

Hitler and Stalin are seen here to be no more than bullies, using their brawn to push people around until a more powerful force—Superman—comes to punish them. When he brings the pair to the League of Nations, their sentence highlights this portrayal, as they stand like two frowning children in front of a judge who announces, "Adolf Hitler and Josef Stalin—we pronounce you guilty of modern history's greatest crime—unprovoked aggression against defenseless countries." The story ends with this proclamation, and Superman stands behind the dictators, hands on his hips in an authoritarian pose.

Outside of this strip, one that wasn't even technically published by DC Comics, Superman was not involved in World War II in any of his contemporary comic book adventures. Instead, he was seen on comic book *covers* encouraging the purchase of war bonds, a real-world application of his popularity rather than a fictional representation of how he might use his powers during wartime. The *Look* short story was enough to show precisely how Superman would end World War II, were he to be involved—quickly and without difficulty.

Superman's compatriots in the Justice Society, however, were on the whole far less powerful than he. As historian William W. Savage Jr. notes, "the credibility, and ultimately the utility, of the heroes were to be maintained" (10), and thus publishers felt the need to explain why their heroes did not end the war. Several writers would meet this question with a variety of answers, each "according to the characteristics of their heroes" (Savage, 10). In the June/July 1942 issue of *All-Star Comics*, the first to be produced after America's entrance into the war, all of the members of the Justice Society (the world's first superhero team) decide to temporarily disband so that they can join the armed forces in their civilian identities.

After the bombing at Pearl Harbor, writer Gardner Fox brought a sense of outrage to the pages of *All-Star Comics* #11, entitled "The Justice Society Joins the War on Japan." The introductory page of this issue proclaims, "The Justice Society of America (JSA) explodes with righteous indignation. They, too, demand their chance to fight for the country they love best" (11). The story that follows portrays what happens when the members decide to temporarily disband the JSA in order to individually enlist in the military. The successes of the heroes leads to the various branches of the armed forces squabbling over which hero is best, until a ranking officer ultimately informs the Justice Society that "the army needs you, but I can't have my officers squabbling because of divisional pride and loyalty—so I have wired Washington for permission to make you a special battalion . . . to be known as the Justice Battalion of America!" (66). With that, the matter, and the issue, is concluded, but not before Hawkman provides the moral of the story for the reader: "We all do the job we're assigned in the best manner we can—and that's all anyone can ask!" (66).

Unlike Siegel and Schuster's short tale of Superman ending the war singlehandedly, in this issue the Justice Society's members actively engage in battle with Japanese forces, coming out the winners in specific, small-scale battles, which, presumably, don't affect the long-term course of the war. Though they are able to help out in certain instances, they don't change the tide of war in the way that Superman could/would. Fox is in this way able to send his patriotic superteam to war for the United States, but in a way that doesn't automatically mean that they would be able to end that war.

However, the problem still remains that any action the Justice Society could take on behalf of the war effort would serve as a fictional distortion of the actual war. As Roy Thomas sees it, to examine these stories, "is to lay bare the problems inherent in the comic books' early approach to total war. In the . . . Real World, of course, the embattled U.S. forces—unlike the JSA in *All Star* #11—didn't manage to save the Philippines or Wake Island from the Japanese, let alone to liberate Formosa" (Thomas 1997, 7). However, he finds an inherent value in these fictional victories: "Still, all that said, the JSA and their fellow super-heroes gave Americans hope—even if it *was* hope laced with a brand of cockeyed optimism [that] was quickly dashed" (Thomas 1997, 7, emphasis in original). The Justice Society's adventures may have been against fictional aspects of the Nazi threat, but there seems to have been a real concern by their creators to use the superheroes in order to keep US morale up and thus aid the war effort (in the same way as those covers of Superman selling war bonds were helping).

The stateside Justice Battalion was thus able to continue to be patriotic, fighting America's foes using their superheroic powers and abilities, while at the same time having little discernible impact on the "real" war being fought by the armed forces, many of whom were becoming avid readers themselves thanks to the comic books that were part of their care packages. Because the Justice Society could not go after the "real" villains of the war, such as the fascist dictators behind the Axis powers or their ideological allies in the United States, Fox was forced to create fictional threats for them to face while the war and its many atrocities continued as contextual background.[1] Readers at the time accepted this, since it would have been more unbelievable to them for the Justice Society to end the war and then continue on with peacetime adventure. As those readers matured and look back on the comics of their youths, however, they began to realize that such a circumstance made the Justice Society appear far less heroic and efficacious, even in the fictional context of the DC Universe. Thus, decades later, fans-turned-pros would come back to the Justice Society and retcon their wartime adventures so as to remove the tarnish from their heroic luster and "explain" why they didn't engage in World War II in any real, meaningful way. Chief among these fans was Roy Thomas.

The Invaders and Conservative Continuity

Though Thomas had wanted the chance to write further adventures of his childhood Justice Society heroes from the moment of his entry into the comic book industry, one major problem stood in his way—he worked for the wrong company. After personal problems with DC editor Mort Weisenger drove him to Marvel Comics in 1965, he worked with a stable of characters that were mostly created earlier in the 1960s. Though he didn't have fond memories of reading their stories as a child, he did his best chronicling their adventures, learning the skills and techniques of a professional comic book writer along the way. Once he had established himself as a successful writer and editor, he was finally able to get as close to the Justice Society as he could while working for Marvel, by creating Marvel's own World War II superhero team, the Invaders.

Prior to Thomas's invention of the Invaders, the Marvel Universe's answer to the Justice Society had been a two-issue run of *All Winners Comics* in 1946 featuring the aptly named "All-Winners Squad," a conglomeration of several of Marvel (then-Timely) Comics' most popular superheroes. However, as Thomas notes, this was an extremely short-lived team-up: "in the late 40's, there were two adventures of an All-Winners Squad, featuring the Big Three [Captain America, the Human Torch, and Namor the Sub-Mariner] (plus their side-kicks Bucky and Toro) plus the super-fast Whizzer and a bespectacled Miss America—then *Zilch*" (1975). The squad was so short lived that, in an article in *Alter Ego* (the first superhero fanzine, cofounded by Thomas and Professor Jerry Bails) published before Thomas became a professional, he called it an "apparently stillborn JSA-type group" (Thomas 1961, 2). As a JSA fan working for Marvel, Thomas was interested in seeing a fully realized Justice Society-type concept for the Marvel Universe, but he would have to wait for a decade into his professional career before that idea came to fruition.

By the mid-1970s Thomas had become Marvel's editor-in-chief, succeeding Stan Lee, the cocreator of most of Marvel's popular characters. When Thomas eventually stepped down from that role, he found himself in the position of being able to create a new title, and he finally saw the opportunity to, in his words, "do the kind of superhero group I'd always wanted to find in those old wartime [Marvel] comics, but rarely did—and I'd do it with (inevitably, unavoidably) a 1970's perspective!" (1975). What this 1970s perspective meant, in practice, was that Thomas would tell stories set in WWII that adhered to the demands of a stricter sense of continuity—a conservative sense of "realism" and a maintenance of the status quo.

Comic book continuity is an inherently conservative notion, concerned as it is with establishing a set of uniform rules of verisimilitude for a fictional universe to which all stories told in that universe must adhere. The desire for consistency and fidelity is what lies at the base of comic book continuity's origins, when the first wave of fans in the 1960s demanded more "adult" and "realistic" explanations for such unrealistic concepts as super powers and alternate dimensions. Embedded within this notion of a consistent continuity is a desire for control. In a world that frequently seems to be providing less and less control to individual citizens, there is a sense of comfort to be found in a fictional world that strictly, even slavishly, adheres to a set of rules. This is part of the appeal of a superhero universe where every story *must* fit into a larger picture and must make sense when held up to other stories in that universe.

However, this can also be burdensome to creators. Writer Lance Parkin notes, in reference to the long-running multimedia *Dr. Who* franchise, which has its own unique set of continuity concerns, "As a series becomes a long-running one, often the involvement of the original creators diminishes, and the weight of internal history and audience expectations begins to affect the stories themselves. Fashions and tastes change, and writers have to make choices about how the series will reflect that" (13). Indeed, as *Doctor Who* novelist Kate Orman admits, "from an authorial point of view, it always comes back to, 'what can I use, what should I try not to contradict?' A practical definition of 'continuity' or 'canon'" (Cornell and Orman, 36). Creators, then, not just fans, find themselves immersed, whether they want to be or not, in the flowing tides of continuity that engulf the fictional realms they are writing for and about. To them, continuity often consists of a system of rules, of what can/can't be used and what can/can't be contradicted.

Perhaps the first sustained reflection upon the nature of superhero continuity in general, and more specifically on its limitations, came from semiotician and critic Umberto Eco, in his analysis of the first superhero, "The Myth of Superman." In the essay, Eco compares Superman to heroes of ancient mythology, noting that a key difference between the two is the fact that, while Superman's story is one of accretion, myths are stories with a beginning and an end, embodying "a law or a universal demand, and therefore must be in part *predictable* and cannot hold surprises for us" (148, emphasis in original). Eco's problem with Superman, then, is that at the end of any given story he "has made a gesture which is inscribed in his past and which weighs on his future ... [and he] has taken a step toward death, he has gotten older, if only by an hour" (150). Thus, "*To act* ... for Superman, as for any other character ... means to 'consume' himself" (150, emphasis in original). In order to avoid this problematic situation, and to keep telling Superman stories in perpetuity, the writers of Superman, according to Eco, have devised a "shrewd" solution in which "The stories develop in a kind of oneiric climate—of which the reader is not aware at all—where what has happened before and what has happened after appear extremely hazy. The narrator picks up the strand of the event again and again, as if he had forgotten to say something and wanted to add details to what had already been said" (153).

When Eco wrote his essay, in the early 1960s, the "oneiric climate" did, indeed, dominate superhero stories, as the earliest form of continuity—things had happened before each issue, and things would happen after each, but the links between events were loosely knit, without relying upon direct cause-and-effect logic. However, this all changed with the advent of the Stan Lee-helmed "Marvel Age" in the mid-1960s, during which Lee (as writer/editor), along with a handful of artists, created a cohesive tapestry out of the Marvel Comics universe, in which change did occur, characters aged, and the events of one comic book were reflected in future stories told within that universe.[2] With this new type of storytelling, the oneiric climate was shattered, leading to various solutions to the thorniest of continuity issues—the aging of superheroes, bringing them ever closer to "death." As fan Kevin Gould has noted, there were a multitude of solutions to this problem—real-time aging, time moving faster or slower than real time at different ratios, sudden aging or de-aging by decree of a writer or editor, or plot points (such as a magical serum or a parallel universe) that give a character extended life. Gould equates Eco's oneiric climate to what he calls "The Suspended Aging Method," wherein characters do not age at all. As he points out, though, since the Superman stories of the 1940s through 1960s, superhero comics have made a greater attempt at realism, and that "a realistic world has replaced a fantasy world, and the reader is somewhat startled when they realize the Superman who was in his early 30s way back in 1938 is still that age (if not younger) 48 years later in 1987" (47). Whether oneiric or suspended, in its limitations on development in both character and plot, comic book continuity is inherently conservative.

Retconning often, though not always, possesses the same conservative sensibility as continuity itself. It can be used to square the fictional history of the comics universe with the history of the real world, despite the immense deviation of the existence, in the former, of beings with superhuman powers. In other cases, retconning allows for a character to stay young despite appearing in decades worth of stories. Thus, Bruce Wayne never ages past the point at which he can still physically perform as Batman, despite the fact that he would likely be dead by now if he were to have aged in real time.[3] Ultimately, superhero readers are fearful of anything that creates too much change to the mythology that they grew up reading, which they cling to nostalgically, and the resultant conservative impulse to embrace the traditional rather than the experimental is one of the hallmarks of continuity, retroactive or otherwise. Retroactive continuity allows for these fictional myths to remain ongoing and never-ending, forsaking the new in favor of the traditional, the fantastic in favor of the pseudo-real, and the historical aberration in favor of the historically accurate. As with the epics of oral societies, changes are made in order to maintain tradition. This is the kind of retconning that would become Roy Thomas's stock in trade.

By the 1970s, comics were beginning to achieve a modicum of artistic and cultural respect, as noted in a 1972 book about the collecting of paper antiques and memorabilia: "You will also find that more and more museums and galleries are featuring the comics as a true art form and exhibiting the works of some of the masters, past and present" (Hechtlinger and Cross 157). However, the superhero revival of the 1960s had grown to such an extent that the costumed figures now dominated the comics industry in a way they hadn't since the early 1940s, with DC's revived heroes and Marvel's new wave of heroes taking the lion's share of both the sales charts and whatever mainstream media coverage there was of the art form. Fans were thus starting to demand more out of those superhero stories, including character developments and elements of soap opera.

As a result, one of the most important aspects of the genre at this time was a more solidified approach to continuity than had existed in the 1930s and 1940s. Fans who had enjoyed superhero stories as children with little concern about where they "fit" into a larger narrative were now demanding that bigger picture. Just as many young radicals age into conservative voters, the children whose imaginations had no limit were becoming older and more conservative in their fantasy lives, and wanted their comics to abide by the set of rules that continuity provided. Particularly in the wake of the turbulence of the late 1960s, the demand for increased continuity in the 1970s was unprecedented.

When Roy Thomas set out to "do the kind of superhero group I'd always wanted to find in those old wartime comics, but rarely did," he meant that he would create a group of World War II superheroes who existed in a superhero universe that lived up to 1970s standards of continuity, more reliant on pseudo-scientific reasoning, logical consistency, and (relative) historical fidelity than the extremely loose continuity of the 1940s. Indeed, in the text page in the back of the Invaders' very first appearance, Thomas notes his abandonment of some of those older stories: "We're ordinarily not going to consider ourselves bound by anything which occurred in the old Timely mags unless we *also* verify it in the 'Invaders' tales themselves" (Thomas, "Another Agonizingly Personal Recollection"). Here, Thomas deliberately sets up the "rules" by which he will be creating the book, indicating an adherence to continuity that had not been present in the "old Timely mags" he's drawing upon as a part of his retconning project.

In the Invaders' first full-length appearance, *Giant-Size Invaders* 1, Thomas sets out to provide an origin for the superteam, and a reason for them to remain together as a fighting force. This is something that the Justice Society itself did not even have at the time. Although initially the Invaders meet by chance, and fight against a common Nazi foe, it is none other than British prime minister Winston Churchill who advises them to stay together. After the heroes save his transatlantic ship, and thus his life, he tells them, "I implore you—swear to me you'll shelve your own petty squabbles for the duration! Surely, until our two nations are ready to invade Hitler's conquered continent—his 'Fortress Europa'—you five shall act as our own unofficial invaders, eh? Yes, yes . . . of course you shall."

In comparison to the Justice Society's original 1940s adventures, these 1970s-penned stories of the Invaders featured the titular heroes actually going to battle in Europe rather than merely fighting threats on the American home front. Their ability to change history, though, is mitigated by three specific factors. First, the Invaders are, on the whole, a less powerful team than the Justice Society. Marvel's characters often fit into real-world geopolitics a bit more comfortably due to their more limited powers, as opposed to the almost god-like heroes published by DC. Second, DC's wartime heroes were far more numerous than Marvel's handful of Invaders. Finally, Thomas created a multitude of powerful WWII-era villains for the Invaders to face; as he noted, in reference to the original Marvel stories of the 1940s, "where were the sensational *super-villains* which are such an integral part of today's comics scene? Except for [Captain America's arch-nemesis] the Red Skull, there was hardly a super-baddie" (Thomas, "Another Agonizingly Personal Recollection"). Thus, the Invaders could "invade" Europe and fight off these super-foes while the rest of the war ran true to history.

Thomas's *Invaders* is a conservative piece of retroactive continuity that establishes a superteam in Marvel's 1940s, but prohibits them, by the "rules" of continuity, from significantly altering the course of World War II in any way.[4] What worked for Marvel, however, would not work for DC, with its more numerous, and more powerful, heroes. When Thomas moved from Marvel to DC in the 1980s, he would craft a different explanation for why the Justice Society did not end World War II. Once again this displays how retroactive continuity can be used by a fan-turned-pro to "speak back" to the stories of his/her youth in a way that maintains the conservative continuity called for by vocal aspects of comics fandom. Thomas, however, favored this conservative continuity while at the same time providing a more radically liberal view of traditional historical narratives.

The Return of the All-Stars

In 1975, Thomas's friend Gerry Conway left Marvel to write and edit for DC Comics, home of the original Justice Society. After this switch-up, according to Thomas, he and Conway were "kicking around some ideas for new projects he could initiate at DC. Gerry had plenty of his own concepts of course—but on a whim, I suggested a revival of *All-Star Comics*" (Thomas 2002, 4). Conway took this idea and ran with it, and in autumn of 1975 he brought back the Justice Society's *All-Star Comics* title, restarting it at issue 58 (the final Justice Society *All-Star* story, before the book changed title and format to *All-Star Western* in 1951, had been issue 57). The series chronicled the adventures of the Justice Society in the 1970s. These stories, however, were set on DC's "Earth 2," an alternate dimension that featured the Justice Society and other of DC's heroes from the 1930s and 1940s, distinct from the present-day, revised versions of the characters who lived on "Earth 1," featured in the rest of DC's publishing line. This distinction would prove important in later years, as Thomas would create stories altering relatively small historical details of World War II, with the excuse that this was how events transpired on Earth 2, as opposed to the more true-to-reality chronicle of history on Earth 1.

Conway, however, was not as interested in the *history* of the Justice Society as Thomas was, but instead concerned himself with continuing their adventures in the present day. As such, the original Justice Society members were older, most of them having come out of "retirement" to join together and fight the forces of injustice once again. They also added three new, younger members to the team. This emphasis on youth and newness, though, did not prevent Conway from pre-soliciting letters for the first issue from two Justice Society history buffs, Professor Jerry Bails and Roy Thomas (cofounders of *Alter Ego*, the very first superhero comic fanzine), standing in as the voice of Justice Society fandom. Bails exclaimed, "You did it! You managed to breathe new life into the Justice Society of America without changing it beyond recognition . . . But I especially like the continuity with past stories. This is most important, and I thank you for it." Conway's run on *All-Star Comics* began with positive notices from the two men recognized as being most closely associated with JSA fandom, allowing him to move forward, with their blessing, in continuing the Justice Society's ongoing story.

Conway's successor on the title was another fan-turned-pro named Paul Levitz, whose work on *All-Star Comics* was among his first professional writing credits. His run on the book proved him to be firmly entrenched in the traditions of fandom, displaying the interest in long-term continuity that was a hallmark of early fans. Within three issues of taking over *All-Star Comics*,

Levitz began to downplay the book's title on its cover, instead making the text announcing the book's stars, "The Legendary Justice Society of America," much larger and more prominent (Wildman 154). Levitz would later remark about this change, "Guess I'm a traditionalist" (quoted in Thomas 2002, 17).

Levitz would prove himself to be not only a Justice Society traditionalist, but also an innovator, as he became the writer who first provided the team with their "Secret Origin." This was an act of retconning at its finest, inserting a story into the narrative fabric of the DC Universe that had not been there previously in order to create a "logical" reason for the superheroes of the 1940s to join together in such a team. Levitz notes that he did "enjoy fitting the retro pieces in," and, just as importantly, that he's "a bit of a history buff" (quoted in Thomas 2002, 17). These two interests collided in his origin story for the Justice Society, released in the summer of 1977 as *DC Comics Special* #29. This was the first time that the story of how the Justice Society came together as a team was "revealed," and it was set in the pre–World War II, New Deal America from which the original *All-Star Comics* stories had emerged. The caption on the opening page, appearing before even the story's title, clearly sets this time frame: "In the winter of 1940, Adolf Hitler abandoned plans to invade England! To this day, no one knows why—no one but the ten heroes who battled across two continents to ruin those plans—and give birth to a legacy!" (1). Levitz culled this opening circumstance from historical fact—in 1940, Germany did, indeed, indefinitely postpone its plan, Operation Sea Lion, to invade the United Kingdom. While in reality this postponement was most likely due to Germany's defeat in the Battle of Britain, Levitz utilizes it as a historical curiosity, a "mystery" around which he could weave his story.

With the benefit of hindsight not available to writers of the original Justice Society stories, who were crafting their narratives as the war unfolded, Levitz was able, for the first time, to retroactively insert a JSA story into the actual fabric of World War II, without creating circumstances that would change the outcome of the war. This clearly displays a change in attitude among writers and readers from the 1940s to the 1970s; in the latter era, we see an increasing demand for realism in superhero stories, where suspension of disbelief allows for an audience to believe that a man can fly, but not that that flying man changed the outcome of World War II. Again, this change can be accounted for based on the fact that comic book audiences of the 1970s, or at least the vocal parts of the audiences (that is, organized fandom), were adult readers whose fantasy realms required an application of logic and realism to otherwise magical thinking and plotting, something which was not an issue for the mostly child audiences of the 1940s.

This is, once again, the inherent conservatism of continuity in action. Fans demand not only fidelity to past storylines within the fictional universe, but also to past events in the chronicle of their own history. The massive superhero universes of DC and Marvel Comics, worlds of escapism for readers and writers both, conservatively reflect the "real world." They never diverge so far as to actually alter the fabric of lived history in the way that stand-alone, out-of-continuity stories are able to.[5] As comics creator John Byrne explains, after years of creating stories and characters for DC and Marvel, he yearned for "a virgin 'universe,' one more like our own—the mythic 'World Outside Your Window.' . . . A world that would have trundled along, just like our own, until the day strange beings appeared—super-heroes for lack of a better term—which would forever alter the course of that world's history. Unlike traditional comic-book universes, it would change, and change drastically" (4–5).

While stand-alone projects are free to take their narratives to whatever extreme imaginable—up to, and including, the end of the world—stories that are set in the firmaments of DC or Marvel's "universes" adhere to a general rule that the events of history unfurled as they did in the world outside the windows of readers. Levitz's "Untold Origin of the Justice Society" is a perfect example of such conservative narratives. In the prologue, he takes great pains to set the historical moment in which the story takes place: "1940: The Nazi juggernaut sweeps across Europe, but 'World War Two' has not officially begun . . . for America has not entered the war . . . yet. Franklin Delano Roosevelt has just been re-elected for an unprecedented third term as president, and he has promised America peace . . . a promise he is hard-pressed to keep" (2). In this context, Roosevelt is visited by a representative of "Intrepid," the code name for William Stephenson, the head of British intelligence for the Western hemisphere during World War II. The representative comes bearing news of "reliable information" about Hitler's plans to invade England and asks Roosevelt for American help. Roosevelt's response, in this pre–Pearl Harbor context, is that, "As God is my witness, you know I want to help, but I am the president of this great nation—not the king. And I have promised my friends, the American people, that I would not lead them into war—not unless we were attacked!" (3). In order to avoid all-out war with Germany, but still provide assistance to Britain, Roosevelt secretly gathers together a group of American superheroes to send into Europe and help stave off invasion. When the heroes ultimately save the day, the grateful president notes that "it's a shame you can't stay together that way—you'd make a snappy Army regiment!" (33). Superman, though, has the final word over Roosevelt, proclaiming, "We're not part of any army. We fight only in the cause of justice . . . and that'll give us our name . . . the Justice Society of America" (33).

President Roosevelt's bookend role as the figure responsible for calling the Justice Society together positions him as every bit as much of a hero as the team's members, with the story failing to question or interrogate his historical policies in any way. While the Justice Society members are fictional constructs who can always follow the most "moral" course, Roosevelt, like any other political leader, was a far more three-dimensional figure. In 1977, though, just after the bicentennial, American exceptionalism would not allow for a story to criticize the president who had "saved" America from the Nazis. This would even mean that stories featuring Roosevelt would downplay his role in initiating the New Deal, a policy that was as controversial to many conservative Americans in the 1970s as it had been during the war.[6] Roosevelt is portrayed as practically a full Justice Society member, using all the resources that he can to help the British while still keeping his "promise" to his "friends," the American people. It would be several more years before readers saw any actual questioning of Roosevelt's policies in a Justice Society story.

Nevertheless, in Levitz's final Justice Society story he *was* able to use the JSA's history to interrogate the politics of a different historical figure—Senator Joe McCarthy. The story reveals the moment of, as the title calls it, "The Defeat of the Justice Society!" This tale is set in 1951, and is used, like the origin story, to add in a retcon, in this case explaining why the team disbanded and "retired" in the 1950s and early 1960s. The JSA is defeated here not by any evil scientist or power-mad supervillain, but rather by the United States Congress. After bringing in a criminal to the Department of Justice, the JSA is summoned before a special hearing by "The Combined Congressional Un-American Activities Committee," who are investigating "the activities of the so-called Justice Society of America" (441). The committee is meant to evoke the Senate Permanent Subcommittee on Investigations headed by Senator Joseph McCarthy in the 1950s, famously used as a "witch hunt" against potential communist allies. Thus, the JSA is concerned when the unnamed senator who calls the hearing to order notes that the criminal they brought in was "a known agent of a hostile foreign power" (442). The senator demands to know their connection to the criminal, claiming that the committee isn't directly accusing them of anything but does want them to undergo security checks. The shadowed figure next to this senator is then revealed as a dead-on likeness of McCarthy, who agrees that "We know nothing about you except the few facts that you've given reporters, and that is not enough. This is a closed session of a Congressional committee—and by that authority I ask you. If you are good Americans, you will show this committee your faces—and then we may begin the process of clearing you" (443).

Aghast at this request, the Justice Society, through their chairman, Hawkman, replies, "We respectfully decline, Senator. Our faces—our names—our lives, are our own business. Don't worry . . . you won't be hearing from us again" (443). With that, the team disappears and officially leaves the public eye for more than a decade.

Whereas Levitz had heroicized President Roosevelt to the point of having him be the founder of the Justice Society, in this story he portrays Senator McCarthy as a villain, the shadowy mastermind behind a vicious plot to attack the JSA on moral grounds. In the following scene, in which two younger members of the 1970s JSA are discussing the historical hearing, one of them notes that "It was a different world then . . . a sick, sad world a few men had twisted out of shape," and specifically calls out McCarthy as "Simply a madman who got himself a little power, and started to use it to crush people" (444). Levitz, like many comic book creators, reveals himself to be politically left leaning, heralding the architect of the New Deal while demonizing the anticommunist crusader.

By 1979, the time this story was published, it was clearly possible for comics creators to use their stories in order to play in the fields of history and memory. In two stories set in different historical contexts, Levitz evokes imagery of a beleaguered-but-heroic president who wants to do what's best for the American people and of a power-mad senator who sets America on a vicious course. Celebration and critique are equally potent aspects of the way a culture remembers and shares its past, and these two stories show that memory at work as a vital part of these moments of retroactive continuity. Such a process would come into play even more solidly in the very book that first printed the term *retroactive continuity*, Roy Thomas's *All-Star Squadron*.

The All-Star Squadron

In 1981, Roy Thomas's lifelong dream finally came true, when he found himself the writer of a new, ongoing DC comic starring the Justice Society, as part of a larger team of "Earth 2" World War II–era heroes, the newly dubbed "All-Star Squadron" (named in honor of the JSA's old home in *All-Star Comics*). The series, also titled *All-Star Squadron*, reflected Thomas's dual obsessions with both the 1940s superheroes and the history of the war. He explains that he "felt most 1940s DC stories should be counted as 'canonical' (i.e., as having 'actually occurred' on Earth-Two), [so] the events of *All-Star Comics* . . . were woven in and out of the *Squadron* issues as the events recounted in them were reached chronologically" (2000, 199). In an introduction to a collected edition of several original issues of *All-Star Comics*, Thomas further notes that "*All Star Comics* and World War II . . . are forever linked in my mind" (1997, 5). When he first discovered the Justice Society in 1950, coming across a used copy of one of the team's early adventures, "two of my main interests of my later life—comic books and history—came crashing together with as much force as a couple of electrons in an atom-smasher!" (1997, 5). Once he was finally given creative control of his boyhood heroes, he continued to collide those two interests, interweaving the JSA's original continuity with retroactive continuity and the actual history of World War II. Fan historian Kurt Mitchell assesses this duel fascination, noting that "The war itself was a major character . . . the series interwove authentic history with explorations of Golden Age continuity and plenty of new storylines, providing the verisimilitude that rooted the Squadron's fantastic adventures in reality" (96). As Thomas would later put it, "Old super-heroes, like old soldiers, never die. They just get redefined" (2002, 26).

Thomas's redefinition of the Justice Society would nevertheless build upon definitions of the past. In the opening moments of *All-Star Squadron*, he carried on the narrative tradition established by Levitz before him that President Roosevelt was a heroic figure, practically an honorary member of the Justice Society. The very first scene of the series portrays Roosevelt attempting to call the JSA at their headquarters, noting to his aide, Harry Hopkins, that "we've already waited as long as we dare . . . perhaps too long! But—why in heaven's name don't they answer? Why?" ("The All-Star Squadron" 1). The captions that close the story expand upon his concern, explaining that, "Meanwhile, from delivery trucks all over the capital, the next morning's newspapers are being delivered to anxious dealers . . . in these first moments of Sunday, December 7, 1941 . . . a date destined to live in infamy . . . !" ("The All-Star Squadron" 14).

As the story continues we learn that a supervillain from the future has traveled back to this "infamous" date specifically in order to kidnap the heroes and prevent them from interfering with the attack on Pearl Harbor. This plot point metatextually gestures to exactly Thomas's purpose with the story, to "finally" explain why the Justice Society, including Superman, were unable to protect Pearl Harbor from Japanese attack despite their massive and varied skills and powers.

This piece of retroactive continuity is emblematic of just how retconning functions, particularly in superhero comics. Here Thomas creates a story that is set in the past—both the historical past of readers and the narrative past of the superheroes he is writing about. In this "newly revealed" story from history, the writer is able to provide an explanation for a question that taxes suspension of disbelief for adult readers. This is ultimately a conservative piece of storytelling, for it is created in order to maintain the equilibrium between the status quo of the fictional world and the real world—this story explains why, despite the ways in which the DC Universe (or, more precisely, DC's "Earth Two" universe) radically differs from the real world, its grand historical narrative of America's direct involvement in World War II remains the same.

Retconning, here as elsewhere, arises out of a desire for continuity, control, and narrative logic, a conservative impulse when compared to the more fantastic and magical elements of stories that eschew reality completely, as many superhero comics in the 1930s and 1940s had. Fans of a world filled with superheroes, especially those fans who become professional/ official chroniclers of this world, demand the narrative closure afforded by explaining inconsistencies such as why those heroes could not prevent the Pearl Harbor attack. To simply have the heroes actually *stop* the attack, and then follow the chain of logic thereafter to a totally changed world, would stretch credulity too much in a superhero universe that touches upon so many different published books and stories, all set in a reality that is ostensibly the same as the one outside the reader's window. Thus the attack on Pearl Harbor *has* to occur. The ongoing narratives of the DC and Marvel universes are not interested in the alternate histories so often explored in science fiction, but rather with creating a "realistic" world in which the superheroes live and interact, but which also strikes a familiar cord with readers as being not too dissimilar from the world they know.

This task of maintaining historical fidelity through retroactive explanations continues in the fourth issue of *All-Star Squadron*, which explains why the Justice Society didn't simply invade Europe and put an end to the Axis forces using their superpowers. During the first storyline, President Roosevelt explains to the three uncaptured members of the JSA, along with several other heroes who have joined up with them on the way to the White House, why he had been trying to contact them the night before:

> I want you of the Justice Society to mobilize every one of this nation's costumed heroes—men and women—into a single, super-powerful unit—a sort of All-Star Squadron, so to speak—responsible to no one but myself! . . . You see, you mysterymen are one of America's greatest natural resources—which we must husband carefully, for the coming struggle with the Nazis! ("The World on Fire!" 23)

Once again, Roosevelt is seen as a founder of a superhero team, this time one that includes *all* of the heroes of the DC Universe active during the 1940s.[7] This becomes the founding concept of the series. The All-Star Squadron is composed of *every* World War II–era Earth 2 hero, and thus has a massive membership, with rotating personnel for any individual mission or in any particular storyline. The speech also places Roosevelt as a heroic central figure in the history of the Justice Society, on par with Superman, Batman, and any of their cohorts.

Thomas was a grand admirer of Roosevelt and his politics, particularly his wartime leadership and the concern for the "everyman" espoused by his New Deal policies. It would seem to be no coincidence, then, that Thomas was heralding Roosevelt's heroism in an era where Ronald Reagan had recently been elected president on a platform that explicitly rejected many of those New Deal beliefs in favor of fiscal conservatism and "trickle down" economics. Part of the iconology that Reagan had used to win the election was associating himself with the mythologized "Good War," even if his own wartime efforts had involved acting rather than fighting. As historian Michael C. C. Adams notes, "Reagan's deep belief in the legitimacy of the movie version of American history made him a living symbol for many Americans of their best war ever and the magic formula for success that they thought was the special possession of the 1940s generation. He was the final embodiment of the movie star as war hero" (16). By espousing this symbolism, "As the grand old man who represented an earlier, simpler, stronger America, Reagan convinced Americans that they could have in the 1980s the world they believed existed in the 1940s, by sheer will" (16). In counterpoint to this image, Thomas associated Roosevelt with the unquestionable heroism of figures like Superman and Batman as a way of defending the politician, heralding him as a superhero among presidents, and recognizing that Reagan and the New Right were in the wrong to assail his legacy.

Indeed, as Thomas would later explain, "It was a privilege to be allowed to show how President Roosevelt would have called every super-hero he could locate into the Oval Office and ask them all . . . to join a single, unified, all-powerful anti-Axis organization 'for the duration.' (Just the kind of thing FDR would've done, too!)" (Thomas 1997, 9). The team, throughout the run of the series, unquestioningly follows Roosevelt's orders, and at the end of the third issue, on his command, they head to Pearl Harbor to examine the aftermath of the Japanese attack. Against FDR's order to investigate only, and to remain on the home front, they head out after the Japanese fleet that they presume the attacking planes must have come from.

The attempt to take the battle to the Japanese forces ends in disaster. While the heroes are flying over the Pacific, Hitler and Japanese emperor Tojo perform a magical rite, utilizing the Spear of Destiny and the legendary Holy Grail, which makes, according to one Japanese agent, "both Hitler's

Fortress Europa and our own Greater East Asia Co-Prosperity Sphere totally impregnable to counterattack by America's most powerful costumed champions!" ("Day of the Dragon King" 17). In practice, this creates a sphere of magical influence over all Axis-occupied territory, anywhere in the world, within which those heroes with magic-based powers, or a special vulnerability to magic, end up turning against their allies and become Axis agents themselves. Unfortunately for the gathered heroes, this includes all of the most powerful All-Star Squadron members, including Superman, Wonder Woman, and the Spectre. As a result, the entire squadron is forced to turn back.

This story serves two purposes. First and foremost, it provides an explanation to the long-held question, on the part of fans, as to why the Justice Society, and Superman in particular, didn't affect or change the outcome of World War II by shortening it significantly. Thomas creates a plot point that prevents the most powerful heroes—those who *could* have a significant impact on the course/history of the war—from entering the battle directly, thus creating a narrative reason for them to remain in the United States and "protect the home front." Once more, we see a piece of retroactive continuity being utilized in order to maintain fidelity to historical reality, yet another moment of continuity as a conservative force. In addition, the story continues the aggrandizing of President Roosevelt, since the Squadron meets such disaster in the Pacific specifically because they disobeyed the president's orders to stay in the United States. Roosevelt is portrayed as knowing better than the heroes themselves—he is their founder and leader, and he directs them to whatever action best serves their country. There are parallels here between how FDR leads the heroes and the ways in which Thomas sees him as having led the country: fairly, justly, and with the best interests of the American people in mind.

Thomas does not stop at Roosevelt in his portrayal of the Allied leaders as the "great men" of history. Early in the run of *All-Star Squadron*, he features several appearances by Winston Churchill, who proves himself to be every bit the heroic leader that Roosevelt is. When Churchill first appears in the series, and meets Roosevelt, a caption explains that, "With the self-assurance that belies his rotund frame, the man [Churchill] strides towards another who half-stands, half-leans against a dark limousine. As he did before, at the signing of the Atlantic charter, the Briton extends a firm hand . . . a hand clasped in friendship" (Thomas, March 1982, 26). The meeting between "POTUS" and "Former Naval Person," as they call each other with tongues in cheek, causes one All-Star Squadron member to remark, "You know, All-Stars . . . I've got a hunch things are gonna go great guns for the Allies from here on" (26). Even the superheroes, it seems, see Roosevelt and Churchill as the two "great men" without whom the war cannot be won by the Allies. Readers who held a different opinion, however, would not let this portrayal go unchallenged.

All-Star Comments

Roy Thomas did not become the editor of *All-Star Squadron* until almost its third year in publication, but from the start, he crafted its letters column ("All-Star Comments"), wrote text pieces, and responded directly to readers' mail. For the first issue, Thomas wrote an "open letter to the readers," wherein he asserts his longtime love for the Justice Society: "ALL-STAR SQUADRON, or something very much like it, is *the* single comic-book I've most wanted to do since I first discovered comics, a good third of a century ago" ("An Open Letter"). He explains that the book will have a focus not just on character and plot, but also on history and, to an extent, education:

> [A] Series set in the early 1940s requires a number of explanatory references not just to comics issues but to everyday events, military/political history of the period, etc. . . . things that might be unclear to many newer or younger readers. . . . [W]e've tried to keep things fairly factual when dealing with the events of the war itself. ("An Open Letter")

It was with such intentions in mind that "All-Star Comments" became a place for debate not just about the history of the Justice Society, but also about the history of World War II. As such, it was a crucial component of the ways in which history was told in *All-Star Squadron*.

It is here, in "All-Star Comments," that we find one of the first printed uses (if not *the* first printed use) of the term *retroactive continuity*: "As for what Roy himself . . . is trying to do, we like to think an enthusiastic ALL-STAR booster at one of Adam Malin's Creation Conventions in San Diego came up with the best name for it, a few months back: 'Retroactive Continuity.' Has kind of a ring, don't you think?" (Thomas, February 1983, 25). Thus, it was within this column that many of the concepts and processes used to create historical revisionism in superhero comics—the very introduction of "retconning" as a term and tool to a fictional universe—were first discussed.

Regarding World War II, though, much of the conversation in "All-Star Comments" would be about minutia, such as makes and models of wartime vehicles and weapons, but Thomas welcomed such discussion. In the sixth issue he notes that "we invite *every* reader of ALL-STAR SQUADRON to send us any . . . goof they spot . . . whether it is a plane flying several years before it was built, or a song played on the radio before its time. Sure, we have to allow ourselves a lot of leeway in order to stop the mag from becoming a history text—but that doesn't mean we're indifferent to our mistakes" (February 1982, 28, emphasis in original).

Whether or not Thomas wanted to prevent the book from becoming a full-on exploration of history, rather than historicized escapist entertainment, the column would quickly become a forum for weightier topics. One issue after the above comment, Thomas discussed how he intended the comic book to be celebratory of American history. In response to a letter exhorting him to not be afraid to "show the utmost pride in our American heritage," Thomas explains, "Despite the well-intentioned and often dead-on-target iconoclasm of the 1960s and early 70s . . . our American heritage is something which we at DC have *never* been ashamed of. And, though ALL-STAR SQUADRON's future issues will deal perhaps with America's lapses as well as her successes, that's precisely the direction which the magazine will continue to go" (March 1982, 28, emphasis in original).

By the tenth issue, though, Thomas was beginning to question this celebratory narrative. Particularly to his credit is the fact that, though he chose which letters would see print, he would frequently run missives that criticized him and the way he chose to portray history. For example, in the first few issues of the comic book, several characters had used the word "Nip" to refer to the Japanese. In issue ten, Thomas notes that

> a Japanese-American co-worker told [me] some years ago that the term was far less offensive than certain others, so it was used in issues #1–5. However, after thinking the matter over, we prefer not to use *any* term which may reasonably seem a racial slur, and sharp-eyed readers will have noted that the phrase has not reappeared since then. Nor will it do so again. We're interested in chronicling the wartime adventures of Earth-Two's greatest heroes—but not in keeping old prejudices and epithets undeservedly alive. (March 1982)

Here we see that Thomas *does* recognize the "prejudices and epithets" of the era in which he has set *All-Star Squadron*, and he evinces an honest desire to avoid such hateful and hurtful language and sensibility. However, and perhaps contrary to his intention, Thomas *is* in a certain sense whitewashing historical reality. In an effort not to hurt or offend contemporary readers, he is ignoring the pervasive linguistic bias against the Japanese during World War II.

Thomas clearly wants to recognize the past for what it was—with a focus on the celebratory, yet an acknowledgment of the regretful—but at the same time he does not want to offend readers' sensibilities. In dealing with such complicated issues, particularly in a popular medium that is meant to provide fictional narratives that are accessible to both children and adults, it is difficult to find a middle ground between historical fidelity and contemporary political correctness.

In a later issue's "All-Star Comments" a reader takes Thomas to task for his portrayal of the Nazi villains in *All-Star Squadron*. Heino G. Moeller, writing from California, argues that

> No one denies the atrocities that were committed by *all* sides during the war, but the persistent focus on the tragic fate of the Jewish people in Europe shows a blatant lack of historical balance. It seems to have become popular in the U.S. mass media to present Germans to the American people as Nazis—brutal, vain, cynical, prejudiced, and above all, *evil*. This simplistic portrayal reinforces stereotypes that defame all Americans of German origin. This type of publicity only provokes a cycle of antagonism and intolerance among ethnic and racial groups. (October 1982, 25, emphasis in original)

In Thomas's response to the letter he does not accuse Moeller of Holocaust denial, but rather explains his narrative choices based on his understanding of the history of the war. He notes that "Pro-democratic Germans, at least in Germany *proper*, had little outlet for their voices or actions in the period covered . . . the battling All-Stars are unlikely to run into non-Nazi Germans" (October 1982, 25, emphasis in original). He then goes on to opine that "the aptly-named 'Holocaust' so dwarfs most other atrocities of World War Two, that we can never apologize for considering, not Germans, but Nazism and those who espoused it, to have been among the greatest curses of mankind" (October 1982, 25). He then finishes his response by explaining that his own ethnic heritage, on both sides, is German, something that has "never been anything he's been either especially proud of *or* ashamed of" (October 1982, 25, emphasis in original). In this exchange, Thomas indicates that he is not blindly following one textbook or another, but rather considering the facts of World War II, as he understands them. From that understanding he has worked to craft a narrative that is at the same time "historically accurate" (insofar as his own interpretations are concerned), inoffensive by contemporary standards, entertaining to readers of escapist fiction, and respectful to those caught up in the many tragedies of the war. That is not to say, however, that he does not end up a bit too traditionalist and celebratory in certain parts of that narrative.

In a later letters column, Thomas is correctly accused of failing to find the middle ground in regards to the two political leaders prominently featured in the early issues of the series—Roosevelt and Churchill. Throughout the run of *All-Star Squadron*, the two men are seen as heroes on par with any of the members of the Squadron, always having the best interests of their countrymen and allies in their hearts and minds. In the letters column of issue 34, reader Carlos Preston calls this portrayal "cloyingly idolatrous," particularly citing the "growing body of historical evidence that suggests that FDR knew in advance that the Japanese were about to attack Pearl Harbor," and that he did nothing in response in order to finally have an "'incident' that he could use as an excuse to draw America into the European war" (June 1984, 25). Similarly, Preston notes a claim from Churchill's secretary that the British prime minister, upon hearing of Pearl Harbor, "shouted hurrah and lifted a toast to his companions . . . and said merrily, 'Now we are saved!'" (June 1984, 25). Preston then criticizes Thomas for his choices in heralding the two men as heroes:

> I realize that you are writing, essentially, fantasy. But I notice what great pains you've taken to render the historical background to your stories as faithfully and exactly as you can (for which you ought to be commended). Perhaps a little more historical research, perhaps a reading of some "revisionist" views of the war and of Roosevelt's and Churchill's roles in it would have shown a very different FDR and Winnie than the ones you have portrayed in your stories thus far. Perhaps not. But I think the real FDR and Churchill were considerably less benign, considerably less noble, than the good people who populate your stories of superheroes. (June 1984, 25)

Thomas responds that, though he thinks "free and healthy exchange of information and opinion is what democracy is all about," he disagrees with Preston's "assessment of many aspects of President Roosevelt and Prime Minister Churchill, that's all. But that's a lot" (June 1984, 25).

Thomas goes on to display his own reading on the subject of World War II, responding to Preston's comments with a specific reference:

> [N]either historian John Toland in his recent book *Infamy* nor the other, earlier accounts of the "Pearl Harbor cover-up" that I have read has really convinced me (or a number of other persons with far more credentials in the field of historical research than either of *us* have, I'm sure) that FDR knew anything more on

December 6–7, 1941, than that the Japanese were about to strike *somewhere*, quite probably against American positions. We're not saying he *didn't*—only that as far as we're concerned, the verdict is still very much *out*. (June 1984, 25, emphasis in original)

However, despite the nuanced understanding of historiography displayed by this statement—a recognition of uncertainty and the subjectivity of personal opinion—Thomas does become a bit overly defensive in claiming that "Far from idolizing Roosevelt or Churchill, especially the former, I find them interesting and important figures whom no one could ever truly 'know.' . . . He could be the most charming and persuasive of men, and that's how I've played him in ALL-STAR SQUADRON" (June 1984, 25). Thomas thus contradicts himself, stating that it is not his intention to idolize Roosevelt, but that he has nevertheless chosen to portray him as "charming and persuasive," to an almost supernatural degree, as we have seen. Thomas's subjective view of Roosevelt, it would seem, errs to the traditionalist opinion of the "great man."

This viewpoint is perhaps understandable given the 1980s context in which Thomas was writing *All-Star Squadron*. Ronald Reagan was being heralded as a similar "great man," one whose conservative values and policies were counteracting the legacy that Roosevelt left behind, a legacy that Thomas admired. By reinstating and reifying Roosevelt's "heroicism," Thomas was attempting to point out that the emperor had no clothes; that is, to hold up a historical "great man" to the present-day one and thereby show that the former was worthy of greater praise.

Such views and conversations show that Thomas was clearly interested in, and educated about, the various facets of World War II and its political and social culture. He may have been accused of being too celebratory in one place, or too derogatory in another, but he certainly showed that he was willing to engage in debate about these issues in the letters column. This debate showcases a tension that is at the very heart of *All-Star Squadron*, and indeed of all historical narratives of the 1980s—the conflict between traditional history and "new history."

The New History of the All-Star Squadron

Throughout his run on *All-Star Squadron*, and its successor title *Young All-Stars*, Roy Thomas was, whether consciously or not, creating an ongoing conversation between traditional historical narrativization and the late-twentieth-century new/cultural historicism in the academy. In the former school of historiography, a narrative is constructed from the "great events" and "great men" of history, using them as a touchstone from which to expound upon the past. In the 1840s, Scottish writer and historian Thomas Carlyle popularized the "Great Men" theory, noting that

> Universal History, the history of what man has accomplished in this world, is at bottom the History of the Great Men who have worked here.... [A]ll things that we see standing accomplished in the world are properly the outer material result, the practical realization and embodiment, of Thoughts that dwelt in the Great Men sent into the world: the soul of the whole world's history, it may justly be considered, were the history of these. (3)

Well into the second half of the twentieth century, it was this version of history, focusing on kings and presidents and prime ministers rather than on the common man, which dominated historical thought and teaching, as well as much historical fiction and drama. Some historians, however, argued that this approach was too narrow. As Robert Brent Toplin explains, in relation to period dramas in film,

> The practice of reporting on good people's struggles against adversity, though it produces attractive drama, raises some problems. Personality-oriented movies give short shrift, for example, to the effect of Collective action or the impact of long-term economic change. Instead of recognizing subtle, complex factors that foster change, these portrayals show progress resulting almost exclusively from the actions of dynamic individuals. (7)

What holds true for historical movies, of course, also holds true for history-minded comics.

Cultural history, however, rejects the concept of a grand narrative, and instead focuses on the broader social/cultural/political picture. This French influence encountered fertile ground in American historiography, as the American Studies movement, which considered untraditional popular sources as a way of understanding American character and the "American mind," had been slowly gaining greater acceptance since its advent around the time of the Great Depression. Historian Eric Foner notes that the "new histories" that emerged from this crucible possessed "an emphasis on the experience of ordinary Americans" and acknowledged that "'politics' now means much more than the activities of party leaders," rejecting the "presidential synthesis," a way of viewing the past that "understood the evolution of American society chiefly via presidential elections and administrations" (ix–xi). In its stead, the new histories "devote attention to the broad political culture or 'public life' of a particular era; others stress the role of the state itself in American history and the ways various groups have tried to use it for their own purposes" (xi–xiii). This new history, focused as it is on fragmentation rather than synthesis, also abandons objectivity as an end-goal, or indeed even a possibility, for historians, preferring instead to point out the subjective point-of-view of any historical narrative.[9]

Thomas's *All-Star Squadron* stories fluctuate constantly between these two ways of viewing the past. In keeping with the inherent conservatism of continuity, and particularly historical retconning used to maintain the "integrity" of real-world history, the stories are obsessed with fidelity to the "grand narrative" of World War II. Stories that explain why the Justice Society couldn't halt Pearl Harbor, or why they didn't fight in occupied Europe, work to establish that real-world grand narrative as part of the DC Universe's history. Similarly, the heroicization of Roosevelt and Churchill, as described above, reflects a conservative, traditionalist respect for the "great men" of World War II whose individual actions were able to shape its outcome.

Thomas's stories *differ* from this conservative historicism, however, when they delve more deeply into the social and cultural history of World War II. While the original Justice Society stories of the 1940s solely told the stories of the superheroes and their various adventures, the *All-Star Squadron* stories, with a perspective of 1980s cultural historicism, explore the impact of the war on not just superheroes, but also average American citizens.

As historian Jill Lenore points out, accounts of wars are particularly fruitful territory in which to explore changing views on historical epochs. She notes that "The words used to describe war have a great deal of work to do: they must communicate war's intensity, its traumas, fears, and glories; they must make clear who is right and who is wrong, rally support, and recruit allies; and they must document the pain of war, and in so doing, help to alleviate it" (ix). Written accounts of war are thus as much of a battlefield as war itself, as most famously reflected in the adage that, "History is written by the victor." Lepore goes so far as to assert that, "wounds and words—the injuries and their interpretations—cannot be separated, that acts of war generate acts of narration, and that both types of acts are often joined in a common purpose: defining the geographical, political, cultural, and sometimes racial and national boundaries between peoples" (x). War is not only remembered in official, sanctioned histories, but also in a culture's broader public memory, which can be and is embodied in popular forms such as superhero comic books.

All-Star Squadron's interpretation of social issues during World War II reflects this sense of redefinition and reinterpretation, particularly in stories touching upon the Detroit Race Riot of 1943 and Japanese internment camps. These two storylines deal with minority groups that were either ignored, or else outright stereotyped, in the original Justice Society stories. The newer stories, with a greater sensitivity to racial inequality and violence, are exemplars of Foner's assertion, "If anything is characteristic of the recent study of American history, it is attention to the experience of previously neglected groups—not simply as an addition to a preexisting body of knowledge but as a fundamental redefinition of history itself" (x). In *All-Star Squadron*, the two "previously neglected groups" that Thomas focuses on are African Americans and Japanese Americans.

In a storyline running from issues 38–40 of the series, a group of the Squadron's heroes watch a newsreel informing them of increasing racial tensions in Detroit, precipitated by "white residents . . . picketing the unoccupied houses of a new negro housing project—the Sojourner Truth homes" ("Detroit Is Dynamite!" 15). The Squadron members take off for Detroit, where they come across a sign in a local diner exclaiming, "Help the white people to keep this district white. Men needed to keep our lines solid" ("Nobody Gets Out of Paradise Valley Alive!" 2). When they confront the locals about it, one man angrily says to them, "We'll see ya around—niggerlovers!" ("Nobody Gets Out of Paradise Valley Alive!" 3).

Despite his earlier promise to keep racial slurs out of *All-Star Squadron*, Thomas is clearly using this vitriolic word in order to portray the depth of the hatred and tensions that ran through Detroit in this era, drawing upon the race riot at Detroit's Sojourner Truth homes in February of 1942. The riot was the result of protest over a government housing project that was moving black workers into a white neighborhood. Violence broke out when black homeowners tried to break through the picket lines that their white neighbors were forming in front of the new houses. Thomas adds the Squadron members into this mix, along with a masked (in this case, the mask of a Ku Klux Klan hood) supervillain named "Real American" (an ironic name meant to pinpoint the hypocrisy of equating racism with what Thomas sees as real American values). Real American incites the crowd to riot and then personally gets into a battle with a local African American hero named Amazing Man. When Amazing Man is defeated, the white police officers arrest him while Real American is allowed to go free. One of the heroes observes, during the riot, "That negro man doesn't even have a weapon—so how come three policemen are on him, and none on the white men who were attacking him a second ago?" ("Nobody Gets Out of Paradise Valley Alive!" 14).

In this story, the "official," celebratory narrative of American solidarity during World War II is called into question. The authorities are seen as being every bit as culpable in the mistreatment of African Americans as the members of the KKK-like group the Phantom Empire are. Such culpability goes all the way to the top as well. In one of the few occasions where Thomas shows Roosevelt in a questionable light, the president explains to the heroes that "My hands are tied, boys. There's a war on . . . that riot, regrettable though it be, is a local matter. Nothing I can do about it" ("Nobody Gets Out of Paradise Valley Alive!" 20). Flying off afterward, Justice Society chairman Hawkman notes that "we may just be working to win one war—while setting the stage for another one—in America itself!" ("Nobody Gets Out of Paradise Valley Alive!" 20).

The final part of the three-issue storyline links the racism of the white crowds, spurred on by Real American and his Phantom Empire backers, with the Nazi threat. The first page of the issue features a quote from a real-life 1942 housing protest placard, stating, "Hitler Supports Housing Discrimination!" ("The Rise and Fall of the Phantom Empire!" 1). When All-Star chairwoman Liberty Belle argues that the racists they have encountered don't represent all Americans, who generally oppose discrimination, teammate Johnny Quick counters with, "Sure—but they're all staying home! That's how a crudhead like Hitler took over Germany!" ("The Rise and Fall of the Phantom Empire!" 9). Thomas is thus not only taking a stand against racist ideology, but also against the passive masses who refuse to take such a stand when confronted by it. Later in the issue, Liberty Belle makes the racist/Nazi equivalency even more explicit, exclaiming to Real American, "We're all Americans—black and white! You're using the same thug-tactics the Nazis used in Austria—Czechoslovakia!" ("The Rise and Fall of the Phantom Empire!" 12).

Though it was easy enough, and noncontroversial, for Thomas to stand against blatant racism in the 1980s, what is more unusual for *All-Star Squadron* is the demonization of World War II victory culture, which is ultimately held responsible for the mistreatment and dehumanization of African Americans on the home front. Because of the singular focus on winning the war, the official state apparatus—from local, possibly racist police, up to a glorified and well-meaning, but ultimately (in this case) impotent president—is not prepared to protect at home the very rights that the country is fighting for overseas.

Thomas was not alone in his reappraisal at this time of the racial politics of World War II. Many scholars, in fact, have traced the beginning of the civil rights movement, which came to a head in the 1960s, with African American struggles and protests during World War II, as "the moment when the structures of Jim Crow began to crack and crumble and a nascent civil rights movement started to take shape" (Kruse and Tuck 3). However, as Kevin M. Kruse and Stephen Tuck argue, African American activist accomplishments during World War II have become embellished over time. It may even be possible that "the war actually marked a *downturn* in black militancy.... because it was followed by the 'bad' years of the Cold War, when anti-communist paranoia at home served to restrict not just the movement of civil rights activists, but their vision for reform itself" (6, emphasis in original).

Nevertheless, African American activists in the 1960s in many ways led the charge for reevaluating the contributions and struggles of American blacks during World War II, and the connection between that movement and the war itself had become part of accepted history by the 1980s. For example, A. Russell Buchanan's 1977 book *Black Americans in World War II* had as its explicit thesis that African Americans during the war "continued their struggle to attain equality of status with other Americans. This narrative summarizes the progress made by Negroes during the course of World War II" (1). Scholars such as Buchanan linked African American gains in the military to the civil rights movement by pointing out that "the war produced thousands of Negro veterans who returned home with a new concept of what life should be like" (134).

In the context of the 1980s, then, Thomas was relying on a body of literature that tied World War II activism to civil rights activism. Much of this focused on the "Double V" campaign advocated by the black press in the 1940s, a movement to fight for victory and democracy not just abroad in Europe, but also at home in the United States. This campaign pushed African Americans to get involved in the war effort and to follow up those contributions with a public relations campaign. Activists used protests and the press to focus on these African American contributions and point out the hypocrisy of a country fighting against racist ideology while at the same time supporting that ideology with its own discriminatory policies and practices. Though, as Kruse and Tuck note, this campaign "did not herald a lasting change in black attitudes" (5), it *was* easy to link to the later 1960s civil rights movement, which employed many of the same tactics, comparing the treatment of African Americans to repressive regimes that were viewed as "the enemy" during the Cold War.

Thomas's storyline recognizing racial unrest during World War II was radical for its time. Although he was relying on a body of historiography that increasingly (and perhaps overly) recognized the value of African American gains during the war, the struggles to achieve those had not yet been widely chronicled in popular culture. Even the now-famed Tuskegee Airmen had not made their way to either the silver or TV screen, nor had they been memorialized or recognized by the "official" culture of government public memory. Thomas's interest in exploring the negative side of the American WWII home front was ahead of its time. It would not be until 1995 that wider American popular culture was to confront the struggles of African Americans during the war, in the form of *The Tuskegee Airmen*, an HBO film.

The Tuskegee Airmen focused on the struggles of African American fighter pilots who had to face not only America's enemies, but also their own superior officers and the politicians who dismissed them as inherently inferior to white soldiers. The film was a critical and commercial success, and for many Americans it provided the first exposure to stories of how WWII victory culture marginalized African Americans while at the same time decrying racism abroad. The script was based on a story cowritten by Robert W. Williams, one of the Tuskegee Airmen, who had been trying to get the film made since as early as 1953 (a further indication of the struggle of black Americans to even have their stories told). According to Williams, he wanted to tell "a story about black people and our struggle as a people to get the right to fight with dignity for our country," and one about "overcoming stupid racially motivated roadblocks and succeeding in spite of them" (quoted in Bodnar 179). *The Tuskegee Airmen* would prove to be just one of several projects commemorating the experiences of black soldiers—including a 2004 book, *Brothers in Arms: The Epic Story of the 761st Tank Battalion, World War II's Forgotten Heroes*, coauthored by basketball superstar Kareem Abdul-Jabbar—and heralding how they overcame racial prejudice. None of these stories, however, chose to focus on the discrimination that black soldiers and citizens faced (especially at home) during and after the war. Roy Thomas, however, was interested in focusing specifically on that home front discrimination in *All-Star Squadron*.

While the original Justice Society stories had been written in the context of a victory culture that wanted to (somewhat literally) whitewash the truth of discrimination on the home front, Thomas's 1980s *All-Star Squadron* tales were written in a post–civil rights context that saw the struggles of African Americans during the second World War as a crucial building block toward the larger movements of the 1960s. His "Real American" story-arc reflects this view of history. With a nod to actual history, the story concludes with disappointment. Real American is revealed as android with a hypnotic ability that has spurred on the tensions of the crowd, though only in part.[10] As Thomas notes, the actual Sojourner Truth housing riot was helped along by miscommunication and mismanagement. Thomas claims that, according to Alan Clive's 1959 book *State of War: Michigan in World War Two*, "on 2-28-42,

Detroit's mayor halted the scheduled move by African-Americans into the Sojourner Truth Homes [until they could be safely escorted into the project], but 'that news did not arrive at the battleground in time to prevent another clash at about 12:15 P.M.' The move was put off till April" (Thomas 2006, 129).

Thomas's research is in full force here, as both the storyline and the actual riot come to an uncertain and unsatisfactory end, with Squadron chairwoman Liberty Belle thinking to herself, "God, I hate leaving here—with so much unrest, so much racial hatred still unsettled. But there's only so much that even an All-Star Squadron can do. Maybe . . . next time . . . next place . . . !" ("The Rise and Fall of the Phantom Empire!" 21). Racial hatred, still an issue plaguing America in the 1980s, was not like a fictional Nazi supervillain that could be subdued through a valiant struggle. Rather, the job of facing down such racial tension is left open-ended and unclear, indicating that each individual reader must do their part in the "next time/place"—that is, the present day—to fight against the menace that even the All-Stars could not defeat.

The other major issue of racial complexity faced by the Squadron is actually presaged in this story, with Amazing Man's fiancée yelling out, in sarcastic anger, "Maybe you ought to put all the other minorities in jail, too, til the war's over—Japanese-Americans, because of Pearl Harbor—Mexican workers, to protect our precious borders!" ("The Rise and Fall of the Phantom Empire!" 7). Thomas uses this line to foreshadow the internment camps for Japanese citizens erected by the US government during the war. The race riot story is, in fact, set less than two weeks after President Roosevelt signed Executive Order 9066, creating Japanese "exclusion zones" along the Pacific Coast. In an earlier issue of *All-Star Squadron*, Thomas had portrayed a conflicted Roosevelt signing the order, feeling, as he does in regard to the Detroit riot, that his hands were tied.[11]

It was much later, in *All-Star Squadron*'s successor title, *Young All-Stars*,[12] that Thomas actually examined the issue in depth. One of the newest members of the Squadron introduced in the series is called Tsunami, a Nisei (US-born child of Japanese immigrants) who was at first an enemy of the heroes but then realized she was being manipulated by imperial Japan into blaming all Americans for the internment camps. However, she comes to think, "I had respected the Americans I had fought . . . and I could not believe they would want to put innocent Issei [Japanese immigrants] and Nisei behind barbed wire. In fact, America and Japan should not be at war at all" ("A Gathering of Heroes!" 5). Though her name is a bit of a stereotype, playing off of one of the few Japanese words that Americans would be familiar with, Tsunami serves as a mouthpiece for Thomas to rail against the internment camps, a historical reality he clearly feels most harshly represents the dark side of America during the war. He would later point specifically to the inhumanity and hypocrisy of the camps: "Many of those in the Los Angeles area were briefly interned at Santa Anita Racetrack, kept in stables that had previously housed racehorses.... Before long, most of these 'enemy aliens' (many of them born US citizens) were sent to barbed-wired camps in the Southwestern Desert" (2008, 202).

When the narrative conspires to bring Tsunami before President Roosevelt, Thomas gives her an eloquent speech denouncing the camps:

> I am an American—and I have come to feel Japan was wrong when she attacked Hawaii without warning. I only want what is best for America—and for Japan—the end of the military dictatorship now governing Japan. But—I must also say this: even though this terrible war must go on, innocent people of Japanese descent—who are nearly all loyal to America—should not be sent to concentration camps, as is now happening on your west coast! I beg of you, Mr. President—rescind your order, which allows your army to place any resident Japanese—yes, even so-called Nisei, born in this country—behind barbed wire! Put me in prison, if you must—but free my people—and give them a chance to prove themselves true Americans. ("A Gathering of Heroes!" 21)

In response, Roosevelt momentarily loses his eloquence for one of the few times throughout the run of the two series, exclaiming, "Uh, nonsense, young lady. I have no intention of putting you behind bars." Recovering himself, he goes on to say, "I don't want any innocent person to suffer—no matter what their ancestry—and I promise to look into this matter, to see if it's really a military necessity, as many of my advisors feel" ("A Gathering of Heroes!" 21–22). Once Tsunami thanks him, though, he immediately changes the subject, moving on to other matters.

In keeping with maintaining fidelity to the actual occurrences of the war, *Young All-Star*'s Roosevelt never does shut down the camps in response to Tsunami's pleas. In the next issue, the young Squadron members travel to California and go to the "relocation center" at the Santa Anita Racetrack where Tsunami's family is being held. The first clear image of the camp provided at the moment of their arrival, as crafted by penciller Howard Simpson, shows a destitute, downtrodden group of Japanese citizens wandering aimlessly behind a barbed-wire fence. Thomas had provided Simpson with a diagram of the racetrack, and of the stables where the Japanese citizens were being temporarily interned (Thomas 2008, 202). In reaction to these abhorrent conditions, Tsunami shouts, "Armed guards—barbed wire—they're being treated like animals. Animals!! Is this how Roosevelt keeps his promise? Turning women—children—old men—into penned cattle?" ("California, Here We Come . . ." 21–22). She dramatically removes her costume and, nude, enters the camp to be with her family, stripped bare as a symbol of the way that America has stripped its Japanese citizens of their humanity. In the next issue, she sits in the camp by herself, noting that "18,000 people of Japanese ancestry are crowded like livestock into the unclean horse stalls of Santa Anita race track, just outside the city of the angels. . . . What good would it do to flee, she wonders . . . seeking peace for herself and for her family? For, when all the world's at war . . . peace is but an illusive dream, with no anchor in either time or space" ("Hollywood Knights (1942 Model)" 24). However, her friendship with the other Squadron members, along with a vaguely described desire to fight "for justice for all people—everywhere," eventually draws her back to the team.

Once more we must make note of the fact that Roy Thomas was crafting this story in the 1980s, in the wake of four decades of Japanese American attempts to, as historian John Bodnar puts it, reclaim "a more critical remembrance of their war experience to seek greater measures of equality and honor" (189). Immediately following the war, they focused less on their victimization at being displaced to these camps (which included the frequent loss of their homes and businesses, even after the war was over) and instead wanted to be publicly remembered for their contributions to America's wartime efforts. With the advent of the modern civil rights movement in the 1960s, however, some Japanese Americans began to demand redress for their internment. In 1974, the Japanese American Citizen League (JACL) formed a National Committee for Redress, designed to get payment for the losses suffered by the interned families as well as to memorialize the camps as historic sites, so as to have official cultural recognition of the injustices suffered there. This sort of political pressure had, by 1980, forced the government to create the Commission on Wartime Relocation and Internment (CWRI). In 1983 (four years before Thomas's internment camp story was published), they released their report, entitled *Personal Justice Denied*, which "concluded that government officials acted not out of military necessity but out of a sense of 'hysteria' and 'racial prejudice,' a public declaration that undermined decades of official and unofficial rhetoric of the virtue of the American war effort" (Bodnar 192). They recommended a one-time, tax-free payment of $20,000 to each survivor of the camps, finally providing official government recognition of the wrongs done to Japanese Americans during the war.

In addition to this official recognition of Japanese American hardships, popular culture had also come to recognize their plight. Miné Okubo's illustrated book relating her experiences in an internment camp, *Citizen 13660* (considered a graphic novel by some critics), had at that point been in print for four decades. The book focused on providing an almost documentary-like portrayal of the experience of the camp, without presenting any anger or bitterness toward the government. As such, it was presented as evidence to the CWRI in 1981. This led to a new edition, including a new preface by Okubo, being printed in 1983. In 1987, Thomas's Justice Society tales were able to reflect this new standpoint of the official US public memory—that the camps had been an injustice and a misstep. The camps, however, though they would be brought up from time to time, would never again return to become the central focus of *Young All-Stars*. Thomas had made his point about the inhumanity of the camps, of their inherent declaration of war upon the United States' own citizens, but his desire to remain consistent with historical happenstance maintained that though characters could complain about the camps, they couldn't put an end to them any more than they could the camps set up by the Nazis in occupied Europe.

When faced not with colorful villains, but with the implacable forces of bigotry and the politics that support it, the superheroes are proven powerless, and all they have to fight with is their words. It is these words, in fact, that are so important to these superhero stories that engage with the past, as they are the words used by writers to "speak back" to both the comic books of their youth and the fictional past out of which those comics emerged.

Speaking Back to World War II

The Justice Society stories of the 1970s and 1980s are among the first examples of a phenomenon that is endemic to comic books—a fictional universe that has propagated for so long and with such narrative multiplicity that creators are able to look back on previous stories with the perspective of history and cultural memory. Writers such as Paul Levitz and Roy Thomas did not come into comics from the science fiction pulps, in the way that the first wave of comics writers did (and often those pulp writers saw themselves as "slumming" in comics). Rather, these new creators had been fans of comic books since childhood, and were eventually able to parlay that fandom into a career in the comics industry. Once they became creators themselves, their work with their favorite childhood characters reflected the memories of the time in which those characters, and their stories, were first published.

This second generation of writers would look back on their own histories, the histories of their characters, and the national/international contexts in which both of those histories took place in order to fashion stories that used contemporary historiography to reenvision the past. Thus, not only did the creators have a stake in working out a tighter sense of fictional continuity, so as to maintain fidelity to changing standards demanding increased "realism," but they were also able to add to this realism by utilizing revisionist views of the Great Depression and World War II. As mostly politically liberal thinkers and writers (this, at least, had not changed from the 1930s and 1940s), comics creators such as Levitz and Thomas wanted to imbue the past of these characters with a sense of contemporary criticism about occurrences such as McCarthyism or home-front discrimination, in opposition to the growing New Right of the 1970s and 1980s that wished to return to postwar values that hadn't yet been "undermined" by the gains of minorities and women during the civil rights era.

This tradition of using these older characters to talk about the past, and through the past to talk about the present, is one that continued into the 1990s, with writer James Robinson's award-winning, critically acclaimed *Starman* series, focusing on a family of superheroes descended from the Justice Society member of the same name. As comics writer/critic Warren Ellis notes of the series, "Robinson, with *Starman*, finds himself at a point in superhero comics where he can actually create a generational saga within the genre . . . set deeply within history itself, telling a tale of 1940s characters with modern skills, using them as a tool to dissect post–World War Two paranoias" (12). Robinson himself would take this a step further, noting in the letters column of *Starman* that the entire theme of the book was to forge a link between the present and the past, both in terms of superheroes and more generally, as reflected in the main character's obsession with nostalgia and his job as a manager of an antiques shop. Robinson explains that the book is "a discourse on the relevance of the past on the present . . . both in terms of actual events 'then' and the rippling ramifications of them 'now,' and in terms of the icons and things of times past that we carry with us into the present time. If the subtext of STARMAN is one of the discourse on value, then it is that value of the past to the present" (26). Such a direct acknowledgment of the influence of the past upon the present, especially in the world of superhero comic books, clearly owes much to Roy Thomas and *All-Star Squadron*.

By the 1980s, the stories that could be told about World War II varied significantly from the original Justice Society stories, enmeshed as they were within a patriotic fervor. In order to craft his narrative, Roy Thomas studied both "classic" and recent historical texts about World War II, and thus was aware of the advent of "new," cultural, revisionist histories. He directly stated that he wanted to answer questions such as "How would such heroes have reacted, in a more realistic world than the early comics mirrored, to the injustices of the Japanese-American detention centers or to Jim Crow treatment of blacks?" (Thomas "Meanwhile . . ."). Though he still maintained an adherence to an overall celebration of American values (and especially the American president) during the war, he nevertheless did not shy away from issues such as racism and bigotry that were a part of those values. In the process, he explored how his contemporary America was still dealing with those fraught tensions and attitudes. He was, in essence, able to examine the past using the present, and vice versa, forging a link between the two that opened doors to new possibilities—such as Robinson's "generational saga"—in superhero comics.

All-Star Squadron directly displays how retroactive continuity and historical revisionism become intrinsically linked in the minds of creators and audiences. Thomas discovered a way of "speaking back" to two kinds of history—both the fictional history/continuity of the DC Universe, and, more important, the actual, lived history of World War II. Through retroactive continuity, creators like Thomas are able to literally rewrite the stories they read years ago as fans. In revisiting the past eras in which those stories were produced, they are able to remember, memorialize, and recreate that past with the narrative and political sensibilities of the present moment. In the case of Thomas's stories in the 1980s, he was able to use these retcons to create an opposition to the right-leaning Reaganite politics of that moment and point out not just the positive, national-identity-building aspects of World War II victory culture, but also its dark shadow on those who stood outside the mass consensus of that particular formation of American identity.

The ways in which the past is remembered in superhero comic books tells us something about the ways in which historical events, and indeed history itself, are viewed over time, and how that view can be influenced by (either directly or in opposition to) contemporary political and social concerns. The retcon is a narrative technique that allows for this shifting view of the past to become embodied in the narratives of popular culture, and thus became a crucial trope in the late twentieth century as what was at first viewed as "historical revisionism" became the de facto mode of "history." In the next chapter, we will see how retroactive continuity similarly moved from being an occasional tool utilized by comics creators to a de facto way of creating a superhero "universe" out of disparate books and stories that were never meant to cohere in the first place.

CRISIS CONTROL
Crisis on Infinite Earths
and the Creation of a
Unified Comic Book Universe

In 1985, DC Comics recognized its fiftieth anniversary.[1] To celebrate this landmark event in comics publishing history, the company put out a twelve-issue miniseries, titled *Crisis on Infinite Earths*, which promised "major and permanent changes to the entire DC line" (*Crisis Compendium* 4). For once, such promises proved to be something less than hyperbolic. *Crisis on Infinite Earths* (referred to hereafter as *Crisis*) brought lasting change to DC Comics from a narrative point of view, and heralded even further-reaching changes for the comic book industry and fan community. As the first multipart, universe-spanning comic book crossover of its kind,[2] *Crisis* showed the two major superhero comic book publishers how they could utilize the continuity (retroactive and otherwise) established by decades' worth of stories to weave together a cohesive, metatextual tapestry that both appealed to longtime readers and made huge profits.

For comics creators working in the industry at the time, the success of the series displayed how epic narratives could be created out of this metatextual history in order to up the stakes for the superheroic protagonists of the stories. Moreover, the series suggested that these same epics could enact lasting change that affected not just individual characters, but entire universes. The series, according to Adam C. Murdough in an in-depth analysis of the metatext of *Crisis*, "functioned as a powerful mythological mediator in the introduction of new ways for superhero stories to interact with their own fictional and historical contexts and with their audience" (13), and ultimately, through "the intermingling of characters from different genres and different 'parallel Earths,' constitutes a violent regurgitation of the entire 'cultural memory' of DC Comics fans, in preparation for the 'new Creation' to come" (66). As a financial and, to a lesser extent, critical success, *Crisis on Infinite Earths* thus taught the makers of superhero comics that the rules were literally being rewritten and that these fictional realms were constantly in conversation with their own histories and past narratives.

Crisis, as perhaps the ultimate example of a comic book universe retcon, deals intimately with the history of DC Comics' characters and its entire universe. *Crisis* writer Marv Wolfman, editor Len Wein, and artist George Perez had all come out of the second wave of comic book fandom, and used their encyclopedic fascination with the DC Universe to craft a tale that dealt obsessively with touching upon all aspects of the company's history in order to create a definitive "DCU" tale. *Crisis* was the first attempt to tell a story about an entire superhero *universe*, rather than an individual hero or team of heroes. As part of creating a narrative about the DC Universe, Wolfman and his cocreators would come to engage with the entire history of that universe—both its publishing history and the ongoing narrative embedded within those publications. *Crisis* used the history of the DC Universe to "forever" change its future, thus engaging in a form of literary cultural memory defined by Renate Lachmann as "the process by which a culture, where 'culture' is a book culture, continually rewrites and retranscribes itself, constantly redefining itself through its signs" (301). *Crisis* was an epic rewriting and retranscription of DC Comics' history, and it turned this kind of retconning of past stories into a tool that defined a new way for comics to engage with their history—by willfully (and retroactively) ignoring, forgetting, and/or negating it.

As a text that stands at the crossroads of corporate interest in redefining a comic book universe so as to make it more salable, fannish interest in creating ordered continuity out of a chaotic publishing history, and readers' interest in understanding what all of these changes meant and how they would come to be, *Crisis on Infinite Earths* must be examined as a crucial moment in the history of how creators and fans of superhero comics consider the past and, via the retcon, engage with that past. *Crisis* shows how the literary sensibilities of superhero comic books, the ways they "rewrite" and "speak back" to their own textual antecedents, aligns with their implementation of history as a part of their narrative, allowing creators to revisit the past with an eye toward crafting new visions of that history, both real and imagined, for use in future narratives. As such, the work of literary theorist Hayden White on historiography can be usefully applied to an examination of *Crisis* in order to display how the crossover serves as a sort of "Rosetta Stone" to understanding the ways in which superhero comic books have come to view the presentation of the past.

Though an attempt to make DC more accessible, *Crisis* also functioned to cement continuity as the most important element of superhero comics, providing the birthplace of modern, obsessive superhero comic continuity. Superhero comics have come to view the past as entirely mutable, which has shaped how they have approached issues of history and memory ever since. In this chapter, I will examine *Crisis on Infinite Earths* as a historical text and as a piece of historical writing (that is, a text relating a history, itself). *Crisis* was a turning point for both of the dual aspects of cultural memory in comics: it showed the fans that there was a new and different way to view comics history, and it did so by showing that continuity, especially retroactive continuity, could, and henceforth would, always be open to massive, often apocalyptic, fluctuation and frustrations.

Crisis on Infinite Earths: A Corporate History

In 1985, DC Comics was feeling its age. After five decades of storylines that involved multiple Earths across a panoply of alternate dimensions, including several conflicting versions of such iconic figures as Superman, Batman, and Wonder Woman, DC's top editorial staff felt that the DC Universe was a confusing mess of contradictory narratives that was gruelingly inaccessible to new readers. They saw the company's golden anniversary as an opportunity to make the kinds of sweeping changes that might draw in new readers and create fresher stories that weren't as directly mired in the past, while at the same time celebrating the parts of the past that long-term fans treasured. The way to accomplish this difficult task, they thought, was through a proposal, then called *History of the DC Universe*, created by two of DC's writer/editors, Marv Wolfman and Len Wein.

From the outset, though, *Crisis* was a project that was driven by editors more than creators. The first inkling that fans and readers of DC Comics got about this project was found in executive editor Dick Giordano's "Meanwhile..." column that ran as a text page in comics throughout the DC line. In the column that appeared in those comics with a June 1984 cover date, Giordano noted that

> We felt it appropriate to save this blockbuster maxi series for this anniversary year because the changes in our universe and the startling events that will unfold within its pages will alter forever the DC universe and provide some wonderful stepping-stones for the next 50 years. Clue: look for odd occurrences in DC titles from now till the end of the year. They'll provide additional clues as to the who, what, where, when and why of the DC universe maxiseries. (*Crisis Compendium* 4)

Behind the scenes, these "odd occurrences" were the cause of a new kind of line-wide editorial wrangling that had not been seen before. In fact, the entirety of *Crisis*, from inception to publication, would include vast amounts of editorial control, imposed from the very top, over the creators of individual DC superhero books. Though in previous decades the relationship between creators and editors had been an extremely collaborative one, *Crisis* was the starting point of a new dynamic, one where creators were often (though not always) made to carry out the story whims of editors who were shepherding an entire "universe" of characters rather than just a single book.

This new era began in earnest with a memo to all DC editors and writers, in which the mandate was given that "Because this series involves the entire DC Universe we do ask that each Editor and writer cooperate with the project by using a character called *The Monitor* in their books twice during the next year" (*Crisis Compendium* 7, emphasis in original). In a follow-up memo to the entire editorial staff, Giordano reiterated that "The need to include the Monitor in your plans is not optional but absolutely required for all designated titles" (*Crisis Compendium* 8). However, only three months later, the editorial staff was notified that plans for *Crisis* had changed: "after you use the Monitor twice, please do not use him again. He'll be gone by next summer" (*Crisis Compendium* 9). *Crisis* thus revealed the full and confusing extent to which editors, and particularly senior editors, were beginning to impose their demands upon the writers of superhero comics, so that the fuller universe of the characters would (ideally) become more united and cohesive.

The conflict of *Crisis on Infinite Earths* lay not just on the four-color pages of the series, but within the real-life offices of DC Comics, where writers and editors struggled both with and against one another to create a single, unified, cohesive "DC Universe," while at the same time maintaining the artistic integrity of individual titles. What these combatants overlooked, or perhaps more accurately simply were not (and could not be) aware of, was that in this battle over the present state of the DC Universe they were shaping not only its future, but also its past.

Hayden White and Continuity in Crisis

Several years before Wolfman and Wein began forming the ideas about DC continuity that would ultimately lead to *Crisis*, literary theorist Hayden White posited a new form of historical analysis that has been extremely influential in the fields of history and literary criticism. White espoused the idea that objective history was ostensibly impossible to write, as every historian would constantly be imposing his or her own biases onto their work, whether consciously or unconsciously. The bare, dry facts of history—the "chronicle," as White calls them[3]—are taken by historians and turned into narratives that are implicitly subjective to whoever writes, and even reads, those narratives. Choosing what facts to take from the chronicle to put into the narrative (because the chronicle consists of every single detail of everything that ever happened, it would be impossible to reproduce it, even for a tiny sliver of history) requires subjective choices that ultimately cause the historian to become a shaper of history. As White points out, "Our explanations of historical structures and processes are thus determined more by what we leave out of our representations than by what we put in" ("Historical Text" 44).

However, in White's view, "history as a discipline is in bad shape today [1978] because it has lost sight of its origins in the literary imagination" ("Historical Text" 62). White was not arguing *against* the literary nature of history, and the process of narrativization that he saw as inherent in the discipline, but rather *for* a recognition of that literariness within the work of his contemporaries and colleagues. He felt that historians should put together their work in much the same way a fiction writer would ("Historical Text" 47). White believed in the "emplotment," the narrativization, of history as a crucial aspect of historiography. Historians, like fiction writers, are telling a story, and they must be aware of that fact if they are to practice their craft while harnessing "its own greatest source of strength and renewal" ("Historical Text" 62).

The reason, White argues, that this is such a strength for the discourse of history is because "the structure of any sophisticated, i.e., self-conscious and self-critical, discourse mirrors or replicates the phases which consciousness itself must pass in *its* progress from a naïve (metaphorical) to a self-critical (ironic) comprehension of itself" (*Tropics of Discourse* 23). For a historian to be properly self-critical, then, and achieve the final stage of his/her discipline's discourse, that historian must be willing to accept the process of emplotment, and be self-critical and self-aware of the process by which an objective chronicle becomes a subjective and personalized narrative.

Crisis was DC's attempt to bring this self-awareness and self-reflection to the realm of its cluttered continuity. As writer/editor Marv Wolfman saw it, by the mid-1980s the obsessive, fan-driven demand for cohesive continuity, combined with the creator-driven desire to constantly devise new scenarios and alternative narratives, had led to a confusing mess in the DC Universe. Wolfman was at this point a senior editor at DC, where he not only wrote his own titles but also oversaw creators on other titles. He was thus not an independent freelance creator, but rather an active part of DC's corporate structure. *Crisis* was Wolfman's brainchild, and he scripted the entire twelve-issue miniseries, which would be illustrated and partially co-plotted by detail-oriented penciller George Perez, with whom Wolfman had already established a fruitful partnership (both creatively and commercially) on the book *New Teen Titans*. In the text page at the back of the second issue of *Crisis*, Wolfman outlined what had become, to him, the problem with DC continuity:

> Writers like to complicate matters, and what began as a dream of a story—"Flash of Two Worlds"—had turned into a nightmare. DC continuity was so confusing, no new reader could easily understand it, while older readers had to keep miles-long lists to set things straight. And the writers . . . well, we were always stumbling over each other trying to figure out simple answers to difficult questions. (*Crisis Compendium* 5)

The story to which Wolfman refers, "Flash of Two Worlds," published in 1961, was in many ways the beginnings of DC's continuity problems.

"Flash of Two Worlds" featured the first appearance of DC's "Earth Two" concept, a theory of parallel universes whereby, because "two objects can occupy the same space and time—if they vibrate at different speeds," it is possible for two earths to be "created at the same time in two quite similar universes! They vibrate differently—which keeps them apart!" (Fox 2005, 13–14). Through the existence of these different earths—"Earth-One," "Earth-Two," "Earth-Prime," and so on—DC was able to create a "multiverse" containing a literally infinite amount of alternate realities, each of which (usually) contained some variation on DC's pantheon of superheroes and villains. Over time, however, as Wolfman indicates, the number of Earths that creators, editors, and fans needed to keep track of became so large as to be intimidating to new readers and confusing even to longtime DC followers. As Wolfman explained:

> For the past several years many people have suggested "fixing up" the DC Universe. Simplifying it. Making it consistent yet in a way which would not prevent experiments that varied with an "established" future . . . Well, *Crisis on Infinite Earths* will attempt such a repair job. By series' end DC will have a consistent and more easily understandable universe to play with. We're pulling out all stops to make *Crisis on Infinite Earths* an epic you will never forget! (*Crisis Compendium* 5)

In addition to explaining the continuity purposes for *Crisis*, Wolfman also provides a mission statement for the series itself—to relate an unforgettable epic that would create a consistent DC Universe. Along the way, this epic would come to redefine how superhero comic creators wrestled with issues of continuity.

Worlds Living and Worlds Dying: The Text and Metatext of *Crisis on Infinite Earths*

The plot of *Crisis on Infinite Earths* is meandering, complicated, and not particularly easy to recount. It begins with a glimpse at the birth of the DC multiverse, slightly reminiscent (at first) of scientific descriptions of the Big Bang:

> In the beginning there was only one. A single black infinitude . . . so cold and dark for so very long . . . that even the burning light was imperceptible. But the light grew, and the infinitude shuddered . . . and the darkness finally . . . screamed, as much in pain as in relief. For in that instant, a multiverse was born. A multiverse of worlds vibrating and replicating . . . and a multiverse that should have been one, became many. (Wolfman 2005, 11, ellipsis in original)

During the course of *Crisis*, the DC superheroes and readers alike learn that the multiverse, indeed, "should have been one"—it was ruptured and fractured into a multiverse, instead of a single universe, due to the scientific inquiry of an alien named Krona who wanted to look back to the dawn of time and learn its secrets.

Crisis opens with an explosive moment of rupture, one that points to the destructive potential of continuity upon creative cohesiveness. This would become embodied in the rest of the story through the roles of two new characters created specifically for the series. In the birth of multiverse a being known as the Monitor was also born. It was his job to learn everything about that multiverse, as well as to protect and maintain it. In addition to birthing the multiverse, however, Krona's actions created an antimatter universe, an evil universe that contained the Monitor's polar opposite, the Anti-Monitor. In *Crisis*, the Anti-Monitor makes his move against the multiverse, attempting to engulf its infinite worlds in an equally infinite wave of antimatter (represented on the comics page by blank whiteness) that literally erases everything in every positive-matter universe that it touches.

The central threat of *Crisis* is actual erasure, from both the page and from existence. The confusing continuity of a multiverse, we are shown, leads to the potential eradication of all storytelling possibilities. As such, *Crisis* opens with the Anti-Monitor's plan already in progress—the antimatter wave is destroying world after world and universe after universe. Despite the best efforts of the Monitor and the various superheroes and villains (working together) whom he assembles, a roster that eventually includes *all* of the heroes and villains from throughout the past, present, and future of the DC Multiverse, the Anti-Monitor manages to destroy all but five of the positive-matter universes. After his plans are halted by the noble sacrifices of Supergirl and the "Earth One" incarnation of the Flash, the Anti-Monitor travels back to the dawn of time, where, following an epic battle with the DC superheroes, the universe is restarted anew, albeit with a significant difference this time:

> In the beginning there were many. A multiversal infinitude . . . so cold and dark for so very long . . . that even the burning light was imperceptible. But the light grew, and the multiverse shuddered . . . and the darkness screamed as much in pain as in relief. For in that instant a universe was born. A universe with mighty worlds orbiting burning suns. A universe reborn at the dawn of time. What had been many became one. (Wolfman 2005, 297, ellipsis in original)

This moment is the central plot/continuity point of *Crisis*—the death of the multiverse, and its rebirth as a single universe, symbolizing the death of cluttered continuity in favor of streamlined storytelling. It takes up the opening page of the eleventh issue and directly resonates with the original birth of the multiverse from the very beginning of the first issue. As a result, certain characters who survived this death/rebirth because they were present at the beginning of time, and yet who contradicted the continuity of the reborn universe—including the Earth-Two versions of Superman, Robin, and Huntress (Batman's daughter)—were erased from the memories of everyone in this reborn universe, such that they, like the multiverse itself, had no longer ever historically existed. Not coincidentally, the most problematic of these characters all died in the final battle of the reborn Earth against the Anti-Monitor, a battle that dominated the final issue of *Crisis*.

The rebirth of the multiverse as a universe, and the attendant rebooting of the major characters in that universe, was originally supposed to provide a springboard for an all-new continuity that did not rely on any prior DC history. Wolfman wanted *none* of the characters to remember what had happened during *Crisis*, and for the entire DC Universe to start from a fresh slate, with new first issues for every ongoing series. According to a DC-published *Crisis* companion volume, though,

> The other editors felt differently. One of them said, "If the heroes don't remember the Crisis it invalidates the book." Exasperated, Marv replied, "The heroes don't buy our comics. It doesn't matter if they remember the stories. The readers do and they'll remember them. Let's not complicate things." But Marv was outvoted. (*Crisis Compendium* 34)

Furthermore, Wolfman's plan for all of DC's superhero comics to reboot with new first issues was similarly shot down.

As a result, the superheroes *did* remember *Crisis*, at least to an extent, and their books did *not* all restart. The outcome, according to DC researcher John Wells, was that, "For the most part, it was as if Earth-One still existed, albeit now peppered with immigrants from Earth-Two. . . . And even this wasn't clear-cut" (*Crisis Compendium* 87). Within a few years, however, Superman, Batman, and Wonder Woman, among other heroes, would all be "rebooted," and given new contexts, origins, and backstories that were consistent with this one, new universe.

This universe, with more complex and morally ambiguous stories and characters, was more in keeping with the "mature" readership that became the prime demographic for the comic book industry in the 1980s. The older readership came to dominance owing to a general shift in the industry from newsstand distribution networks to what was known as the direct market, which revolved around specialty comics stores. Publishers like DC and Marvel soon came to realize that the major source of their revenue at such stores was the dedicated comic fans, rather than casual buyers. As a result, Paul Levitz, who had ascended to vice president and publisher at DC, stated that publishers were "Consciously aiming their efforts directly at the fan market as their chief area of growth" (quoted in Wright 261). In addition, this system of direct-market distribution allowed publishers to create books with greater sophistication and more violent and/or adult content, because comic book specialty shops, unlike newsstands, drugstores, and supermarkets, were by and large not patronized by children. Even more importantly, they were not covered by the strictures of the Comics Code Authority. Comic book stores were destinations that adult fans specifically journeyed to and were far less local and ubiquitous than the corner drugstores that children purchased their comics from.

Crisis, with its complex, solipsistic plot, its apocalyptic tone, and its unprecedented body count, was itself only possible thanks to the direct market. This new type of market allowed publishers to utilize a new kind of storytelling: the "event" or "crossover" series, that asked readers to pick up multiple tie-ins to a central miniseries and promised lasting, permanent change to the fictional universe. *Crisis*, the first of these stories, was geared toward a specifically fannish, collector's mentality, which was far more prevalent among adult readers than children. Similarly, once the narrative line was drawn between the "pre-*Crisis*" DC Multiverse and the "post-*Crisis*" DC Universe, those "post-*Crisis*" stories were aimed squarely at this adult readership. Not only were DC's stories more mature in and of themselves—such as Frank Miller and David Mazzucchelli's dark Batman origin, *Batman: Year One*—but they also reflected, from their outset, the kind of shared continuity that Wolfman and Wein had argued for. Comics writer Paul Cornell notes that such continuity is "one big and very complex story, that rewrites and contradicts itself. That was always the case. Only now it does it with purpose, rather than by accident" (Cornell 2007).[4]

As was seen in the build-up to *Crisis*, this kind of a shared universe is only possible under the hand of firm editorial control across the entire publishing line. The post-*Crisis* DC Universe, and the superhero comics being produced at DC and Marvel from the mid-1980s up to the present, is a landscape where editors hold supreme power. *Crisis* changed not just the narrative DC Universe, but also the way of doing business for publishers of comic book "universes." Narratively, for the next two decades DC continuity would be a continual reflection of the changes wrought by *Crisis*.[5] The creators of DC's superhero tales, working under strict editorial demands, would constantly be negotiating with the fact that fifty years' worth of storytelling was now "pre-*Crisis*" and had to be rewoven into the ongoing post-*Crisis* tapestry through the process of retroactive continuity.

By creating a new, cohesive universe that combined characteristics of the various worlds of the multiverse, *Crisis* was, itself, the ultimate retcon. It completely rewrote the entire history of the DC Universe, making it so that those stories that occurred pre-*Crisis* had, for the characters, never actually happened. Although, the readers and creators still remembered those stories, as Wolfman rightly pointed out, the characters within the fictional realm did not. The massive retcon of *Crisis* erased their original history and replaced it, rewrote it, with a new one.

Crisis was a project that deliberately set out to draw together the ragged strands of various continuities into one larger metanarrative. As such, it was an example of superhero comics achieving Hayden White's "final stage"[6] of historical self-criticism and self-awareness. White, in trying to unite "scientific *and* artistic insights in history without leading to radical relativism and the assimilation of history to propaganda," posits that a historian, "like the modern artist and scientist," should "exploit a certain perspective on the world that does not pretend to exhaust description or analysis of all the data in the entire phenomenal field but rather offers itself as *one way among many* of disclosing certain aspects of the field." Thus, "we should recognize that *what constitutes the facts themselves* is the problem that the historian, like the artist, has tried to solve in the choice of the metaphor by which he orders his world" (*Tropics of Discourse* 46–47, emphasis in original). Furthermore, the organization of whatever facts a historian chooses to put in his/her record must conform to a certain mode of storytelling—a particular genre. White explains, "What the historian must bring to his consideration of the record are general notions of the *kinds of stories* that might be found there, just as he must bring to consideration of the problem of narrative representation some notion of the 'pre-generic plot-structure' by which the story *he* tells is endowed with formal coherency" (*Tropics of Discourse* 60).

White goes on to summarize this entire process of historical discourse: "The historical discourse should be viewed as a sign system which points in two directions simultaneously: first, toward the set of events it purports to describe, and, second, toward the generic story form to which it tacitly likens the set in order to disclose its formal coherence considered as either a structure or a *process*" (*Tropics of Discourse* 106, emphasis in original). What White is pointing toward here is, again, a larger self-awareness on the part of a historian, recognizing that every organization of facts, and every choice made in what facts to present and what to leave out, creates a subjective history, "one way among many" to make meaning out of a series of events.

With *Crisis*, DC Comics reached this stage of self-awareness in regards to its own history and continuity. It was an intentional narrative that attempted to wrestle with the problematic, confusing "chronicle" of continuity that preceded it. According to Wolfman:

> *Crisis* was created to solve a specific problem: to make the confusing DC universe accessible to new readers. I had thought it would do its job and the focus of attention would then be on the new books and not the title that changed them. . . . But

its sales is what made everyone suddenly decide to copy the concept. Unfortunately, from what I know, most of the mega-crossovers that followed didn't have a core reason for their existence as *Crisis* did.... In a way, *Crisis* spawned an industry of mega-events when it should have only given birth to those kinds of events where something vitally important had to be achieved. (quoted in H. Siegel)

It is important to note, here, that Wolfman's focus in regards to *Crisis* was placed firmly on what it was trying to specifically "achieve." Thanks to its commercial and critical acceptance (though it certainly had its share of criticism, explored below), along with its achievement of that goal of forming a massively important continuity shift, it became a central text of the DC Universe "canon," one that has been widely copied, particularly in format, in the years since.

What was unique about *Crisis*, though, and certainly part of what spurred on the interest in it, was the fact that it was deliberately created for the purpose of altering and rebooting an entire comic book universe's continuity—as critic Harry Siegel calls it, "the comic book equivalent of Noah's flood." *Crisis* was the first superhero comic to make continuity the central concern of the text. As such it altered the way that continuity could and would be used by superhero creators. Retconning became much more commonplace, allowing stories to visit the past more freely. The idea that a superhero's origin could be directly revisited, and even rebuilt from the ground up, inspired a multitude of texts that delved into the past.

For *Crisis*, this obsession with the past was a necessity for shaping the publishing line's future. Wolfman freely admitted that *Crisis* only incidentally became "quite good beyond serving its purpose," but, more importantly that it "had a reason to be done; it solved a major problem DC was facing" (quoted in H. Siegel). This problem, he notes, was not only one of continuity, but also that "certain characters no longer work because they've gone as far as they can in terms of sales, and of writers who can work up stories with them.... So you can either let the character just fade away into oblivion, or you can do something special with him" (quoted in Waid 1985, 30). On top of this, he explains, "The reason for doing it? We thought the DC Universe was cluttered, it made no sense. There were so many stories that set up so much, it was too much for anybody to understand" (quoted in O'Neill 17). For Wolfman *Crisis* was initially intended to "fix" continuity and recreate characters for a new audience and for fresher stories, part of the outgrowth of his personal belief, formed from a life in fandom and in professional comics, that every generation needs the comics recreated for them. This happened by accident in the past: Comics were created in 1938 with Superman. About 25 years later, between 1956–1961, the Silver age was created with no direct regard for what happened before. About 25 years after that, I did Crisis with George Perez and that once again updated the DCU. (quoted in H. Siegel)

What had been done accidentally with earlier reinvigorations of older character concepts was now being done purposely by Wolfman, Perez, and Wein. Years later, DC's editor-in-chief Dan DiDio would note the importance of this purposeful rebooting:

Over the years, individual characters have changed directions, and origins have been rebooted to keep more in line with the times, but up until 1985, stories like that never occurred on a universal scale. [*Crisis*] changed that . . . The original Crisis became a seminal event for all comics fans, one cosmic series that touched upon every book and showed the DC universe to be one shared universe. (DiDio 2012, 5)

Going forward from *Crisis*, DC's editors and writers did not forget this lesson.

Crisis's Critical Reception

Crisis intentionally serves as a crucial moment of continuity change, a continuity node rewriting the fictional history of the universe, one created by fans-turned-pros who felt that this reinvigoration was necessary to attract a new generation of comics readers. The key members of the *Crisis* creative team (writer Wolfman, editor Wein, and artist Perez) had all arisen out of fandom, and possessed a fascination with older stories and continuity that fed their desire to create this massive "house-cleaning" story. They were creating a story for readers like themselves, who were enchanted not just with individual characters, but with entire fictional universes, and, at least according to Wolfman in the letter column of the fourth issue, they successfully reached that audience:

The CRISIS was created solely to make the DC Universe more accessible to the largest number of readers, which means our concerns are towards story, plot, and characterization . . . To date we've received no—repeat NO—negative mail on issue #1, and although I'm sure somebody out there didn't like it, we're incredibly gratified to all those who wrote to say they cared. (Wolfman 1985, 27)

Even if taken at face value, Wolfman's statement that "we've received no negative mail on issue #1" should by no means imply that *Crisis* was universally praised at its time of publication. Indeed, his need to claim such praise may have been a defense against the controversy that the series generated among DC's fans. Longtime fan Mark Waid, in an issue of the professional fanzine *Amazing Heroes* dedicated solely to *Crisis*, noted, "In *Crisis*, readers were witness to the deaths of major characters (like Supergirl and Flash), as well as a few 'trivia deaths' . . . If you're a long-time fan, that may have bent you out of shape somewhat—but it's a sad Rule of Collecting that nothing attracts the diehard fans of today like the smell of carrion, pal" (Waid 1986, 4). It was, however, not just the deaths that proved controversial, but also the rewrite/retcon process itself, which made some readers feel that the comics they had grown up enjoying no longer "counted" or even "existed." This was noted in an editorial cartoon, in the issue's letter columns, with the caption, "Across the country, readers are seeing the effects of the conclusion of *Crisis*!" Beneath that caption is a startled reader who, holding a copy of *Batman* that is fading from view, is screaming, "My 1950's *Batman* comic . . . It's fading like it never existed!" (Grandinettie).

The letters column of *Amazing Heroes* itself showed a variety of responses to *Crisis*. Reader Christopher Day compared the series favorably to Marvel Comics' *Secret Wars*, stating that "*Crisis* was everything that *Secret Wars* should have been. . . . I am sorry that *Crisis* is over while I am relieved that *Secret Wars* is over" ("Amazing Readers" 110). However, Robert Plunkett Jr., in the very next letter, states that "*Crisis on Infinite Earths* was the most wrongheaded work DC has produced in memory. The balance sheet on the series probably looks very good right now, but these short-term profits will be purchased dearly, at the cost of alienating the long-term readers and potential readers, and of inflicting havoc on a once strong comic mythos" ("Amazing Readers" 110). Meeting these two opinions in the middle was *Amazing Heroes* critic R. A. Jones, who reviewed all twelve individual issues of *Crisis* and found that "a major flaw in the series" was that "It is such a confusing amalgam of contrivances, back-peddling, miscommunications and general disorder that it is nearly impossible to make any point with complete certainty" (108–9). Because of this, he ultimately feels that "the scope of this particular story simply proved to be too much for Wolfman. And he did truly *have* a story—something which cannot be said for . . . *Secret Wars*. It was indeed more story than he was capable of telling. His literary reach exceeded his grasp" (109).

Jones came to the conclusion that *Crisis*'s impact on DC, and on the entire comics industry, was perhaps more important than its literary merits: "In terms of story alone, *Crisis on Infinite Earths* melts beneath the glare of critical scrutiny, but that does not diminish its importance in my eyes. In this instance, the fact that DC dared attempt to scale the heights far and away overshadows the fact that it stumbled and fell halfway up the slope" (109). This is, in fact, how *Crisis* has been remembered in the decades since its publication. As Hilary Goldstein, a reviewer for the pop culture website IGN, noted in 2006,

> *Crisis on Infinite Earths* is a crucial turning point for DC Comics. Originally a celebration of the 50th anniversary of the company, it became a savior. . . . Marv Wolfman had the bold idea to cleanse the burdens of 50 years of continuity, with an event unlike any seen before . . . And once the *Crisis* ended, DC spent the next several years slowly reintroducing and revamping its characters. It was a long, arduous process that . . . helped put DC back on the map.

Goldstein shows how, with the passage of time, the series is frequently framed by its historical value rather than as a discrete literary entity unto itself. Today, *Crisis* serves not only as a historical text, but also as a text that, quite literally, created DC's contemporary history.

The Chronicle and the Narrative

With the advent *Crisis*, the process of creating a meaningful narrative out of a chronicle of previous events in the DC Universe came more fully to the forefront of fans' minds than it ever had before. The review of this chronicle was so important, in fact, that in the preplanning stages of the story DC hired a researcher, Peter Sanderson, to review the entire history of its comic book universe. History was a crucial component of the *Crisis* project, and the hiring of Sanderson shows that the creators themselves were deeply invested in the history of their own cultural product, as an integral part of *Crisis*'s literary content. Though they were almost certainly not thinking about the kind of historical framework provided by theorists like White, the creators of *Crisis* were clearly engaged in what they saw as a process of historical storytelling.

Sanderson spent three years reading all the comics that DC had published since 1935, taking extensive notes along the way. Wolfman then took the reins from Sanderson, and instead of research-historian, worked as storyteller-historian. He grabbed the various narrative threads of DC history and tied them together into a larger narrative tapestry, one that took a group of disparate concepts created by multiple writers over half a century and turned them into a single, cohesive universe. Wolfman displayed a self-consciousness about this aspect of *Crisis* in a memo cowritten with Giordano and Wein where he told all DC staffers that *Crisis* "will establish which characters exist in the [new DC] universe, and therefore, by inference, which don't ... [Those that don't] do not exist in the one cohesive timeline the 'DC Universe' represents ... The series will correct 'mistakes' made in the past, eliminate repetitive concepts and generally make the DC Universe easier to understand for both us and our readers" (*Crisis Compendium* 7).

Crisis was not just about telling an epic story and simplifying DC continuity, but was also, in part, a project geared toward taking control of the DC Universe with a firmer hand, deciding which stories and characters did or did not exist within that universe, and creating a single "cohesive timeline" out of the characters who did. Wolfman and his coconspirators were, in a sense, narrativizing comic book history, a process he likened to "a giant, 1000-piece jigsaw puzzle, with 1000 characters running around, and my job is to take those pieces, along with George Perez, and make the complete picture with no seams. If George and I are successful, you won't know there was ever a puzzle" (quoted in O'Neill 15). This kind of project, in one sense, was nothing new, since readers had been nitpicking continuity for years, finding a certain pleasure in doing so. In terms of one of the comic book *publishers* engaging in the continuity game on such a massive scale, though, *Crisis* was revolutionary, and heralded a new era in which comic book creators were forced to adhere to the demands of readers and create a cohesive sense of continuity.

In *Crisis*, DC's panoply of multiple earths, instead of an editorial jumble of continuity, were retroactively made into a single story of how "a multiverse that should have been one, became many" (Wolfman 2005, 11) and then how, through the retconning events and plot/continuity twists of *Crisis*, "What had been many became one" (Wolfman 2005, 297). The narrativizing of the multiple earths' history was in effect a retconning of reality. Wolfman took what had been creative and editorial inconsistency and turned it into a story that led up to a specific end point (or rather, given how the DC Universe continued forward after *Crisis*, to a specific midpoint). At the moment in *Crisis* where the Anti-Monitor has caused the restarting of reality that will turn the multiverse into a single universe, a caption box notes, "It is the end of all that was" (Wolfman 2005, 295). *Crisis* was, in the context of its time, literally an end to the story of the DC Multiverse—a *narrative* that Wolfman had created out of a *chronicle* of previous parallel earth tales—and the beginning of the narrative of the DC Universe, or, as Adam C. Murdough phrases it, "a dynamic, albeit tragic, 'character arc' for the DC Universe, from old continuity to new" (63).

From its very beginnings, this new DC Universe *would* have a strong sense of its own history. During the course of *Crisis*, the Monitor's assistant,

Harbinger, taking note of all of the events of the story through the Monitor's hi-tech machines, states that "the HISTORY OF THE UNIVERSE—from the dawn of fiery creation to its last smoking ember—will be recorded here for all posterity" (Wolfman 2005, 294). While *History of the DC Universe* (hereafter referred to as *History*) was the original title for *Crisis*, it ultimately became its own entity, a two-volume illustrated prose story, written by Wolfman and illustrated by Perez, that told the history of the new, solitary universe. In the process, *History* also served as a re-narrativization of pre-*Crisis* (multiversal) stories into a post-*Crisis* (universal) milieu. Whereas part of the goal of *Crisis* had been to create a big, sprawling, superhero crossover epic, *History* did not have the same drive behind it, and was intended instead, according to Wolfman, to "be an epilogue to the *Crisis*," and thus "to tell readers which heroes and worlds still lived and which were consigned to the double-bagged depths of their collection" (Wolfman 2002, 1). He elaborated, "It's a history, it's not a story. It's a chronological retelling of DC's history in order. I think it's very exciting, because we can finally put all our characters in order for all the readers. *Crisis* is not a history, because we're changing history. A lot of readers will not be sure where everything fits now. The history will let them know" (quoted in O'Neill 24).

History was an attempt to provide a direct, clear-cut narrative of the new, unified DC Universe, one that would be accessible both to longtime fans and to new readers attracted by the streamlined post-*Crisis* DC. This is reflected not only in Wolfman's introduction to and quotes about the book, but also within the text itself. *History* is narrated by Harbinger, at some undefined time after *Crisis* has ended. Her in-story purpose for crafting such a text is "because I must, because change must be recorded" (Wolfman 2002, 5). Like Sanderson and Wolfman, Harbinger is taking on the guise of historian in order to craft a narrative of the DC Universe and, specifically, its superheroes. This is a narrative of "the History of the Universe as seen through my eyes. Its concerns are with those men and women who fought and sacrificed their own lives to save the universe, whose courage and determination altered the past and future" (Wolfman 2002, 5). She further refines her purpose in writing such a history (while at the same time making a nod toward real-world heroes, not just super-powered ones), explaining that:

> Throughout the history of the World there were freedom fighters, and this is their history, whether uniformed or not, whether powered or ordinary . . . I have been able to place them chronologically and thus show a continuity of events. . . . What began many years in the past will be remembered and acted upon many centuries from now. What *was* affects what *is* and what *will be*. This, more than

any other reason, is why this history of the universe is needed. To look at the heroic age without perspective, to understand one element without seeing the whole, is to do it a vast injustice. (Wolfman 2002, 54)

In this speech, Wolfman seems to be speaking, through Harbinger, about the nature of continuity itself (note the use of the phrase "continuity of events"). The purpose of *History* is to give an understanding of DC's continuity to readers, creators, and editors alike, so that they can "see the whole" instead of just "one element," and thus avoid recreating the confusing morass of contradictions that led to the need for *Crisis* in the first place.

In order to make such a text palatable, though, the chronicle (in White's usage of the term) of events that made up DC continuity had to be turned into an entertaining story, a narrative. Wolfman, via Harbinger, states this directly: "This is not a chronological retelling of historical events which can be read in any text—this is the history of heroism" (Wolfman 2002, 55). This statement serves several purposes. On a surface level, it provides Wolfman with a narrative excuse for Harbinger to relate only the events that separate the DC Universe from the real world, rather than providing a full textbook of world history. It also, however, structures the entire fictional universe around the concept of "heroism," making it clear that the DC Universe revolves around heroes and heroines as the pivot-points of its history. It places the *characters*, rather than specific *events*, at the center of the universe, something that was crucial to a text that was erasing many of those events from its own history in order to focus on presenting streamlined characters and stories to discerning, mature fans.

Both *Crisis* and *History* were direct attempts by DC to expand their market share in a culturally marginalized industry. Since the rise of Marvel's popularity in the 1960s, DC had been seen both by both fans and cultural critics as a secondary company. The publisher's focus on mythic god-like heroes, multiple universes, and clear-cut tropes of good versus evil had made it lag behind Marvel in terms of both sales and critical success. Because Marvel's heroes were created to be better-rounded characters with more relatable problems, the older audience that made up the readership of the 1980s gravitated much more strongly to their line than to DC's. The post-*Crisis* DC Universe, the one solidified by *History*, was a direct response to this, providing a mission statement for the publisher to focus on more mature stories with richer characters.

In order to create a universe that appealed to older readers, though, creators had to pick and choose from prior continuity. As Wolfman explained in an interview given at the time that *Crisis* was still being released, "anything we do not state happened, did not happen, unless it's brought back. So all the stupid stuff has to be brought back again" (quoted in O'Neill 24). He went on to state exactly how this process worked, editorially:

> What we're trying to do: If it's not restated, it did not happen.... All of the dumb stuff is gone, and somebody's really going to have to go out of his way to bring it back ... *It's corrective history.* There's a big eraser that's gone over all of it. If an editor deems a character or storyline worthy enough to bring back, okay—but I don't think we should be held responsible for past mistakes. Starting in January [of 1986], we only use the past that was good. (quoted in O'Neill 24, emphasis mine)

This is not only a corrective history, but also a selective history, one specifically constructed by Wolfman, Wein, Perez, and DC's other editorial and corporate staff. It reflects what *they* viewed as not falling into the realm of "dumb stuff," and thus worth keeping in a post-*Crisis* DC Universe.

This sort of cherry-picking of past events is remarkably similar to what White describes as the process of historians: "there are always more facts in the record than the historian can possibly include in his narrative representation of a given segment of the historical process. And so the historian must 'interpret' his data excluding certain facts from his account as irrelevant to his narrative purpose" (*Tropics of Discourse* 51). Once more we can see how *Crisis*, and its follow-up *History*, was a project of literally rewriting the narrative history of the DC Universe, one which utilized the decades of stories that made up a large part of the body of comics' cultural memory in order to create a new future. As Perez stated, "We're focusing on change ... *Crisis* is establishing [continuity]" (quoted in Waid 1985, 27–28). The establishment and maintenance of clarity and consistency in the continuity of the DC Universe firmly relies upon a narrativization of its history and events, as created in *Crisis* and elucidated in *History*.

By turning disparate stories about various characters and settings from DC's past (the chronicle) into one ongoing universal narrative, Wolfman and his compatriots forever changed the way superhero comics worked. Every single story from now on would be seen as a building block toward the publisher's larger universe, allowing editors to steer the entire line toward predetermined "events" and crossovers, the many descendants of *Crisis*. What's more, creators were suddenly far less free in the way they could treat iconic characters, or even second-tier characters. Whereas prior to *Crisis* a writer of Superman could have the hero partake in whatever adventure that could be imagined, no matter how outlandish (so long as it did nothing to tarnish the character's brand and stayed within the basic confines of his established personality), now the stories involving Superman had to cohere to the universal continuity established and overseen by DC's editorial team.

This would come to have a dual impact on those writers and artists interested in exploring historical narratives featuring corporately owned characters. On the one hand, creators now needed to adhere to the historical reality established by the editorial staff and by previously published stories. Any new stories set in World War II or during Vietnam, for example, needed to fit within the larger picture of how those wars functioned within the DC or Marvel Universes *plus* cohere with real-world history. Writers needed to juggle an increasing multitude of story elements if they wanted to write a series, or even a scene, with a historical setting, and everything in that series needed to make sense in the context of everything else that had been established about that time and place in the "universe."

On the other hand, though, the new focus on a universal narrative brought with it an obsession with continuity not just in the present, but also the past. Fans wanted to know how all of the stories in the publishers' long histories fit together, and this demanded a repetitive return to the past in order to provide explanations. Roy Thomas's *Young All-Stars* story featuring internment camps, for example, was made possible by the universal *Crisis* retcon erasing the 1940s Aquaman from DC history, allowing Thomas to "replace" him in World War II with a young Nisei woman.

The relationship between continuity and historical narratives is a very fraught one. Continuity tears at historical stories because its demands dictate that the fictional universe's history must constantly be updated such that everything makes sense in the context of both other stories and real-world history; meanwhile, historical stories can wreak havoc with that continuity through the addition of new events and characters. Ultimately, this back-and-forth can lead to a situation where the fictional universe's continuity becomes every bit as confused and confusing as it was at DC in the years leading up to *Crisis*.

Crises of the Twenty-First Century

Creating a solid, unchangeable continuity that doesn't accept any retcons or new historical narratives is functionally impossible for DC or Marvel. If, as established after *Crisis*, Superman, Batman, Wonder Woman, and the rest of the major superheroes were definitively said to have started their careers in the late 1980s, then in the present day they would all be pushing fifty (at least). Because the major publishers are unwilling to age the characters, most of the heroes are still said to be somewhere in their twenties or thirties, thus negating *Crisis*'s continuity. As a result, a new story must arrive to explain these new continuity entanglements.

In short, once there is one *Crisis*, there must ultimately come another. This next *Crisis*, whatever narrative form it takes, needs to explain the nagging continuity issues created by the first story and by the many other comic books that follow it in the ensuing years. As a result, the process of meta-narrativization-via-universal-cataclysm initiated by *Crisis* and *History* has become a repetitive trope used many times by DC Comics in the years since those books' publication. The publisher is constantly working to fight back against the slow accretion of backstory that might discourage new readers, while at the same time servicing fans who find that continuity to be part of the appeal of the books. DC and Marvel are both engaged in a struggle to maintain their loyal readership even as they attempt to expand their audience base, a tricky balancing act that is often achieved through line-wide revamps in the mode of *Crisis*.

The continual repetition of *Crisis*-styled plot points and themes has not been without its share of complaints, however. Fans often complain of "event fatigue" in relation to these large-scale events. Comics critic Douglas Wolk, for example, argues that the continual use of the universal retcon by DC Comics as well as other publishers is merely an expression of the problematic fact that "significant, lasting change is almost impossible to get past the marketing department, or past sentimentally attached readers. If the new way doesn't work out—and it almost never does—it's time for the 'cosmic reset button,' as fans call it; a contrivance that restores things to their original state" (102).

Beginning in 2004, in fact, DC Comics *did* hit the cosmic reset button once more. In the fifteen years following *Crisis on Infinite Earths*, DC had published a stream of semiannual crossovers, some of which were creatively and commercially successful and some of which appeared to be no more than uninspired, diluted versions of those that had come before. In the aftermath of the events of September 11, 2001, though, DC focused instead on more character-based storytelling that didn't involve much cross-title continuity. This began to change with the increasing influence of editor Dan DiDio, who had a background writing and editing for both soap operas and children's cartoon programming. When DiDio took the reigns of DC editorial, he brought back the primacy of the crossover event as a storytelling vehicle. From 2004 through 2011, DC's entire line would be defined by a series of one crossover "event" after another, which all attempted, on an ongoing basis, to tie together universal continuity as *Crisis on Infinite Earths* had done in the 1980s.

The opening salvo of this long list of events was, initially, one of the most independent of them—the seven-issue miniseries *Identity Crisis*, released between June and December of 2004, by best-selling prose novelist Brad Meltzer (who had previously written a *Green Arrow* arc for DC) and artist Rags Morales. The series was touted as a Justice League murder mystery that would reveal deep-seated secrets of the team, but as it went along its ramifications were felt wider and wider across DC's publishing line. The story does, in fact, begin as a murder mystery, with the brutal death of Sue Danby, wife to lighthearted hero Ralph Dibny, the Elongated Man, who together had formed a sort of superhero version of *The Thin Man*'s Nick and Nora Charles. That Sue Dibny was the first death in *Identity Crisis* was not incidental. It was an indication that darker times were coming for the DC Universe, where even genial, innocent creations from when the comics were more geared toward children (Ralph and Sue were meant to be likable parent figures) were subject to violent, adult forces.

As *Identity Crisis* continued, its body count rose, and its grim nature became more and more apparent. The deaths would come to include the superhero Firestorm, the supervillain Captain Boomerang, and Jack Drake, the father of Batman's young sidekick, Robin. The darkness of the story, however, did not just extend to these deaths. Although Sue Dibny's murderer is revealed to be Jean Loring, the ex-wife of superhero the Atom, during the investigation several younger heroes discover a long-hidden secret kept from them by their mentors and predecessors—years earlier, in the wake of Sue's rape at the hands of supervillain Dr. Light, several Justice League members began a campaign to alter the minds of some of their worst villains.

This piece of retroactive continuity is used by Meltzer as a way of "explaining" the somewhat goofy tone of the superhero stories of the 1950s and 1960s, stories meant for children and produced under strict Comics Code guidelines that limited the amount of violence or action that could appear in a story. Meltzer argues,

> You look back on those stories now and they're wonderful—nothing tops them—but I think a lot of people chuck them to the side and say, *That's fun, that's cute, but they're a coloring book and we don't need them anymore*. I love those stories. I grew up on those stories, and those stories changed my life. They taught me my values. They engaged me when no one else did. And in my own selfish way, I wanted them back.

Meltzer does not appear to realize the paradox he was creating—in order to "get back" the simple, moralistic stories of his childhood by bringing them into contemporary DC continuity, he needed to add a dark and horrific backstory of sexualized violence and morally compromised heroes. From the outset, the project initiated by DC with *Identity Crisis* was mired in this obsession with justifying continuity at the expense of the values and intentions of the older stories that were being revisited.

Identity Crisis was ultimately a story about the darkness at the core of even the greatest of heroes. The most significant secret that gets unearthed in the miniseries is that several Justice League members erased Batman's memory when he discovered them altering Dr. Light's mind, an event that the finale of the story hints he is starting to remember. In a special commentary included with the collected edition of *Identity Crisis*, Meltzer notes that the series was intended to show the clay feet of DC's superheroes, revealing their dark history as well as ramping up the focus on the constant threat of death faced by both them and their loved ones: "In this story we look at death in all its manifestations—not just the death of a person, but the death of an ideal, the death of a dream, and . . . the death of self . . . So many superhero comics look at things through a telescope trying to find giant monsters and whole worlds to punch. *Identity Crisis* is designed to look at these characters through a microscope, pulling in so tight, we can see all their flaws and imperfections." The series proved so successful at revealing the cracks in the foundation of the DC Universe—or, rather, at *creating* those cracks, retroactively—that it led to multiple years' worth of stories about what it would take to heal those wounds and get the heroes working together again, acting heroically rather than selfishly, in new storylines that pitted them against more extreme villains. Meltzer explains that "DC told me they were going to build a year of stories on this moment [of Batman remembering the Justice League's betrayal]," an indication of how *Identity Crisis* was going to be used by DC as a launching point for a much darker continuity.

Spinning out of *Identity Crisis*, DC's editors, headed by DiDio, took a more prominent role in the creative process, tightening the continuity of the entire publishing line so that all of the titles worked together to build toward a series of continuity changes that would impact the entire DC Universe. As a result of this, the entire DC line—which typically was upbeat and filled with the fantastic as opposed to Marvel's more grounded, and often grimmer, superhero stories—took a darker turn. This was a way of both reflecting national anxieties and appealing to a more mature readership than had been the original audience for superhero stories. Though the storylines involved bore no resemblance to the events of 9/11, the tonal shift can certainly be linked to the uncertainty permeating the American consciousness in the years following the attacks, years filled with unwinnable wars, an increasingly polarized political divide, and the ever-present fear of future attacks.

As a reaction to 9/11, DC's tightened continuity seemed to serve two purposes. First, it created a sense of editorial certainty and control in the fictional universe, something that could be comforting to readers in comparison to the seemingly chaotic, out-of-control real world. Second, the crossover stories that punctuate this tighter continuity required a greater-than-usual threat to the superheroes and their universe, which reflected the greater sense of threat permeating the American psyche after the 9/11 attacks. This, at least, was what DiDio believed, arguing that the comics provided a therapeutic and cathartic force for readers. In his words, these stories were

> crafted in a post-9/11 world at a time when most Americans were feeling vulnerable and in need of heroes. We saw a world where the human spirit was pushed to the limit and against overwhelming odds, people persevered and heroes emerged—sadly, at the cost of their own lives. And although we work in fantasy, the questions became, "Should we expect less from comics' greatest heroes?" The answer, of course, is "No." So, while the [stories have] all the requisite death and destruction, the true story is the measure of determination and self-sacrifice necessary to be a hero in the DC Universe. (5–6)

DiDio indicates that bigger threats ultimately provide a larger cathartic release by showing how the heroes overcome those threats in order to save the day and save lives.

Scholars Phillip Smith and Michael Goodrum go even further in talking about superhero comics' responses to 9/11 and their role in creating a sense of control: "In terms of clinical psychology, a sense of control is key in preventing trauma . . . The superhero genre allows . . . attacks to be contained within the familiar and its outcomes are evoked but resolved without any adverse effects" (490). The large-scale, cosmic, epic stakes of DC's crossovers are a way of reliving the trauma of attack and destruction, but with the creators (and to a lesser extent the readers/fans) in control and able to create a positive outcome.

DC's continuity-driven storytelling of this era can thus be seen as a response to the events of 9/11 and its aftereffects. The stories provided readers with an increased sense of narrative tension while at the same time releasing their real-life tensions through the cathartic experience of a genre where, eventually, the good guys always win. As a result, the increased level of continuity that began with *Identity Crisis* brought with it a dark and dour tone that would spread throughout in the DC Universe in the years to come. This darkness first presented itself in stories throughout 2004 and 2005 that addressed the dangling plot lines of *Identity Crisis*, such as Batman's reaction to finally recalling his memory-wipe. Though initially appearing in various storylines of ongoing series, these plot points came to a head in March 2005 with a special one-shot issue, *DC Countdown*, crafted by prolific DC writers Judd Winick, Greg Rucka, and Geoff Johns, along with a series of popular artists. The issue tells the story of a widespread conspiracy to take advantage of the ways in which the various corners of the DC Universe were in disarray following *Identity Crisis*. This conspiracy is uncovered by B-level superhero the Blue Beetle, who pays the price with his life. It is important to note that Blue Beetle had his highest level of success in the 1980s as a member of a humorous take on the Justice League; as with *Identity Crisis*, *Countdown* implements contemporary continuity by actively destroying the lighter moments in DC's history.

Equally as crucial to DC as the plotlines that spun out of *Countdown* was the role Geoff Johns played in creating the book. Johns was a young writer with a rising profile both within DC and within the larger comic book industry. In a generation of comic book writers who had started out as fans, Johns stands out as a different sort of figure, one who had not created fanzines but who nonetheless was a voracious comic book reader with an almost encyclopedic knowledge of the DC Universe. His fandom "credentials," so to speak, can be seen in several letters columns from the early 1990s, which the young Johns wrote to before getting his first professional break (even suggesting plot points to editors and writers that he would follow up on himself once he broke into the field) (see Cronin). It was while working as an assistant to film director Richard Donner (who had directed *Superman: The Movie*) that he began a career in comics, creating the series *Stars and S.T.R.I.P.E.* for DC before moving on to successful and well-received runs on titles such as *The Flash*, *JSA*, and *Teen Titans*, for which he received multiple fan awards. His popularity with the fans, which was thanks in part to his immense knowledge of DC's characters and continuity, led to a higher and higher profile within the company, which culminated in being handed the opportunity to helm 2005's seven-issue crossover "event" *Infinite Crisis*, the official twenty-year anniversary/sequel to *Crisis on Infinite Earths*. Tellingly, this was a project initiated by DiDio and DC editorial rather than by the book's creative team, which Johns would later admit: "Dan always had the plan to do a sequel to the original *Crisis on Infinite Earths*, and then he just got the rest of us involved" ("Infinite Discussions").

Four miniseries had spun out of *Countdown*—*The OMAC Project*, *Day of Vengeance*, *Villains United*, and *Rann/Thanager War*—that were each disparate in tone and created by different teams of writers and artists. However, thanks to DC's tight editorial control, each series was designed to reach a common endpoint—the beginning of *Infinite Crisis*. Johns describes how at the outset of *Infinite Crisis*, "the universe was going to hell in a handbasket, all of the DC mini-series . . . had pushed our world into such chaos" ("Infinite Discussions"). The books' primary artist, penciller Phil Jimenez, explains how this dark opening, one which all of DC continuity had been pushing toward, was intended to be the starting point of a redemption arc for DC's heroes: "It set up our heroes in this dark place . . . and it gave us a great starting place to take our heroes back to their iconographic status" ("Infinite Discussions"). The presale hype for *Infinite Crisis* was of such a great extent that the comics-centric *Wizard* magazine followed Johns and Jimenez to various comic book stores in Los Angeles and New York on the day the series was released, gauging fan reactions about everything from confusion over continuity issues, to fear about what characters might die, and even to recognizing the presumably "undercover" creators (Casey and Cotton).[7]

Much of the advertising and advance hype for *Infinite Crisis* focused on the story's darkness, explaining the series as portraying "the worst day in the history of the DC Universe" (Ward "Crisis Confidential," 51). However, *Infinite Crisis* was also advertised as being the culmination of very careful planning on the part of DC editorial, along with top creators like Johns and Jimenez. Johns explained in an interview that "There's a reason everything's happening the way it is now. It's not arbitrary. Everything's been planned really carefully" (quoted in Ward "Crisis Confidential," 52). The same interview noted how the planning and the increased darkness went hand in hand, as Johns "prefers to think of each ripple in the DCU—be it *Identity Crisis* or the original *Crisis*—as part of one enormous story, rather than self-contained events. In a way, this allows him to justify the unspeakable pain about to befall the bravest and boldest of the DCU" (Ward "Crisis Confidential," 52).

Johns, who was quickly becoming the main architect of the DC Universe, wholeheartedly subscribed to the concept of a universal narrative, a way of viewing DC's publishing line that had been initiated with the original *Crisis on Infinite Earths*. The planning that went into this endeavor was on such a scale that, according to another interview, the chief DC editors and creators laid out "the tricky and intricate story pacing . . . via giant blueprints, charts, and Post-It notes DiDio . . . keeps locked in his office, to keep tabs on the story as it progresses" (Ward "Crisis Almighty," 81). These story beats were then farmed out to various DC books and creators: "The core Crisis architects strived to provide enough story and character options for the rest of the

DC talent, so that tie-ins weren't forced and previously planned storylines weren't undermined or tossed. The character and story links would ultimately result in a more cohesive universe and add to the already epic quality of the event—stretching across all books in the DCU" (Ward "Crisis Almighty," 83).

The darkness that all of this universal planning sets up for the first issue of *Infinite Crisis* is meant to affect not only the audience, but also a set of characters within the story itself—the Superman, Lois Lane, Superboy, and heroic Lex Luthor of several alternate dimensions, all of whom had gone into a limbo-like zone at the end of the original *Crisis on Infinite Earths*. In *Infinite Crisis*, this Superman—the original Superman of Earth-2, the one who had initiated the DC Universe as well as the very concept of the superhero in *Action Comics* #1—has finally seen enough darkness overtake the world, and he breaks free of limbo to return home, bringing with him his memories of the pre-*Crisis* multiverse.

After twenty years of a single DC Universe with an entirely rewritten and retconned history, the DC Multiverse returned, providing a fresh link between current stories and those going back to the 1930s, a link which had been severed by the original *Crisis* in the mid-1980s. This reemergence of the multiverse, a retcon of a previous retcon, was perhaps a reflection of the post-9/11 desire to return to "simpler" times of the past, in this case via a multitude of fanciful worlds and stories that need not be slaves to reality or continuity. By this point, too, creators like Johns who had grown up reading DC's comics but never had a chance to utilize the idea of the multiverse in their work wanted to bring that story possibility back into the publisher's fold. Thanks to *Infinite Crisis*, after twenty years these fans-turned-creators were, like Roy Thomas in the 1980s, able to write back to the stories set in a DC Multiverse that they had grown up with.

On a deeper level, though, in the estimation of literary scholar Geoff Klock, the reemergence of past narratives has psychological connotations. In analyzing the "revisionary superhero narrative" of the late 1980s through mid-1990s, Klock posits that "any given superhero narrative stands in relation to its conflicted, chaotic tradition, and continuity as the ego stands in relation to the unconscious" (5). Relating these narratives to Harold Bloom's theory of "anxiety of influence," Klock argues that "superhero comic books are an especially good place to witness the structure of misprision [active/critical reading/misreading], because as a serial narrative that has been running for more than sixty years, reinterpretation becomes part of its survival code" (13). Though Klock uses the "anxiety of influence" to examine a specific set of revisionist superhero texts, his larger point here is valid to the heavily "influenced" *Infinite Crisis* as well.

During the course of its story, *Infinite Crisis* becomes a fictional embodiment of the battle over that multiverse: the alternate Lex Luthor and Superboy have gone mad during their time in limbo, and want to destroy the current DC universe in order to create a more "perfect" one. These two characters' manipulations behind the scenes turn out to have caused much of the terrible circumstances that the series opened on, and the world's heroes—especially the "trinity" of Superman, Batman, and Wonder Woman, who begin the series barely on speaking terms—must come together to defeat them. In the process, the Earth-Two Superman and Lois Lane both die, and the DC Universe's continuity is given something of a "soft" reboot, where certain aspects of its history are tweaked or recreated (such as whether or not there was ever a Superboy, or whether Wonder Woman was a founding member of the Justice League) while leaving much of the overriding structure of the universe intact (which differentiates it from the "hard" reboot of the original *Crisis* that altered the very core and history of the DC Universe, rewriting its basic format, setup, and structure).

While *Identity Crisis* established a darker, more serious tone for DC, one created through editorial oversight of the entire line, *Infinite Crisis* started a second thread of control—that of obsession with DC's history and continuity. The follow-up "event" series to *Infinite Crisis* was *52*, a year-long weekly series set in "real time" telling the story of what happened to the DC Universe in the year following *Infinite Crisis*, a year in which Superman, Batman, and Wonder Woman were all inactive. *52* was a critically acclaimed series, due both to its unique narrative structure as well as the four "all-star" writers helming it, which included Geoff Johns and longtime comics superstar Grant Morrison. Though composed of a variety of character-focused narrative threads, the "big reveal" of the series in the fifty-second issue is that the events of *Infinite Crisis* resulted in not just the return of memories of the DC Multiverse, but the full-on recreation of that multiverse as fifty-two alternate worlds and dimensions. Many of these were reminiscent of worlds from the original multiverse, while others were home to popular out-of-continuity stories (called "Elseworlds") from the previous few decades that imagined scenarios such as Batman becoming a vampire or Superman landing in Soviet Russia instead of Kansas. This recreation of the multiverse further shows DC's continuing obsession with its own history and continuity, in essence retconning the retcon of the original *Crisis on Infinite Earths*. One of the characters in the series sums up the feeling of the creators and editors behind *52* when he exclaims, "Look around you . . . There's so much more happening out there than we could ever have imagined . . . That's the way things should be. Welcome to a multiverse of possibility . . . Welcome home" (Johns et al. 2008, 25–26).

DC followed up the well-received 52 with another weekly series, *Countdown*, which was poorly received by critics and fans alike. What DC's editors failed to realize was that 52 had been a success not just because of its attention to continuity, but because of its attention to character and story. 52 was crafted by four of the finest writers working in superhero comics, veritable experts in bringing together action, characterization, and continuity tidbits within a meaningful overarching story structure. *Countdown*, however, was driven by editors rather than writers, and was concerned with tying all of DC's books into one massive continuity rather than exploring nuances of character. Its focus on continuity as the star of the title led to flat, undifferentiated character arcs that provided little emotional depth for readers to latch on to. Eventually it was revealed that *Countdown* was only ever "counting down" to yet another major "event," *Final Crisis*, a book helmed by writer Grant Morrison in what was intended to be the finale of the "crisis trilogy."

The goal of *Countdown*, narratively, was to get the DC Universe into position for the beginning of *Final Crisis*, and yet in the end it failed at this because neither Morrison nor the writers of *Countdown* were even aware that this was DC's goal. Morrison would later explain that *Countdown* had little to do with what he was crafting for *Final Crisis*:

> *Final Crisis* was partly written and broken down into rough issue-by-issue plots before *Countdown* was even conceived, let alone written. . . . The *Countdown* writers were later asked to "seed" material from *Final Crisis* and in some cases, probably due to the pressure of filling the pages of a weekly book, that seeding amounted to entire plotlines veering off in directions I had never envisaged, anticipated, or planned for in *Final Crisis*. (quoted in C. Eckert)

This certainly seems to support the idea that *Countdown* was, rather than a creator-driven book, one that was micromanaged by DC editorial as a way to keep up the feeling of an ongoing "event" in the DC Universe while Morrison prepared *Final Crisis* for the following year. Indeed, DiDio himself would admit that "I'd say about 75% of the concepts that are being created [at DC Comics] are editorially driven." However, he clarified that "The role of the editor is to assemble and be responsible for whatever project they are in charge of . . . please understand that whatever book you hold in your hand, at the end of the day, is there because of an editorial mandate to create that book" (quoted in C. Eckert). Nevertheless, even DiDio would come to admit that many fans and reviewers felt that *Countdown* suffered from too much editorial interference, forcing it to reflect too much of what was happening in other DC books: "If you're creating stories just for the sake of having events to tie things together with no real meat on the bones, then you're going to have event fatigue because you have all this promotion and drive and anticipation, but you've under-delivered on what the expectations are" (quoted in C. Eckert). *Countdown* served as a lesson to DiDio and the rest of DC editorial that even they could only control the DC Universe so much before the stories and characters, not to mention the creators, suffered from being stifled.

In Morrison's *Final Crisis*, those characters suffered in a different sense—they were subjected to "the day evil won," when the superheroes failed to stop the physical, psychological, and emotional invasion of earth by the dark "New God" Darkseid. Morrison had a long history working for DC Comics, beginning in the 1980s when he was part of the "British invasion" of creators brought to DC from the world of British comics. Over the two decades since then, Morrison had become a critical darling as well as a blockbuster sales force, whose postmodern, intellectual take on superheroes reflected an outsider, counterculture ethos that he brought to such seemingly staid characters as Superman, Batman, and the Justice League. He was also known for his creator-owned properties, such as *The Invisibles*, which brought him an audience that wasn't much interested in superheroes, generally, but did avidly follow his work on any project. With *Final Crisis*, Morrison, along with artistic collaborators J. G. Jones, Carlos Pacheco, and Doug Mahnke, among others, finally brought to a head plot threads that he had been seeding into his DC work since the 1990s, in order to tell his version of the ultimate story of good versus evil in the DC Universe. Perhaps having learned something from *Countdown*, DC did not force *Final Crisis* tie-ins upon every one of its books and creators, but rather let it stand alone with a few related miniseries and crossovers.

Final Crisis is a solipsistic, metafictional, and surprisingly philosophical superhero magnum opus for Morrison. It suffers, however, from its own cleverness—to truly understand the series requires not only a knowledge of DC's extensive continuity (even though the series does not tie into any ongoing series, it draws upon decades of previous stories), but also an ability to parse out the metatextual message Morrison implants into the series about the force of creation versus the blank page, and the hope inspired in readers by the inevitable fact that DC's superhero stories never end, are always "to be continued." By the end of the series, Morrison experiments with new storytelling techniques, distilling entire story beats down into single iconic panels, and telling the story from multiple points of view in both time and space. As Morrison himself describes the series,

> The "final crisis," as I saw it for a paper universe like DC's, would be the terminal war between is and isn't, between the story and the blank page. What would

happen if the void of the page took issue with the quality of material imposed upon it and decided to fight back by spontaneously generating a living concept capable of devouring narrative itself. . . . I tried to show the DC universe breaking down into signature gestures, last-gasp strategies that were tried and tested but would this time fail, until finally even the characterizations would fade and the plot become rambling, meaningless, disconnected. Although I lost my nerve a little, I must confess, and it never became disconnected enough. This, I was trying to say, is what happens when you let bad stories eat good ones. (Morrison 2011, 368)

Though an interesting postmodern exercise in creating a comic, this stylistic flourish did not sit well with many readers. Some felt that Morrison was making a simple superhero story too complex and difficult to read, while others felt that such complexity was wasted on the subject matter of superheroes. The reviews of the series were, at best, mixed. Critic Graeme McMillan, writing for the website io9, noted that

Like the majority of Morrison's superhero work, this isn't a story that will satisfy fans of the literal; it's very much an allegorical, lyrical story . . . with narrative clarity sacrificed on occasion for artistic effect. It's very much a story you feel as much as anything, and because of that, re-reading it becomes a strange celebration of the successful moments with an increasing awareness of its faults.

The blog Collected Edition similarly described *Final Crisis* as a story that had both flaws and moments that soared, summarizing that, "Though the storytelling within *Final Crisis* is perhaps at times unnecessarily complex, it is at its heart an ode to comic books." In essence, Morrison was trying to please both superheroes and "alternative" comics readers, and was unable to find a happy middle. The metanarrative of creation/destruction, good story/bad story, comic book/blank page ultimately *becomes* the narrative of *Final Crisis*, a concept that was not as pleasing to fans as either the "universe/multiverse"-based storytelling of *Crisis on Infinite Earths* and *Infinite Crisis* or the character-driven story of 52. As Morrison himself notes: "*Final Crisis* was a bestseller, but it divided the Internet crowd like Alexander's sword" (Morrison 2011, 368).

Superhero comics, as we have seen, walk a tightrope between the pleasures of escapism and the strictures of continuity and historical reality. *Final Crisis*, in a sense, eschewed *both* of these poles, by being both densely philosophical and yet also unconnected to real politics or history. Fans and critics were only somewhat willing to follow Morrison in this strange direction, and thus it received neither the sales success of *Infinite Crisis* nor the critical acclaim of *52*. Though Morrison showed that comics can utilize their form and structure to create new ways of understanding story and new modes of looking at reality, he also learned that these concepts do not sit well with average superhero fans.

However it was received, with *Final Crisis* DC reached the apex of its post-9/11 continuity obsessions. Morrison created a story of the DC Multiverse that is ultimately not about the individual heroes or their struggles, but rather about the living multiverse itself, and the power of superhero comics as a vehicle for instilling hope and awe in readers. The end of the series reflects this, explaining that Superman, at a point in the story where he was given an all-powerful "God machine" with which he could do anything, "wished for a happy ending." However, the very next page explores, via the voice of a newscaster, how that happy ending is merely a beginning for new stories: "You've just joined WGBS on a beautiful day in Metropolis! With more on those newly discovered parallel worlds and how they could change our lives forever! This is one story that's only just beginning" (Morrison 2009, 34–35). Thus, even when evil wins, in the DC Universe the figure of the superhero—represented by the iconic Superman—can "wish" it back to a happy ending, as a place for new narratives and new comic books to emerge from.

Final Crisis shows just how different the DC Universe is from the real world. After September 11, 2001, there was no way of magically wishing things back to the way they were before. On America's own "day evil won," tragedy and trauma prevailed, despite the narratives of superheroic emergency workers. *Final Crisis* is, fittingly, the final reaction by DC (whether consciously or not) to the events of 9/11, a statement of the power of heroic fiction to always lead to another adventure and never give in to defeat or surrender. Just as ancient societies created pantheons of gods in order to explain the natural workings of the world, including horrific tragedies, Morrison is saying that modern writers of superhero comics can craft mythologies that can be every bit as inspiring to readers as the older myths were to their inventors, enabling their respective societies and cultures to get over great tragedy.

With *Final Crisis*, Morrison and DC affirm the value of escapism and hope in superhero stories as a valid way of responding to tragedy, showcasing how such escapism can be tied into the ongoing narrative of a comic book universe with a tightly controlled continuity. Retconning—which was central to all of this—was thus useful as a tool to reinvigorate that universe with new values, replacing a decade of despair and fear with a new ethos of hope and wonder.

It wasn't until the tenth anniversary of 9/11, however, that DC Comics finally shed its focus on the past, with a massive half-reboot/half-retcon that they called "The New 52." Following a crossover event entitled *Flashpoint*, written by Geoff Johns (who by this point had gone from simply an influential writer at DC to an executive in the company, serving as its chief creative officer), the entire DC publishing line was canceled, with fifty-two titles—some classic, some brand new—receiving first issues as part of an entirely rebooted DC Universe. As a *New York Times* article published just prior to the release of the first of these new issues explained, "The success or failure of this plan will have far-reaching implications: it could alienate longtime fans at the cost of new readers" (Itzkoff). As the *Times* article rightly points out, this reboot was a bold move. Though the publisher had previously restarted its continuity in the mid-1980s in the wake of *Crisis on Infinite Earths*, that was a gradual process in which individual characters' backstories were retconned and retold over a period of months and even years. DC editorial had rejected Marv Wolfman's idea to start all of the publisher's books anew with first issues. Twenty-five years later, though, faced with ever-shrinking sales and an increasingly vocal group of hardcore fans who were resistant to change, DC decided it was time for just such a risky move.

Although officially DC would note that not *all* of the prior continuity was thrown out (hence the classification of the New 52 as both a partial reboot *and* a massive retcon), the company went to great effort to streamline its books. All of its iconic characters were much younger than they had previously been portrayed, with the modern DC Universe having started with Superman's first appearance about five years in the past. Dan DiDio, who by this point was DC's copublisher alongside artist-turned-businessman Jim Lee, explained in a *USA Today* article officially announcing the relaunch, "We really want to inject new life in our characters and line. This was a chance to start, not at the beginning, but at a point where our characters are younger and the stories are being told for today's audience" (quoted in Truit). In this way, DC hoped to retain fans who would see links to the previous continuity, while at the same time gaining new readers who may have been interested in DC's books but were looking for a jumping-on point: "Not only will this initiative be compelling for existing readers, it will give new readers a precise entry point into our universe" (DiDio and Lee).

The New 52 was at first a smash success for DC, in large part because it served as a very public jumping-on point to an otherwise increasingly impenetrable fictional universe. Not only did the company market their new books to comic book readers at conventions and on popular industry websites, but they also made an attempt to capture a broader audience through mainstream media coverage in such outlets as the *New York Times* and *Entertainment Weekly*. Initially, this move seemed to work. The initiative increased their sales by a significant amount and gave them a majority of the market sale for Diamond Comic Distributors (the nationwide comic book distribution network) for the first few months of the new line, a position that Marvel had traditionally held for years (Melrose). As would be expected from fifty-two discreet books, critical reaction was mixed, with some series receiving rave reviews while others failed to find critical and/or sales footing. Comics journalist Rich Johnston, for example, provided brief reviews for all of the first issues, ranging from a pan of the series *Stormwatch* ("A bunch of characters, some known, some new, that stand around saying that they are not superheroes, but not acting... any differently. It's not just been neutered, it's been castrated") to a glowing review of the book *Animal Man* ("If *Stormwatch* seems to abandon what made it special, *Animal Man* has preserved it... concentrated it and portrayed it with a writer and artist working like one").

By eight months in, however, analysts began to question just how successful the initiative really was. Comics translator and critic Marc-Oliver Frisch, in crunching the numbers of the first eight months of sales, concluded that the New 52 stopped DC's drop-off in sales from 2011, but in the end only by returning to sales amounts from 2010:

> All told, the "New 52" seems to have stabilized DC's sales right in the middle of the spectrum. Whether or not that's good or bad, given the massive logistical and promotional efforts and incentives that went into the "New 52" relaunch... is a matter of interpretation. The good news is that DC managed to boost and stabilize its line after a very tough couple of years. The bad news is that DC took its best shot and it bought them a reset to 2010, basically.

This is about the most up-to-date assessment of DC's New 52—a moderate success, but not exactly a game-changer in terms of sales.

Meanwhile, from a narrative standpoint, this regeneration of the DC Universe did not derail Grant Morrison's continued plans to explore the complex continuities of the publisher's vast history. In 2009, prior to the New 52, Morrison revealed that he was working on a new series, called *Multiversity*, specifically meant to map out several of the worlds of the new multiverse. This project, which ultimately would not see release until late 2014, is (whether explicitly stated or not) a sequel to the now-misleadingly-named *Final Crisis*. Morrison himself has said, "I want this to be big. I kind of thought 'Final Crisis' would be the big one and then I realized I had to tell this Multiverse one.

So this is the real big epic that comes up next" (quoted in Renaud). His hope for the series was that it would explore these new Earths, one per issue for seven issues, and then, "in the eighth issue, I would tell a new big story to link things up in into one big epic" (quoted in Renaud).

All of this shows how the ongoing cycle of repetition regarding the DC multiverse, and the "big events" and "crises" that threaten it, continues more than a quarter of a century after *Crisis* was meant to clean up the continuity confusions that such stories have the strong potential to produce. Once creators saw the narrative potential of the retcon, for both individual characters/books and for an entire comic book universe, they wanted to utilize that potential to continually rejuvenate stories and characters that were not reaching their full critical or sales potential.

Given the vast success of retconning in the world of comic books, it should be no surprise that other media would come to seize upon retroactive continuity as a storytelling tool of their own. In the next chapter, we will see how this was utilized on both the small screen of the television set and the silver screen of major film franchises.

MOVING IMAGES, MOVING HISTORY
Retroactive Continuity in Television and Film

When one thinks about continuity on television, perhaps the first genre that comes to mind is the TV soap opera. Certainly, as decades-long ongoing storylines, soap operas have much in common with superhero comic books, including complex continuity, a huge cast of characters, a dedicated and vocal fandom, and the occasional evil twin. Because they are continuity-dense long-form narratives, soap operas have been engaging in retroactive continuity for decades now, nearly as long as comic books have been doing so, and with similarly varying degrees of acceptance from audiences.

Soap operas are not the only television genre to develop such a complex level of continuity, though. Genre programming—much of which has been collated under the heading of "Cult TV"—has evolved over time from episodic, character-based serials to ongoing narratives with an emphasis on long-term, dangling plot lines. What's more, this type of storytelling has, in recent years, jumped from the small screen to the silver screen, taking over billion-dollar movie franchises.[1] Comics historian Robert Greenberger, in an article discussing *Crisis on Infinite Earths*, notes this transposition of storytelling techniques between media:

> It's interesting to note how the evolving method of telling comic-book stories, owing in equal parts to the ancient mythology and radio soap opera, has spilled beyond its four-color pages. You could see it infiltrate science fiction with shared universes such as Robert Lynn Aspirin and Lynn Abbey's *Thieves' World* and George R. R. Martin's *Wild Cards* in the 1980s. In time, the serialized nature also found its way into primetime television as dramas got richer and deeper, an early example being Steven Bochco's *Hill Street Blues*. It took time, but in recent years, it finally made it to the movies starting with subplots spun across the *Star Wars* and *Star Trek* films and finally, the team-up film—Marvel's *The Avengers*. (53)

As a result of this movement, both television and film have more and more become sites of retroactive continuity, as the technique has moved beyond the page and been embraced by many of the transmedia empires of the twenty-first century.

This chapter will begin by examining how retroactive continuity has functioned in soap operas, a genre with as rich a narrative complexity as the superhero universes discussed in the previous two chapters. From there, we will examine how retconning—thanks in no small part to comic book fans becoming TV writers and producers—has slowly moved from the television soap opera to the primetime television drama, becoming progressively more self-conscious, intentional, and eventually integral to many popular "cult TV" programs. Finally, we will look at how retconning has gone from the small screen to the silver screen, forming an integral part of many of the dominant film franchises of the early twenty-first century.

As the World Turns Backward: Retconning in Soap Operas

The soap opera is a genre that debuted on radio networks in the 1930s. The often-daily shows were aimed at a primarily female audience, particularly housewives who spent their afternoons in the home. The shows featured large amounts of dialogue, a focus on female characters/concerns, and melodramatic plots and characterizations. Most importantly for their continued production, they proved to be potent avenues through which to sell products.

Often they were sponsored by soap and detergent companies, leading to the name of the genre.

Jennifer Hayward notes in her study of serial fiction, *Consuming Pleasures*, that "Broadcasting regulations did not yet forbid the plugging of particular name brands, and in fact shows were usually sponsored by a single manufacturer. Audiences demonstrating an astonishing loyalty to 'their' shows—as soap audiences overwhelmingly did—could be encouraged to transfer that loyalty to a sponsoring product" (139). She defines these early soaps as "serial[s] aimed at a female audience and marked by a domestic setting, emphasis on emotional and interpersonal concerns, and continuing narrative" (139). The soap opera was thus, in its very title, defined both by the "operatic" content of its melodrama, as well as by the advertising possibilities of its form.

For this reason, the format was easily transferable to television—the emphasis on dialogue, and on extreme emotion rather than complicated action, made for shows that were cheap and easy to produce for a weekday afternoon slot, bolstered by extensive advertising support. With the transfer to television, the emphasis shifted away from domestic situations and toward complicated plot. According to Hayward,

> Television's added visual dimension introduced complications, among them the need for a greatly expanded cast since viewers could now identify characters by appearance as well as voice. Larger casts required more involved plots, which in turn demanded lengthened segments, and this development eventually worked to encourage multiple subplots and to complicate plots even further. (139)

By the time that the soaps transferred completely from radio to television in the 1960s, they were fully reliant upon complicated plots in addition to melodrama, creating a serial narrative situation very much akin to the kinds that Stan Lee and his artistic cohorts were developing at Marvel Comics in the 1960s. As the soaps continued over the ensuing decades, they developed continuities every bit as complicated as those established in the superhero comics, and often found themselves in need of a retcon in order to reflect or prepare for present and future narrative contingencies.

As with superhero comics, in order to maintain an ongoing narrative that denies closure, and continually cycles subplots into main plots while developing new subplots ad infinitum, complications arose in soap operas regarding the shows' continuities. A shifting history became required simply because so much detail had been added to that history over time that inconsistencies naturally arose. This lead to a reliance upon a vacillating notion of both history and identity, resulting in some of the now-clichéd plotlines associated with the genre. As Hayward explains,

> The ubiquitous "cliff-hanger" endings and secrets combine with the plot devices of amnesia, long-lost relatives, mistaken identity, and so on to expose the shifting and subjective nature of "fact." All attest to the ways in which soap plots are impelled by exploration of the difficulty or impossibility of *knowing*, of keeping "facts" straight despite the shimmering distortions of memory and subjective desire. (152, emphasis in original)

Though Hayward is speaking of soap operas here, it is hard not to read that description as being equally apt for superhero comics. Just as the fans of those comics can become unnerved when the history/facts with which they are familiar change, the same is true of fans of soaps, according to Hayward: "[E]xigencies of production may lead to viewers feeling betrayed by sudden shifts in clearly established storylines that effectively deny what the viewer experienced as narrative *fact* in previous episodes" (154, emphasis in original). It hardly needs to be added that the same is true of superhero comics and other types of long-form narratives that experience retroactive continuity. Hayward, herself, positions this textual/historical instability in the context of serial fiction, generally:

> Producers' frequent rewriting of soap history and ignoring of soap chronology or real world temporality are necessary consequences of soap creation. In narrative terms, interminable serial reproduction requires that each small, temporary "conclusion" shift, give way to a new instability. In production terms, the sheer volume and longevity of each show, coupled with the imperative of maintaining at least the illusion of newness while preserving favorite characters, introduce ... instability of memory, personality, and history. (154–55)

Soap operas, as the first television shows to rely upon longtime, complicated continuities, thus provide some of the earliest examples of retroactive continuity on TV.

As in the realm of superhero comics, retcons in soap operas were often met with mixed audience response, as was the case with the characters of Luke Spencer and Laura Webber on the soap *General Hospital*. In an October 1979 episode, Luke drunkenly rapes Laura, whom he has been stalking. However, audiences responded well to the pairing of the two actors, and so the writers of *General Hospital* were faced with a conundrum of making a believable, likable couple out of a rape victim and her attacker. As Hayward explains, their solution involved a retroactive rewriting of the show's history:

> [The] writers rewrote past history to the extent that as far as Luke and Laura themselves are concerned, the rape was "semi-consensual" (whatever that means).... [T]he fact that the rape had to be erased from collective memory indicates that in the minds of the writers, a rapist *could not* become a good character and therefore the rape itself had to be denied and dissolved. (177, emphasis in original)

Hayward underscores this last point to provide a counterpoint to a different example she analyses in depth—the redemption of the character of Todd Manning, who had instigated the gang-rape of a woman by three fraternity boys on the soap *One Life to Live*. Hayward notes that "viewers so vehemently and publicly expressed their horror at the thought that *One Life to Live* might be heading in such a direction that the executive producer issued a statement . . . to the effect that a Luke/Laura style romance—explicitly so labeled—between Todd and Marty was 'absolutely, categorically out of the question'" (178). Clearly, audiences had had mixed reactions to the rewriting of Luke and Laura's history. Todd, however, was kept as a clear-cut rapist, who was "redeemed" (albeit only to some members of the audience) via traditions taken from Victorian sentimental fiction rather than by any rewriting of his past. The retcon is thus not the only tool available to soap opera writers in order to handle messy continuity, and in fact it is often *not* the best tool to use. This is particularly true because—evil twins and occasional demonic possessions aside—most soap operas occur in a real-world setting, rather than one where fantastic magic or advanced science can account for a *Crisis*-style rewriting of history.

Nighttime soap operas—distinguished from their daily forefathers by a weekly primetime slot and higher budgets—were no stranger to the convention of the retcon, either. Infamously, the television show *Dallas* completely retconned an entire season into being "just a dream," a sloppy-but-popular retcon trope. Just as infamous was the ending of the long-running hospital drama *St. Elsewhere*, which concluded with a surprise revelation that the entire series had taken place in the mind of an autistic child.[2]

These two examples, though, are often heralded as being two of the worst moments of "shock-value" plot twists in television history. Their extremity is worsened by the fact that they occurred in shows that were otherwise mired in naturalistic (if melodramatic) character relations. It would be in a different sort of television show, the genre-enmeshed program that has often been called "Cult TV," that retroactive continuity would find its way more permanently onto primetime in a manner that audiences were willing to accept.

Where No Retcon Has Gone Before: *Star Trek* and Continuity

In the 1960s, Gene Roddenberry's science fiction show *Star Trek* was groundbreaking for a variety of reasons. Not only did it showcase international cooperation during the Cold War, and was the first show to feature an interracial kiss, but it was also one of the first programs to attain a cult fan following (similar to the fandom that developed around science fiction program *Doctor Who* in Great Britain). *Star Trek* was thus one of the originators of Cult TV, a genre described by media scholar Matt Hills as shows that evolve a cult following over time, "through audience routines and repeated viewing, as well as through organized fandoms, reading protocols, textual forms, the situated agency of media producers, and media-institutional contexts such as syndication or prolonged seriality" (522). However, Hills also situates Cult TV within the context of three other proposed definitions. The first of these—"Cult TV can be defined through textual analysis, and depends on texts"—looks to the genres from which cult television programs tend to emerge (science fiction, fantasy, and horror) for shared textual qualities. The second—"Cult TV can be defined through an analysis of secondary texts or inter-texts, and depends on these inter-texts"—relies upon the existence of secondary texts talking about the cult program. The third proposed definition—"Cult TV can be defined through an analysis of fan practices, and depends on fan activities"—focuses not on the program, but on the fan activity engendered and inspired by that program.

For the purposes of this discussion, I will be taking Cult TV to mean all three of these definitions. The shows I discuss share generic conventions, possess numerous intertexts (some of which prove vital toward understanding the shows' retcons), and feature active fandoms, all of which developed, as Hills defines it, "within the institutional contexts of US and UK media industries, by producers placed within the institutional contexts of production companies and professional bodies, and by fans placed within the institutional contexts of organised and online fan communities" (522). Though there is a long history of Cult TV shows, from roughly the 1960s through to the present, I will focus on only a few examples in order to show how retcons have moved from the realm of "subcultural" artifacts like comic books and soap operas to primetime shows with a mass (if "cult") following.

Star Trek, when it first aired, was unable to maintain a viewership strong enough to keep it in NBC's lineup. Initially conceived as a five-year program (referenced in its title narration as a "five-year mission"), the show's ratings were low, and NBC threatened to cancel it after its second season. However, an unprecedented letter writing campaign by its die-hard fans convinced the network to keep it on the air, but ultimately only for one more season. Reruns of *Star Trek* continued in syndication throughout the 1970s, and led to an increased popularity and growing cult following, helped along by an animated spin-off series in 1973–74. The resurgence of the franchise was cemented with the 1979 *Star Trek: The Motion Picture* and its critically acclaimed 1982 sequel, *Star Trek II: The Wrath of Khan*. This revived interest in the franchise allowed Rodenberry to cocreate (prior to his 1991 death) a new television series, *Star Trek: The Next Generation*, which ran from 1987 to 1994. Simultaneously, the *Star Trek* films continued with multiple sequels featuring the cast of the original series (followed by four more with the *Next Generation* cast). Several other *Star Trek* television series and films would follow, leading to a blockbuster reboot of the franchise with J. J. Abrams's 2009 film simply titled *Star Trek*.

As this brief history of the franchise shows, the *Star Trek* universe consists of a long-lasting, extensive narrative, which has often created messy bits of inconsistent continuity. For almost forty years, *Star Trek* stories have spanned multiple media, including the aforementioned television and film series, alongside fanzines, official companion books, novels, comic books, and multiple other productions of various levels of canonicity. It is no surprise, then, that *Star Trek* has utilized multiple retcons in its long history—particularly in the last few decades—to help keep that continuity straight, as well as to cement the "canon" of what is and is not considered an official part of the universe's timeline (something that is of great concern to many fans).

Star Trek is also somewhat unique among television franchises in that it spans multiple decades in real time, but even longer than that in story time. *The Next Generation* takes place about a century after the original *Star Trek* series does, which allowed the later series to create its own identity separate from the shadow of the original. However, the time jump was not the only significant difference between the two shows. *The Next Generation* also features an infusion of soap opera elements into the story, with a greater focus on character development and a series of melodramatic relationships, both romantic and platonic.

In its initial incarnation, the original *Star Trek* series had more in common with traditional westerns than it did with soap operas. Episodes tended to be self-contained, and the characters had defined, rarely changing relationships, which they maintained from episode to episode. The focus was, instead, on the problem they were encountering on a particular foreign planet each week. As media scholar Henry Jenkins explains,

> Part of what distinguishes an episodic series like *Star Trek* from a serial . . . is the degree to which each *Star Trek* story remains self-contained. A typical *Star Trek* episode poses a problem needing to be solved by the episode's conclusion and that solution restores equilibrium on the ship; the established relationships must end exactly where they begin. (98–99)

As Jenkins points out, though, fans of the series read seriality into it anyway:

> No episode can be easily disentangled from the series' historical trajectory; plot developments are seen not as complete within themselves but as one series of events among many in the lives of its primary characters. For the fan, it is important to see *all* of the episodes "in order" in a way that is not for the average viewer of that same program. The character's responses to a particular situation are seen as growing from that character's total life experiences and may be explained through references to what has been learned about that character in previous episodes. (99)

This kind of seriality, largely developed by fans, was more directly part of the text itself in *The Next Generation*, where interpersonal relationships changed and developed (albeit slightly) over the course of the series. By the time that future *Star Trek* spin-offs were airing—*Star Trek: Deep Space Nine*, *Star Trek: Voyager*, and *Star Trek: Enterprise*—they were focusing on season/series-long story arcs, which required previous knowledge on the part of viewers in order to understand what was happening from episode to episode. The *Star Trek* franchise had absorbed the seriality of soap operas and superhero comics and made it a crucial part of the shows' texts, not just the fan-driven intertexts.

As serial continuity became more important to the franchise, so too did maintaining consistent continuity. At first, this was a primarily fannish concern, expressed both in discussions and in fan fiction that "fixed" those errors, frequently through retconning. Jenkins explains:

> Episodes are viewed negatively if they contradict information fans assume to be true about the series world or if they develop the program in directions frustrating fans' own sense of its "potentials." . . . [Some] contradictions, while unpopular, may be more tolerable than others. . . . Other changes cut too close to basic assumptions about what constitutes a good or credible *Star Trek* narrative to be so accommodated and must be rejected outright as "unforgivable" transgressions and unjustifiable infringements on the pleasures fans find in the program. (103–6)

Over time, though, particularly as the producers and writers of the various *Star Trek* shows came to be fans who grew up watching the original or *The Next Generation* (similar to what happened in the comic book industry, with Roy Thomas leading the way), that continuity moved beyond fan discussion/speculation and became an important concern of the series.

For example, in between the original television series and the first films in the franchise, the makeup that was used for the alien Klingon race changed drastically, moving from simple skin darkening to full prosthesis. In the real world, this was of course due to the fact that the budget for the films was much higher than that for the television series. This was even made into a joke on an episode of *Star Trek: Deep Space Nine*, "Trials and Tribble-ations." The episode, thanks to the always-handy plot device of time travel, finds the crew of the space station *Deep Space Nine* sent back to the starship *Enterprise* of the original series. During the episode, the *Deep Space Nine* characters notice the difference between the older and contemporary Klingons, causing the Klingon character of Worf (one of their crew) to mention that it is a matter never discussed with outsiders. This is a tongue-in-cheek moment, meant to appeal to longtime viewers and fans of the franchise who knew that the reason for this change was a matter of budget. However, according to the website TV Tropes, it was those very fans who reacted most vehemently in opposition to the joke: "The writers expressed total bafflement over how much of an uproar it had created with the fandom. Reactions in Usenet newsgroups ranged from 'can't you guys relax and take a joke,' to 'we demand answers NOW!' to 'We were fine ignoring it until you morons brought it up" ("Retcon"). To appease these fans, the producers of the franchise crafted an actual answer in the prequel series *Star Trek: Enterprise*, which explained that the change in Klingon physiology was the result of a cure being found to the viral pandemic that had initially created the more human-like Klingons.

By 1997, retroactive continuity had become such a self-conscious trope for the *Star Trek* writers that *Star Trek: Voyager* was even able to use it as a direct part of the plot of a two-part episode. In "Year of Hell," the villain is a scientist named Annorax, who has developed a weapon that can cause temporal paradoxes and thus change the course of time. This is, in essence, a "retcon gun," which weaponizes the ability to rewrite history and places it in the hands of a character within the reality of the show. The story takes place over the course of a year—the titular "Year of Hell"—until the weapon explodes and erases history such that the two episodes are retconned so as to have never actually happened.

The 2009 big-budget *Star Trek* film, directed by J. J. Abrams, uses a similar kind of in-universe logic to allow for its plot (and sequels) to utilize the familiar characters from the original *Star Trek* series while remaining unbeholden to all that had gone before. In the film, a villain named Nero travels back in time in order to revenge himself upon Spock, the science officer and first officer of the *Enterprise* from the original series. Blaming Spock for the death of his people, Nero's revenge relies upon destroying Spock's home planet, Vulcan. When Spock follows Nero back in time, the two create an alternate timeline, one where events flow differently than they did in the original series. In the metatext of the film, this allowed for Leonard Nimoy, the actor who originally played Spock, to meet his younger self, played by Zachary Quinto, and symbolically hand off the reigns of the franchise to this new, younger version of the *Enterprise* crew. Although more of a full-on reboot of the franchise than a retcon—the sequels and tie-in media are explicitly set in an alternate timeline, rather than the one in which all of the stories in the franchise had previously been set—the complicated plot mechanics of the film show how the franchise has come to value explanations for historical rewrites that come out of the world of the story itself.

Cult TV shows are, due to their generic makeup, often able to create in-world reasons for moments of retconning. According to Matt Hills,

> [C]ult TV, unlike most realist soap operas, or indeed much contemporary serial and "quality" drama on TV, does not only accrue a kind of "series memory." Given its emphasis on fantasy and the fantastic, cult TV can also play diegetically with its own narrative rules and norms without necessarily breaking the frame, slipping into parody, camp, or producing overtly displayed markers of reflexivity. (512)

Although Hills does not precisely say so, I would argue that directly addressed retcons—of the kind that involve a fantastic or science-fictional reason for a historical rewrite rather than the "just a dream" or "misremembering" of soap operas like *Dallas* and *General Hospital*—provide just this kind of "marker of reflexivity." On *Star Trek* this involved science fiction tropes, such as time travel and reality-erasing weapons; on a different cult program, *Buffy, the Vampire Slayer*, retconning was based on the even simpler plot device of magic.

Retcon Dawning: *Buffy, the Vampire Slayer* and the Self-Conscious Retcon

Writer/director/producer Joss Whedon comes from a prestigious television pedigree, as both his father and grandfather before him wrote for a variety of TV shows. Joss Whedon first made his name in the film industry after a short-lived run working as a writer on the sitcom *Roseanne*. Though he became known as a hotshot script doctor, working on such films as *Speed*, *Twister*, and *Toy Story* (for which he netted an Academy Award nomination), his big screen breakthrough was the comedy *Buffy, the Vampire Slayer*. Whedon's script played with and subverted tropes of the horror genre, turning a ditzy, blonde, Los Angeles cheerleader into a fearless "slayer" chosen by fate to heroically battle vampires. However, the film itself took a more broadly comedic approach to the material, which Whedon was less than thrilled with. When he was approached by fledgling network The WB to revive the concept as a television show, he jumped at the chance, working to separate it as much as possible from the film version (most crucially by changing both the setting and the actress portraying the titular Buffy Summers). In the very first episode of the series, Buffy makes vague reference to the events of the film, but Whedon has her specifically mention moments from the screenplay that didn't make it into the film version.[3] This, an offhand retcon, helped to set the series apart from the film, creating a darker and more horror-based tone that focused on character over comedy.

Whedon was no stranger to continuity changes, as he had grown up an avid comic book reader, particularly of Chris Claremont and John Byrne's run on Marvel's *Uncanny X-Men*. It is perhaps no surprise, then, that Whedon agreed to license *Buffy* to publisher Dark Horse Comics, who produced a series of noncanonical comic book tie-ins that played off of the show. Over time, though, Whedon became more directly involved in the series, leading to a few special projects that he wrote himself, culminating with the launching of an official comic book continuation of the show's story following its final television season. Whedon also tried his hand at writing other franchise's characters, taking over as writer for the Marvel title *Astonishing X-Men* for several years. He not only had television credentials, but he also had geek credibility as a proven comic book "fan boy." Whedon was thus well aware of the concept of retroactive continuity and purposefully played with it as a part of *Buffy*'s narrative.[4]

For the first four seasons of the show, Buffy Summers was an only child. Her father appeared very sporadically, and her family unit consisted of only herself and her mother (although her close friends—nicknamed the Scooby Gang—were essentially family, as well, and she had a surrogate father in the form of her overseeing "Watcher," Rupert Giles). It came as a great surprise to viewers, then, when at the end of the first episode of season 5 Buffy suddenly had a little sister named Dawn. Nobody, including Buffy and her mother, seemed to notice that there was anything strange about this; it was simply presented as a fact, both to the audience and to the characters in the show, that Buffy had, and always had had, a younger sister.

As the season wore on, it was slowly revealed that Dawn was the physical embodiment of a force of energy that could open the gate to a hellish dimension of evil gods. A group of concerned monks had sent the energy to Buffy in the form that she would be most likely to protect—a "helpless" little sister. As part of the monks' spell, Buffy and everybody else remembered Dawn as *always* having been a part of their lives. Dawn, in this sense, was a walking, talking retcon, who even became *aware* of herself as a retcon.

Many fans criticized this move, claiming that Whedon had added Dawn merely to infuse the show with a younger character now that its initially high-school-aged cast was growing older, a move on par with adding a precocious new child to a long-running sitcom. However, Whedon had somewhat loftier goals with the creation of Dawn. *Buffy, the Vampire Slayer* was ultimately a show that was as much about growing up and finding one's own identity as it was about a powerful girl kicking vampire butt. Adding Dawn into the equation allowed him and his writing team to show Buffy accepting a new level of responsibility over a child, without having her become a mother, herself. Similarly, in a series that was about taking genre tropes and twisting them to various effect, the writers were able to take the trope of the retcon and explore its emotional impact upon the show's characters as they learned that Dawn was not a "real" person, and that all of their memories of/with her had been magically implanted. Whedon could thus explore issues of memory and identity and of emotional truth clashing with historical truth. *Buffy*, in short, anthropomorphized the very concept of a retcon in order to discuss how the slipperiness of memory and history has a realistic influence over people's lives.

As much as the show played around with this retroactive continuity, the Dark Horse *Buffy* comics were able to take it even further. Comics that came out after the fifth season, but that were set in earlier seasons, inserted Dawn into those stories. Scott Allie was the Dark Horse editor who made this decision, which, he explains, "met with some criticism from fans. Dawn wasn't *really* there during these events, but as the show had explored . . . Buffy would *remember* her having been there" (Allie 2007, 5, emphasis in original).

The comic book explored this issue even more directly in a storyline called "False Memories," which, according to Allie,

> played with the idea that the characters would remember Dawn having been there in earlier adventures. I felt I was finally understanding what Joss was doing to elevate this genre stuff, so we took that supernatural notion of the false Dawn

memories and explored the idea in more emotionally real ways for the characters. We re-created earlier scenes, giving Dawn significant roles in those scenes, thereby changing the spirit of what had happened. Readers have always been a little uncomfortable with the way the comic had inserted Dawn into the early years, but for me, not only does it make sense that characters would remember her being there, but it allowed us to do something the show never could—to go back. (Allie 2009, 5)

Here, Allie shows precisely how and why retconning was formulated most thoroughly in superhero comic books: the nature of the comics medium allows for a return to earlier stories in a way that television shows at the time were unable to do. Thus, in "False Memories," we see flashbacks to scenes from the first four seasons of *Buffy*, but retconned to include Dawn at key moments. In the present, Buffy is struggling with her own memories, trying to figure out what is/was "real" now that those memories feature Dawn, even though the events must have played out differently in her "actual" history. A frustrated Buffy exclaims,

> Why do the supernatural forces think it's just perfectly okay to come along, hide a mystical key in the form of a sister I've never had, then plant false memories in all our heads, leaving me to take care of everything! Vampires I can handle, but a little sister... How do I sort out the truth, Giles? I mean, all the stuff that really happened? I can't do it alone. (Fassbender and Pascoe 305)

Later she adds, "As if being the slayer wasn't enough... my sister and these memories are going to drive me crazy" (Fassbender and Pascoe 359). The storyline examines the nature of memory and how it interacts with identity, an exploration that is made possible by the fact that Dawn physically embodies the process of retroactive continuity and its potential emotional aftermath.

Part of the reason the comics proved so crucial in exploring the nature of Dawn's retconned history was because the television show, as Allie explains, was never going to address this issue, since it was moving forward rather than looking backward. Television at that point in the late 1990s was structured on pushing the narrative ever forward; although longer story arcs had become de rigueur in cult shows like *Buffy*, *The X-Files*, and the later *Star Trek* series, they still emphasized forward momentum and progression, rather than looking back to the past (save for the occasional flashback). However, while *Buffy* was unable "to go back," by the mid-2000s the extremely popular primetime action-adventure drama *Lost* upended the conventions of the genre by boldly declaring, "We *have* to go back!"

Lost in History

When *Lost* debuted in 2004, it was an immediate critical and commercial success, gaining huge ratings for the ABC network and winning the Emmy Award for Outstanding Drama Series. The series told the story of the survivors of a plane crash trapped on a tropical island filled with an increasing amount of strange and frightening mysteries. Although future seasons would receive mixed critical reception and slightly lower ratings, the show nevertheless remained a blockbuster hit, and (despite a controversial final episode) still makes a variety of lists recognizing the top television shows of all time. If nothing else, *Lost* was certainly influential. A swath of shows followed in its wake, filled with high-concept science fiction fueled by a variety of different character types. Shows like *Heroes*, *Flash Forward*, and *The Event* all tried to be "the next *Lost*," with varying degrees of success (although none proved to be the blockbuster force that *Lost* was).

Many of *Lost*'s writers were either influenced by comic books or were comic book writers themselves, and they drew upon techniques developed in those comics over the prior half century. *Lost* was thus the first of a group of primetime dramas that actively practiced the process of world-building, consciously creating complex continuities whose shifting histories were an important part of the unfolding narrative. This was seen not only in the narratives of these shows, but also in their format.

For the entirety of its run, *Lost* was as reliant on its unique formal structure as it was its characters and mysteries. Those story elements were in fact partially cocreated *by* that format, which (in the first few seasons) featured flashbacks to the lives of the characters prior to the plane trip that brought them to the island. Although at first these flashbacks merely provided character backstory that tied in thematically with the present-day events of a particular episode, over time they slowly began to show how the characters shared mysterious ties with one another. As the show went on, and filled in the characters' lives, it would switch to providing "flash forwards" that the main story would eventually catch up to and, finally, "flash-sideways," showing an alternate timeline (which would prove to be a sort of afterlife, much to many fans' dismay).

Although the idea of a flashback was hardly original to *Lost*, what was unique about the series was that each episode of the first three seasons was structured around and reliant upon those flashbacks. Thus, *Lost* focused an equal amount of importance on the past as it did on the present. Characters were constantly returning to their pasts, both emotionally and psychologically, as well as occasionally literally (thanks to the introduction of time travel into the plot of later seasons). Unlike *Buffy*, then, *Lost* actually *was* able to go back and revisit both the past of its characters as well as, occasionally, its own past. This enabled the show's writers and producers to weave retroactive continuity into the fabric of the program, presenting the narrative technique to an audience that went far beyond the "cult" following of soap operas and shows like *Star Trek* and *Buffy*.

Lost never featured a retcon as big and obvious as that of Dawn in *Buffy*, but it did deliberately play around with its own narrative history and continuity on multiple occasions. For example, the third season episode "Exposé" focused on two characters who had previously appeared largely only in the background, a couple named Nikki and Paulo. The pair had first shown up earlier that same season, in response to criticism that the show focused only on a handful of characters rather than exploring all of the survivors of the plane crash. However, Nikki and Paulo proved enormously unpopular with fans, in part because they were so abruptly introduced into the show's narrative. As a result, the writers decided to send them off in the form of a rather unusual episode that—rather than flashing back to the life of one of the main characters—focused on the couple's life both before and on the island. The episode featured a series of retconned flashbacks showing Nikki and Paulo as being present for important moments in the show's history, before mercilessly killing them off by having them get accidentally buried alive. Though Nikki and Paulo's story was something of a cul-de-sac on the road of *Lost*'s main narrative, it did provide the show's writers with an opportunity to display just how much the flashback format could be used to integrate the present-day narrative with the characters' backstories.

In the wake of *Lost*, many other popular and acclaimed television shows, from crime stories like *Breaking Bad* to historical dramas like *Mad Men*, utilized flashbacks and complex backstories in order to show how the past interplayed with the shows' ongoing storylines in the present, often revealing new information about those backstories several seasons into the shows' runs. Although none used this to as much effect as *Lost* did (and, in fact, these were not always actual retcons, as they did not recontextualize previously given information, even on a level of reinterpretation), the influence of the show was widely felt in the ensuing years. Perhaps most importantly, *Lost* presented the concept of a fluctuating history, with a floating idea of what the "truth" actually is/was, to a wider audience than possibly any television show prior to it. At roughly the same time, however, a bigger audience still was being introduced to the concept of retroactive continuity in the form of long-running blockbuster film franchises.

Film Franchises and Complex Continuity

Film franchises were nothing new in the early 2000s. The popular James Bond series of films, for example, had been successfully in production since the 1960s. However, it was during the first decade of the twenty-first century that the multi-sequel franchise came to so dominate Hollywood that film studies—as well as entire multimedia empires—began to rely upon them for their economic survival. Though it is outside the purview of this book to examine precisely how and why such franchises came to rule the film industry, what is important to recognize in this context is how those franchises utilized retroactive continuity as a way to tie various films together to form a cohesive, salable story universe.

One of the earliest mega-blockbuster film franchises was the *Star Wars* films, created by George Lucas. The original trilogy of films came out in the 1970s and 1980s, capturing the imaginations of children and adults alike for decades to come. *Star Wars* was thus still a hot brand in the late 1990s (thanks in no small part to expansive multimedia and licensing deals) when Lucas decided to write, direct, and produce three prequels set before the original films. Despite derision from fans and critics alike, these prequels proved financially successful, and the first—*Star Wars Episode I: The Phantom Menace*—became the second-highest-grossing film of all time upon its release. The *Star Wars* prequels were seen by millions of people worldwide, as were the digitally altered re-releases of the original trilogy that were in theaters prior to *Episode 1*—and for some of that audience they provided an introduction to the realm of retroactive continuity.

The three original *Star Wars* films told the story of Luke Skywalker, a farm boy from a backwater planet who becomes a galactic hero and leads an interplanetary rebellion against an evil empire. During the course of this grand adventure, he discovers that the second-in-command of the empire is none other than his own father, Anakin Skywalker, who has taken on the name Darth Vader after succumbing to the "dark side" of a mythical metaphysical power known as the Force. Ultimately, Vader saves Luke from the wicked Emperor Palatine, therefore redeeming himself in his son's eyes. The prequels would come to focus on Anakin's story and how he was seduced to the dark side by the Emperor. In doing so, however, they totally recontextualize—and thus retcon, to a greater or lesser degree—certain key elements related as canonical backstory in the original trilogy.

One of the biggest retcons to *Star Wars* continuity as revealed in the prequels is that C-3PO, one of the two robotic comic relief "droid" characters from the original film series, was built by a nine-year-old Anakin, who was a young mechanical and flying genius. The original series gives no hint of this connection, especially since the droids are only incidentally—and rather by chance—drawn into Luke Skywalker's life. What was happenstance in the course of the original trilogy has been retconned into something akin to fate or destiny, particularly since the prequels indicate that C-3PO's memories of the earlier events have been wiped. The fact that no mention is made of R2-D2's memories being similarly erased has led to a popular fan theory that the droid, along with the character of Chewbacca (neither of whom speak in a language the audience, nor the majority of the characters, can understand without interpretation), were secret agents for the Rebellion during the course of the original trilogy (see Martin). The intricacy of this theory, just one among many, shows how this retcon—as with most in the *Star Wars* prequels—is of the least stringent sort, a reinterpretation that relies, in part, on audience members' ability and willingness to decide what remains "true" or canonical.

Similarly, Luke's wise mentor, Obi-Wan Kenobi, is revealed to have told Luke multiple lies in *A New Hope*, since many things he tells him are retroactively revealed to be untrue by the events of the prequels. For example, Obi-Wan presents Luke with a laser sword, called a lightsaber, that he claims Anakin wanted him to have when he was old enough. However, the prequel films reveal that Obi-Wan and Anakin's final encounter comes in the form of a duel where Obi-Wan leaves his former comrade to burn to death in a sea of lava (which he ultimately survives). This is where Obi-Wan obtained Anakin's lightsaber, with no such caveat regarding passing it on to Anakin's son, who Anakin did not even know about.

This is a minor bit of retconning, on the level of reinterpretation—easily explained away by saying that Obi-Wan was an unreliable narrator who lied to Luke for his own protection, or was simply describing things from a metaphorical point of view—but it nevertheless shows how the *Star Wars* prequels play around with the history revealed in the original film trilogy. Fans of the *Star Wars* franchise, thanks both to the prequels and to numerous tie-in media (canonical or otherwise) that expand upon the story world, have grown very accustomed to unsteady historical grounding, accepting that the past in the *Star Wars* universe is constantly and frequently open to some kind of change in order to explore new story ideas and potentials. In fact, in re-releasing versions of the original trilogy with updated CGI and new/different scenes, George Lucas was able to change the *original* films as well, something that has played with the memories of real-life fans and not just fictional characters.

Star Wars, though, is not the only popular film franchise to deal in retroactive continuity, nor is the use of this technique limited to science fiction and fantasy films. The highly popular *Saw* series of horror films, for example, utilizes a massive amount of narrative complexity for a franchise that is, ultimately, part of the "torture porn"/slasher subgenre of horror. Matthew Belinkie, contributing editor to the pop culture analysis website *Overthinking It*, claims that "This is far and away the most plot-heavy, convoluted horror film series ever.... Seemingly minor characters return in later films, suddenly thrust into the spotlight. We flash backwards and forwards, revisiting the events of past films from multiple angles." As the series goes on, the *Saw* films reach a level of complex, interweaving narratives and character arcs—particularly utilizing extensive flashbacks—that rivals the confusing continuities of comic books and soap operas. Belinkie links the films even more closely with a different popular narrative from the same time period as the franchise—*Lost*:

> The lesson everyone in Hollywood took from [*Lost*'s] runaway success was that audiences could be enthralled, not repelled, by huge mysteries that unfolded over years.... The *Saw* producers took this lesson to heart, and built the *Saw* sequels to be full of twists, complete with *Lost*-esque flashbacks and lots of loose ends.

As Belinkie goes on to point out, though, this convoluted framework was *not* the result of a master plan that the writers and producers of the franchise had established from its inception. In fact, "*Saw II* started out as a completely non-*Saw*-related story before being adapted into a quickie sequel. This kind of after-the-fact plotting leads to some inconsistencies that can't be explained away."

Many of the *Saw* sequels utilize deliberate retcons in order to create the complicated story universe that has become the heart of the franchise. Later films frequently flash back to scenes from earlier films, completely recreating those moments for the purpose of twisting their narrative. Belinkie notes, "the latter movies recreated earlier sets and brought back actors who were chronologically deceased, to show us new information about things we'd already seen." This is, in some ways, the epitome of a retcon—revisiting a past moment for the explicit purpose of rewriting that moment in order to allow for new narrative potential in the present and future. Retconning has become so much a part of mainstream media that it is even a staple of what is, on the surface, a schlocky horror film franchise dedicated to portraying splattered blood and horrifically creative deathtraps.

Retroactive continuity is no longer solely the terrain of superhero comic books, soap operas, or "cult" media. It has become a ubiquitous part of modern forms of mass entertainment, a technique that most audience members across a variety of media are familiar with, in action if not in name. To further prove just how much retconning has come to be accepted as a natural part of popular imaginary worlds and fictional narratives, we next turn to a classic metric of just how much any idea has permeated popular culture and public consciousness—the realm of satire, parody, and play.

PUTTING IT ALL TOGETHER
Retroactive Parody and Play

In his study of how cultural hierarchies developed in the United States, *Highbrow/Lowbrow*, historian Lawrence W. Levine explains how he was surprised by a discovery he made while analyzing antebellum minstrel shows: "What arrested my attention was the ubiquity of Shakespearean drama in the humor of the minstrels" (3–4). Because these Shakespearean parodies and jokes "were popular with the extremely heterogeneous audiences which attended minstrel shows," Levine arrived at the conclusion that "Shakespeare must have been well known throughout the society since people cannot parody what is not familiar" (4). In his book, Levine uses these humorous Shakespearean pastiches as evidence for Shakespeare's mass popularity in nineteenth-century America.

Literary theorist Linda Hutcheon takes this exploration of parody even further. In her landmark study on the topic, *A Theory of Parody: The Teachings of Twentieth-Century Art Forms*, she describes parody as "one of the major forms of modern self-reflexivity; it is a form of inter-art discourse" (2). It is thus a form of artistic expression that relies to some extent upon the previous expression(s) of others: "In transmuting or remodeling previous texts, it points to the differential but mutual dependence of parody and parodied texts. Its voices neither merge nor cancel each other out; they work together, while remaining distinct in their defining difference" (xiv). For a parody to work, then, it must engage in a relationship with a previous text, or set of texts, and the audience must be aware of that relationship, as well as the base text(s). Along those lines, this chapter will explore how retroactive continuity has been parodied and played with in recent mass culture, in order to show just how much it has permeated the awareness of audiences.

The chapter will begin by looking at moments of direct satire and parody, particularly from comics writer Alan Moore and from the long-running, influential animated television show *The Simpsons*. From there, I will move on to examining the history of a subtler form of play, one that turns continuity—retroactive and otherwise—into a metatextual literary game played by creators, fans, and fans-turned-creators, alike. As such, rather than providing one long case study, this chapter will jump (sometimes achronologically) between disparate examples in order to provide a broad overview of the various and sundry ways that retroactive continuity has become culturally ubiquitous not only as a frequent narrative tool, but also as a form of play for creators and their audiences.

Never Mentioned Again: Parodying Retconning

Since retroactive continuity, as a specific narrative technique and a defined term, evolved in important ways out of superhero comic books, it comes as no surprise that the comic book medium is rife with parodies of retconning. Several of these come from Alan Moore, acclaimed writer of *Watchmen* and other highly regarded superhero stories. Moore is both a crucial component in the history of superhero narratives, pointing the way in the 1980s toward a more mature style of storytelling, as well as a frequent critic of the genre, who often bemoans stories that become mired in the juvenile roots of superheroes while still presenting dense continuities that are inaccessible to children. Some of this ire has come forth in the form of superhero homages and parodies, some of which impishly comment upon what Moore views as the inherent silliness of retconning.

When Moore took over the Image Comics series *Supreme*, for example, he changed it from a dark, violent parody of Superman into a loving pastiche to the zaniness and excess of the Superman stories he had grown up reading.

To enact this change, his first issue tells the story of a "revision wave" that serves as an in-universe form of cosmic retconning, much like that seen in *Crisis on Infinite Earths*. Here, though, various versions of Supreme have survived their own revisions in a limbo-like realm called the Supremacy, and are able to explain to the current version that he is the latest product of this metaphysical rearrangement of reality: "We don't have long before you leave us. The flickering . . . the indeterminate state that precedes a revision . . . will soon subside. Then you'll return to your newly-revised Earth and your life will begin" (Moore 1996, 17). Moore goes further than just utilizing this retcon as a rationale for his extensive changes to *Supreme*, but also comments upon how retconning is frequently used when creators have run out of ideas on how to follow up with a character's continuity: "Multiple variants . . . seem to arise just before the flickering starts and a new revision begins. It's as if the universe is desperately trying different variations to get things right, before it gives up and starts again!" (Moore 1996, 18). Ironically, it could be argued that this kind of "giving up" is just what Moore himself is doing, fundamentally altering the nature of the dark character of Supreme as originally envisioned by his creator, Rob Liefeld. Moore's satire, though biting, also reflects upon his own tropes and techniques as well.

Somewhat later in his career, Moore created his own comic book line, America's Best Comics,[1] including several pulp/superhero-inspired comics that featured a variety of different genres and tonalities. The book *Tomorrow Stories*, for example, consisted of a rotating group of stories that deliberately pastiched classic comics and creators, including "The First American," a series cocreated with artist Jim Baikie that parodied, in a form similar to early *Mad* comics, generic patriotic superheroes. "The First American" would take its superheroic conceit to ridiculous heights, including a revelation of the hero's "origin" that was inconsistent, incoherent, and incorporated "various ill-advised makeovers," ending with the caption, "So, like, that's who he is and how he come to be became! Read about him every month here in Tomorrow Stories! Frankly, we'll probably change the origin next month anyway" (Moore 2000, 7). This humorous conclusion is a quip about the inconsistencies in the origin stories of most superheroes, the majority of whom have had their histories retconned at some point or another.

Moore makes a similar dig at retconning in another of his America's Best Comics series, *Top 10* (cocreated with artists Gene Ha and Zander Cannon), a police procedural drama set in a city where everybody, from cop to criminal to civilian, has superpowers. *Top 10* is far more serious than "The First American," yet it still features moments of parody and satire, such as when one police officer's mother faces an infestation of super-powered "ultramice," which escalates into "a secret crisis crossover war, with cosmic powers involved" (Moore 2001, 4). They call in *Top 10*'s version of an exterminator, named the Ex-Verminator, who is shocked when he is suddenly no longer recognized, realizing that the animals "must have altered time itself! . . . Cosmouse must have changed the entire continuity, so that the whole catmouse crisis never happened! . . . How am I supposed to live, huh? Those little bastards, they're always pulling #@*& like this!" (Moore 2001, 4–5). More explicitly than in "First American," in *Top 10* Moore has reduced retconning to its silliest extreme, with the Ex-Verminator standing in for a confused, and sometimes angry, audience.

Moore is not the only creator to have fun with—and poke fun at—retconning. Writer Bill Willingham, in his long-running series *Fables* (about fairy tale characters all living together in contemporary New York), frequently strayed into satire and parody, including a storyline wherein a god-like character intends to literally rewrite reality through a magic pen. His son directly explains that this god intends to destroy "Not just the world . . . The universe and everything in it. And not only will everything cease to exist if my father has his way, everything we know will never have existed at all," to which another character replies, "Retroactive reality?" and is told, "Something like that" (2). Willingham is playing with generic conventions here—as he does throughout all of *Fables*—to indicate his characters' awareness of their impending erasure through retcon, and provides a humorous aside that relies upon readers knowing the term "retroactive continuity" and its incorrect formation here as "retroactive reality" (though to be fair to the characters, that continuity actually *is* their reality).

However, these—and others much like them—are in-jokes, nods to fans of superhero comics who are already immersed in the complexities of their style of storytelling. Perhaps more important to proving that retconning has become known to a wider audience than just superhero readers is the half-hour animated sitcom *The Simpsons*, which has played on the Fox Broadcasting Company since 1989, making it the longest-running American sitcom, longest-running animated program, and longest-running primetime sitcom of all time. Even during periods where the show hasn't been a ratings juggernaut, it has maintained a steady enough viewership to keep it on the air as a decades-long touchstone of popular culture.

Unlike previous examples in this book, however, *The Simpsons* takes place in an atemporal setting. Because the characters are animated (and the children voiced by adults), there is no need for them to ever age, and so they have remained in relative stasis over the course of the show's run. As a result of this, the continuity of the show—such as it is—has provided its writers with an opportunity to play around with the idea of retroactive continuity without worrying about it altering the status quo. The results show that *The Simpsons*' media-savvy writers and audience understand how retcons traditionally work, and what may be both attractive and frustrating about them to fans and audiences.

In the ninth-season *Simpsons* episode "The Principal and the Pauper," which first aired in 1997, a strange man (voiced by guest star Martin Sheen) comes to the town of Springfield and reveals that he is the real Seymour Skinner, the elementary school principal who is a regular character on the show. The Skinner we have seen for nine seasons, it turns out, is actually an imposter named Armin Tamzarian, who decides to leave town and let the real Skinner resume his life. However, the citizens of Springfield discover that they preferred Armin to Skinner, and so they convince him to come back to town. Upon his return, some of the townspeople express confusion and disbelief, leading Homer Simpson (the father of the titular family) to proclaim, "All right, all right, so he's a fraud. I don't care. His mom doesn't care. Do any of *you* care?" He then convinces the town to literally run the real Seymour Skinner out of town on a rail, and has the town's judge legally change Armin's name and identity to that of Seymour Skinner. The judge then adds, "And I further decree that everything will be just like it was before all this happened. And no one will ever mention it again, under penalty of torture."

The main gist of "The Principal and the Pauper" is to explore the character of Seymour Skinner, adding a sordid backstory to the straight-laced, uptight principal who so often serves as the foil to the precocious young Bart Simpson. The writers do this through a low-level retcon, a reinterpretation of past assumptions about Skinner. However, because *The Simpsons* exists in a timeless continuity where typically nothing significant changes from episode to episode,[2] the writers knew that the events of this episode had to be reset to the show's stable backdrop by the end of the episode. In essence, they had to create a plot point that would invalidate neither the contents of the individual episode nor any other given episode where everybody treats Armin Tamzarian as though he actually is Seymour Skinner. Their solution, in essence, is to pre-retcon (or perhaps it should be "proconning," for "proactive continuity") their own retcon, creating a satirical narrative reason for the episode's revelations to never be mentioned again.

The original retcon in this episode, boiled down, is that the man we have previously known as Seymour Skinner is actually Armin Tamzarian. Since the writers knew this plot point would not be mentioned in subsequent episodes, they directly address that fact at the end of "The Principal and the Pauper," having a character metatextually declare that these events would never be mentioned again and everything would return to exactly how it was before the real Skinner came to town. In this way, *The Simpsons* recognizes how and why retroactive continuity is typically implemented (changing the story's past in order to create narrative potential in the future), and then humorously turns that convention on its ear (by directly stating that this changed past will *not* have any influence on the future). Because this is the punch line of the entire episode, it relies on the fact that the audience is aware of, and even familiar with, the retcon conventions that are being subverted.

The Simpsons, of course, is not the only place that has parodied retroactive continuity. In the NBC sitcom *Community*, for example, comedian Jack Black guest starred in an episode as Buddy Austin, a student at Greendale Community College (the show's setting) who knew all of the series' main characters but yet was unfamiliar to them. Buddy explains that he has a tendency to blend into the background, leading to a montage of "flashbacks" to previous episodes that insert Buddy into important events from the course of the series thus far. Played for laughs, this sequence is a self-conscious parody of retroactive continuity that inserts a new character into an ongoing narrative by shoehorning him or her into the backstory.

Another comedic take on retconning came in 2015, in the form of a widespread online debate about how to spell the title of a popular series of children's books, *The Berenstain Bears*. Many readers grew up believing—or at least remembered growing up believing—that the books, and its titular bear family protagonists, were spelled *The Berenstein Bears* (Siede). One online blogger posited a (presumably joking) theory that this was because of real life retroactive continuity: "[A]t some time in the last 10 years or so, reality has been tampered with and history has been retroactively changed. The bears *really were* called the 'BerenstEin Bears' when we were growing up, but now reality has been altered such that the name of the bears has been changed post hoc" (Reece, emphasis in original). In a humorous sense, retconning has begun to leak out into reality itself.[3]

In a very different vein, and with a very different tone, the *Doctor Who* science fiction spin-off series *Torchwood* features a drug called "Retcon" that can erase, alter, and/or implant selective memories, thereby changing the past as far as the user is concerned. Though the drug is played to serious effect in the show—there are Retcon abusers and overdoses—its name is an obvious humorous allusion to the narrative technique. In an even earlier example—one that plays on horror more than humor—the protagonist of Stephen King's 1987 novel *Misery* is forced by a crazed, violent fan to write a new manuscript wherein he brings back to life the heroine of his previous book series. This is a horrific take on fan obsession with serial fictions and continuity/retconning, to the point of a fan literally forcing an author to create a retcon in order to keep telling future stories about her favorite character.

The above examples are just a few that show how retconning has become a well-known trope among mass audiences of popular media, and not just the "cult" readers of comic books and viewers of soap operas. In fact, retconning has become so popular that it has bled out of the boundaries of fiction into some real-world fannish activities (inspired by historical examples) of playing with the boundaries between the fictional, the historical, and the real.

Don Quixote and Sherlock Holmes: Early Continuity Play

When Miguel de Cervantes published *The Ingenious Gentleman Don Quixote of La Mancha* in 1605, it is unclear whether or not he had a sequel in mind. Upon reading the novel, however, somebody else certainly felt it was worth a second part; in 1614, an anonymous writer published an unlicensed sequel—entitled *Second Volume of the Ingenious Gentleman Don Quixote of La Mancha: by the Liciendo (doctorate) Alonso Fernández de Avellaneda, of Tordesillas*—without Cervantes's knowledge or assent. Indeed, when Cervantes found out about this book he wrote his own, official sequel, more reasonably titled *Don Quixote, Part Two*. In that continuation, Cervantes criticizes the false sequel, through the words of the fictional/metatextual Moorish author Cid Hamet Ben Engeli, who serves as Cervantes's alter ego: "For me alone was Don Quixote born, and I for him . . . and in despite of that scribbling imposter of Tordesillas, who has dared, or shall dare, with his gross and ill-cut ostrich quill, to describe the exploits of my valourous knight" (quoted in Ndalianis 31). The existence of this false sequel in fact becomes a main aspect of the narrative of *Part Two*. As media scholar Angela Ndalianis explains, *Part Two* spends a great deal of time on this kind of metatextual game:

> Creating fact out of fiction and blurring fictional space with the reader's space, at numerous points throughout the second part, Cervantes's fictitious character Don Quixote meets other fictitious characters who act as if they inhabit a material realm of existence that parallels the reader's own. . . . Throughout Cervantes's own sequel to *Don Quixote*, his protagonist continually defends his authenticity to characters in light of the other Quixote. For some characters who have read the Tordesillan sequel, however, it is the "imposter" who constitutes the authentic version of the hero Don Quixote. (31)

For Cervantes, the fictional world of *Don Quixote* becomes a literary playground in *Part Two*, wherein various characters are aware of differing layers of falsity or reality (which is, in turn, only a "reality" within the fictional realm of the novel itself).

This is something of a game, allowing Cervantes to playfully mix history and reality. In that sense, he is not dissimilar from later "historical novelists" like E. L. Doctorow, who created intricate novels that weave together fictional creations with the real lives (and fictionalized lives) of famous Americans. However, Cervantes was less interested in discussing "real" people and more concerned with poking at the boundaries between fiction and reality. Ultimately, though, he came up against one particular, impossible boundary—the one between author and audience. *Don Quixote* was one of the earliest examples of the novel in Western literature, and was published in the earliest days of what could be considered "mass media." Cervantes's readers would have little to no opportunity to "speak back" to the text in the way that modern fandoms have been able to.

The prime exception to this, of course, is the unauthorized sequel, which may be considered one of the earliest pieces of fan fiction (or, perhaps, anti-fan fiction, as the author of the sequel used it as an opportunity to insult Cervantes). *Part Two* takes up the dialogue with this text and responds to it, but otherwise Cervantes has no way to interact with his readers, and can merely pose questions without a format for answers, as Ndalianis points out: "Cervantes frequently and self-reflexively invites the reader to engage in a dialogic relationship with the novel's characters on issues dealing with artistic production in light of historical and economic transformations" (32). Yet those transformations, strange and new as they may have been to Cervantes, were not of the level that allowed for authors and their readers to create an *actual* dialogue, whether that conversation appeared on the page itself or in other media and para-texts.

By the time Sir Arthur Conan Doyle was writing, however, the mass media had evolved to the point that he was able to respond to readers' and fans' reactions and opinions (not least of all by bringing Sherlock Holmes back to life, although an economic motive was equally responsible for that). Perhaps more important, his readers and fans were able to respond to *him*, in magazines and newspapers and within Sherlockian fan clubs. The love for Holmes, one of the most popular characters of all time, inspired what has become known as "The Great Game," wherein fans pretend that Holmes and Dr. Watson are real figures to whom Conan Doyle was a literary agent. With that as a basis, they seek to reconcile all of the inconsistencies within and between the stories in order to "reconstruct" what "really" happened, as well as to create a clear continuity within which new Holmes stories and pastiches can exist. Leslie Klinger, editor of an annotated edition of Conan Doyle's Holmes stories, explains that "it's just for fun. . . . We all know we're having fun. It's serious fun, but it's fun" (quoted in Cole). This aspect of "The Great Game" has a long heritage and pedigree, Klinger notes: "Dorothy Sayers famously said, 'The game must be played with one's tongue firmly in one's cheek, but with all the seriousness of a cricket game at Lords'" (quoted in Cole).

Though not strictly retroactive continuity as I have defined it, the Great Game certainly *contains* elements of retcon, particularly in stories/scholarship that propose to alter the narrative of the original texts. A National Public Radio story about the Great Game explains how Klinger, in his annotations, "even second-guesses Watson the narrator's account of the story, saying he might have sent a telegram to his wife and failed to mention it" (Cole). The Game has also expanded beyond fan speculation into seemingly endless new variations of the original Holmes stories, in such recent iterations as the BBC's Holmes-in-the-twenty-first-century *Sherlock*, CBS's Holmes-in-twenty-first-century-America *Elementary*, director Guy Ritchie's action-comedy *Sherlock Holmes* films starring Robert Downey Jr. and actor Ian McKellan's turn as an aging Holmes dealing with his own mortality in the film *Mr. Holmes*. Sherlock Holmes has proven to be endlessly mutable to a variety of contexts and media, due in no small part to the ways in which the Great Game have shown the plasticity and potential of the character and his original stories to be constantly toyed with and remixed.

However, the Great Game is also retroactive continuity of a different kind. By positing that Conan Doyle's stories really happened, players in the Great Game are able to create a *new* kind of continuity, one that never existed nor was intended in the original tales—a continuity between fiction and reality. This also creates a sense of continuity between fictional character and real reader/fan. Participants in the Great Game get to interact with the character (and deceased author) whom they so admire, and to retroactively interact with his continuity as well. In this sense, retcon becomes a kind of play, a game that brings together a community of fans, readers, and writers in creating a new, shared text (similar, as we shall see in the next chapter, to how various hands came together to create Wikipedia). In more recent years, this game has gone beyond simply focusing on one character or author, and has created a plethora of dense texts and para-texts that make play out of retconning in order to create vast, metatextual worlds that incorporate the continuity of thousands of pieces of fiction.

Extraordinary Worlds: Creating a Universe of Crossovers

In the spirit of play, I share the following anecdote from my childhood. One April Saturday when I was seven years old, I awoke more excited than usual for that morning's roster of cartoon shows. On that day, April 21, 1990, all the major television networks were simulcasting a special program, *Cartoon All-Stars to the Rescue* (see Bernstein). This unprecedented (for me, at least) event was meant to educate children about the dangers of drug abuse. What excited me about the show, though, was the way that it was going to go about teaching this lesson—by featuring *all* of the characters from my favorite cartoon shows in one adventure together. I could hardly believe it. What would happen when Papa Smurf met the Teenage Mutant Ninja Turtles? Would the cat-eating ALF prove a danger to the lasagna-eating Garfield? Most importantly, what tremendous circumstance could possibly cause so many of my favorite characters to team up?

Though the moral, antidrug lesson of *Cartoon All-Stars to the Rescue* may have been the show's impetus, it was the teaming up of these cartoon heroes from my favorite shows, all of which ostensibly existed in entirely different universes, which stuck with me. In hindsight, *all* of my favorite movies and shows from this period featured seemingly disparate characters meeting each other in some kind of crazy, shared realm. In Robert Zemeckis's feature film *Who Framed Roger Rabbit?*, the animated characters of a half-century of cartoons all lived in one city, called Toontown, and interacted with real-life human beings just like me. In the made-for-TV holiday special *A Muppet Family Christmas*, I got to spend Christmas Eve with not just the Muppets, but also with my friends from *Sesame Street* and *Fraggle Rock*. If the goal of my young, overactive imagination was to escape into a fictional world where the ordinary rules of my life did not apply, then I wanted that world to be one populated by as many of my favorite characters as possible. As it turns out, I was not the only person to feel this way. Though I was certainly unaware of this at the time, there was already a kind of variation of the Sherlockian Great Game, known as Wold Newtonry, which was attempting to create a world that united all fiction together into one massive, exciting universe of adventures and ideas.

The Wold Newton concept belongs to science fiction and fantasy author Philip José Farmer, originally introduced in his 1972 novel, *Tarzan Alive*. The book purports to be a biography of Edgar Rice Burroughs's famous jungle hero, Tarzan, using the premise that Burroughs wrote fictionalized memoirs and Farmer was now revealing the "true story." Farmer was influenced by the

Sherlockian Great Game, and decided to apply it, in this case, to a different character. However, Farmer goes beyond simply reconciling the chronology of Burroughs's stories, and adds to the mix a whole slew of other fictional characters, all of whom he genealogically links to Tarzan as part of what became known as "The Wold Newton Family."

The basis for this linkage is a 1795 meteor strike in Wold Newton, Yorkshire, England (an actual event that Farmer brought into his narrative), near two coaches carrying "five married couples and a brother of one of the wives" (Farmer 235). The effects of this explosion would be felt not only by the passengers, but also their offspring: "The bright light and heat and thunderous roar of the meteorite blinded and terrified the passengers, coachmen, and horses. But they recovered quickly, thanking God that they were unharmed by the near-hit. They never guessed, being ignorant of ionization, that the fallen star had affected them and their unborn" (Farmer 236). Farmer even went so far as to list all of the characters who, belonging to this genealogy, are members of the Wold Newton Family:

> The mutated and recessive genes would be reinforced, kept from being lost, by the frequent marriages among the descendants of the irradiated parents. And this reinforcement and reshuffling of superior genes resulted in at least fourteen great detectives, scientists, and explorers, some of whom bordered on the superhuman. These would be Dupin, M. Lecoq, Arsène Lupin, Mycroft and Sherlock Holmes, Professor Challenger, Lord John Roxton, Denis Nayland Smith, A. J. Raffles, Tarzan, Monk Mayfair, Bulldog Drummond, John Drummond (Korak), Nero Wolfe, Lord Peter Wimsey, Richard Wentworth (who was also G-8 and Kent Allard), and Doc Savage. (247)

The Wold Newton Family would expand beyond this list over time, in works both by Farmer himself (including another fictional biography, *Doc Savage: His Apocalyptic Life*) and by other writers who set their stories in the Wold Newton Universe. That universe would come to also include characters not directly part of the genealogy of the Wold Newton Family but linked to them by various crossover stories. Farmer expert Win Scott Eckert explains,

> Popular characters who Philip José Farmer concluded were members of the Wold Newton Family (both pre- and post-meteor strike) include: Solomon Kane; Captain Blood; The Scarlet Pimpernel; Harry Flashman; C. August Dupin; Sherlock Holmes and his nemesis Professor Moriarty (aka Captain Nemo); Phileas Fogg; The Time Traveler; Allan Quartermain; Tarzan and his son Korak; A. J. Raffles; Arsène Lupin; Professor Challenger; Richard Hannay; Bulldog Drummond; the

evil Doctor Fu Manchu and his adversary, Sir Denis Nayland Smith; G-8; Lord Peter Wimsey; The Shadow; Sam Spade; Doc Savage, his cousin Pat Savage, and one of his five assistants, Monk Mayfair; The Spider; Nero Wolfe; Mr. Moto; The Avenger; Philip Marlowe; James Bond; Lew Archer; and Travis McGee. (W. Eckert 2005, 2)

As these extensive character lists show, the Wold Newton Universe came to include almost all of the great heroes and villains of pulp fiction.

Farmer's ability to include all of these characters was aided by their original mechanism of publishing, in the pages of serialized pulp magazines. Like the comic book superheroes who would be their literary descendants, the pulp heroes were owned by publishing companies, rather than individual authors, and their adventures were chronicled by various and diverse writers. Their fictional timelines, then, were already cobbled together piecemeal from many different stories and perspectives, which encouraged interplay among both writers and readers in the creation of these characters' histories. Farmer simply took this one step further and began to tie those separate histories together, retroactively creating a unified fictional universe that contained *all* of these pulp characters' diverse stories.

Adding ever more characters into the Wold Newton Universe became part of a new game, called Wold Newtonry. This game, much like the Sherlockian Great Game, is one that combines literature and history in order to retroactively create a sense of continuity among originally disparate texts. As comics scholar Peter Coogan explains, it is akin to a kind of archeological project:

> As "literary archeologists" we map and investigate the unknown history of the literary universe as revealed in novels, pulps, films, comics, legends, myths, epics, and other literary and cultural texts. We treat these texts as archeologists treat the artifacts they dig up, as clues to a larger understanding of the world that must be guessed at and constructed from incomplete pieces. Wold Newton scholars seek to create connections between texts in a game that supposes creative works to be merely an archipelago representation of a world more exciting and interesting than the one we live in. Creating these connections recreates the "sense of wonder," in the terminology of science-fiction fandom, that we felt when we first read the pulps and other texts we work with. (Coogan 2005, 21)

The key to the Wold Newton game is thus the same as the key to the Sherlockian game—fun. Playing with these texts give fans/writers/scholars a chance to dive deeper into their favorite works of fiction, interacting with the text in a way that makes them part of the process of creation. They join with others who share their interest to cocreate a consistent continuity between these works that evoke a collective sense of wonder.

In order for such a project to exist in any objective sense, however, it requires more than just whimsy. As with any game, there are rules, and these rules are what (for those who participate) separate it from fan fiction. Coogan explains,

> as with any game the pleasure of playing comes from performing well within its rules. In the case of Wold-Newtonry, scholars choose their own rules; but there does exist a group of scholars . . . who generally work with the same basic assumptions and through their articles have created a kind of consensus version of the [Wold Newton Universe] that is essentially consistent with Farmer's (occasionally contradictory) vision of the Wold Newton Universe and Family. (Coogan 2005, 35)

In this way Wold Newtonry is separate from fan fiction: "Despite some surface similarities, Wold-Newtonry is not a form of fan fiction. Rather it is parascholarship" (Coogan 2005, 35). While fan fiction is one method of "writing back" to a text and interacting with it, Wold Newtonry is a different approach to doing the same thing. The difference, though, is crucial, because it turns what would otherwise be the solitary activity of one writer into a group activity that relies upon sources, evidence, footnotes, and an evolving canon of what is and is not accepted as "factual."

This reliance upon a structured set of rules is what ties Wold Newtonry in with retroactive continuity. In the Wold Newton game, these "literary archeologists" weave together a continuous tapestry out of disparate pieces of fiction, retroactively enforcing a continuity upon them that had not originally existed, nor been intended. To do this requires a set of rules that Wold Newton scholars generally agree on (though, as Coogan notes, those rules may vary from person to person). This is reminiscent of how Wolfman and his cocreators took the disparities of DC Comics' fifty years of continuity and turned them into one semi-cohesive narrative, via *Crisis on Infinite Earths*. Once again, we here have an example of the ways in which different fans and creators have differing views about continuity, and how stringently it must be enforced in long-form narratives. The retcon is a tool frequently utilized and appreciated by the most continuity-obsessed, those so intent upon enforcing the rules that they will literally rewrite (fictional) history in order to maintain cohesion.

Many other creators—both professional writers and fans/scholars alike—have gone on to create their own versions of the Wold Newton Universe, playing a metatextual game where they can create and define worlds that are inspired by, but also differ greatly from, Farmer's. Win Scott Eckert, for example, has taken Wold Newtonry a step further, to create what he has called "The Crossover Universe," or CU for short. Eckert explains that he has created the CU from a core list of "fictional biographies," akin to Farmer's *Tarzan Alive* and *Doc Savage* books, all of which treat imaginary characters as if they were real. From that list, he has expanded the CU based on a series of ever-expanding crossover stories:

> The Crossover Chronology builds a universe using the fictional biographies listed above as its platform. Put another way, the Crossover Chronology plays a "six degrees of separation" game, with the characters from the fictional biographies as the first degree. . . . The Crossover Chronology is a timeline of crossover stories in which two or more literary characters, situations, universes, or, in some rare cases, actual historical personages, are linked together. (W. Eckert 2011, 14)

As with the Great Game and Wold Newtonry (both of which inspired and contributed to the CU), Eckert's Crossover Chronology is structured around a series of rules, such as honoring "the basic tenant of fictional biographies, treating the universe it documents as a series of real, historical events" (W. Eckert 2011, 14). Out of this, Eckert has created a massive two-volume (with more promised) timeline, entitled *Crossovers: A Secret Chronology of the World*, an attempt to reconcile all of the crossovers from all of literature with the CU framework (and, by extension, with the Wold Newton Universe and the Sherlockian Great Game). The fact that there is an audience for such a work, even a cult audience, shows how much of an interest there is in this kind of metatextual play.

Win Scott Eckert may be the biggest proponent of Farmer's game, but he is not the only writer influenced by it. Horror and science fiction writer Kim Newman (who not coincidentally wrote the introduction to the first volume of Eckert's *Crossovers*) has cited Farmer as one source of inspiration for his popular *Anno Dracula* series of novels, which create an alternate history based on the concept that Count Dracula, the titular villain of Bram Stoker's classic vampire novel *Dracula*, conquered England instead of being defeated by the novel's heroes. Newman's books are meticulously researched in order to include fictionalized/alternate versions of real historical figures alongside period-appropriate fictional characters. As Newman describes,

> With *Anno Dracula*, I had the background and the two lead characters . . . plus the notion (inspired by Philip José Farmer) of a large cast list which would include not only real Victorians (Oscar Wilde, Gilbert & Sullivan, Swinburne) but famous characters from the fiction of the period (Raffles, Fu Manchu, various Holmesian hangers-on, Dr Moreau, Dr Jekyll).

Newman also notes that it is his fandom, and his love of the original stories, characters, and figures that he retroactively weaves together into an alternate reality, that has seen him through four books in the series so far: "I am only able to keep this work up—the books demand an awful lot of nit-picking research and detail-gathering—because my enthusiasm for *Dracula* is undimmed." Like comic book fans who obsess about continuity details, and comic book creators who implement retcons to fix that continuity, it is love and playfulness that carries writers along through these sometimes-arduous metatextual creations.

Possibly the most well-known iteration of this game (thanks in part to a mediocre action film that was very untrue to the source material) is the comic book series *The League of Extraordinary Gentlemen*, by writer Alan Moore and illustrator Kevin O'Neill. *League* began as a high concept idea to create a Victorian-era "Justice League" out of the heroes of the earliest science fiction, fantasy, and horror novels. However, in the hands of Moore (perhaps the most influential and well-regarded writer in the history of the medium) and O'Neill (a stylized artist with an obsessive attention to detail), the series evolved out of this initial concept and turned toward a greater one: creating a world wherein every piece of fiction ever written is able to coexist. Many of the later volumes of *League* eschew the action-adventure narratives of earlier stories to focus instead on the nature of stories and fictional creations themselves and how they have evolved in the years between the Victorian Age and the present. In this endeavor, Moore recognizes Farmer as one of his inspirations:

> I can remember very definitely being excited by the thrill of linking up all of these disparate stories. Even if it was a kind of obsessive, fannish, mad thing to do, to work out the exact relationships between Tarzan, Doc Savage, and the Scarlet Pimpernel, I thought that you had to admire Philip Josè Farmer's fortitude and obsessive passion in working it all out. (quoted in Nevins 217)

As it did for Farmer, Eckert, and Newman, this type of work requires a vast amount of time and research by Moore and O'Neill in order to uncover obscure and minor works of published fiction (generally of the fantastic/romantic variety) that can be integrated into the increasingly complex world of *League*. Though the game may have at first been merely between themselves, readers soon caught on to it, organizing online annotations that allow those less familiar with the history of British literature (and increasingly French and American literature, as well as film and television) to enjoy the references and sight gags crammed into almost every panel of the comics. Historian and librarian Jess Nevins arose as the primary wrangler of these annotations, ultimately printing them as a series of unofficial companion books to the various volumes of *The League of Extraordinary Gentlemen*.

That these books are met with approval by the creators is indicated by the fact that Moore and O'Neill have each been involved with them, providing interviews and introductions. Moore even explains, in one of those introductions, that Nevins's annotations are precisely what *allow* the creators to go as far as they do in their metatextual game:

> As *League* itself has grown more complex and ambitious since its first conception, so too have I become obsessed with expanding the book's remit to include even the most remote and obscure corners of the fictional landscape. At the same time, I've grown concerned that this might eventually serve to alienate the readership, if they came to feel that we were showering them with unrecognisably arcane literary winks and nudges for no greater purpose than to demonstrate how much research Kevin and I have done. With Jess at hand to field even the wildest lobs over the ballpark gates of audience comprehension, these anxieties melt away. Thanks to his tireless work and enthusiasm at the academic margins of our project, unpacking the increasingly densely referenced thesis that our comic book and its collected volumes have become, then there is no reader, of whatever age or background, who need feel excluded. (Moore 2004, 11)

Moore, then, is explicitly aware of how *League* has become a game with various different participants: himself and O'Neill, Nevins and the other annotators, and the readers who want to fully understand the richness and complexity of the text. Nevins's annotations thus become a para-text to *League*, a separate but necessary part of enjoying the comic books. To Moore, the metatextual game of creating a sort of retroactive continuity for the entirety of fiction and literature is one that relies upon many hands, and not just a solitary authorial voice (though that voice, of course, does have ultimate authority when it comes to what is and is not part of the world of *The League of Extraordinary Gentlemen*).

These examples brush the surface of a steadily growing subgenre of literature that plays with metatextuality in order to bring together characters from a variety of sources and create a retroactive sense of continuity between them. Others include Jasper Fforde's "fiction police" series of Thursday Next novels; *League of Extraordinary Gentlemen*-inspired British-American horror drama *Penny Dreadful*; Disney and video game publisher Square Enix's *Kingdom Hearts* video games, which cross over characters and settings from a huge variety of Disney properties; Bill Willingham's *Fables*; and the *Fables*-influenced television series *Grimm* and *Once Upon a Time*.

Literature is not the only medium that finds itself subject to these kinds of retcon games. The "Tommy Westphall Universe" theory, for example, combines the ending of the television series *St. Elsewhere* (wherein the entire show is revealed to have taken place in the mind of an autistic child named Tommy Westphall) with the series' frequent crossovers with other television programs, to posit that almost four hundred different TV shows all take place within Tommy's mind. Mark J. P. Wolf calls this "Probably the most elaborate example of retroactive linkages resulting in a multiverse," and explains that "Noting crossovers from one television show to another, fans in on-line forums have linked together 282 television shows, from *I Love Lucy* (1951–1957) to new programs still on television as of spring 2012, with lists and a chart demonstrating how all the shows are connected" (218). Yet again, we see retroactive continuity becoming a communal game.

Sometimes, this kind of metatextual play can literally come in the form of a game. Shades of *Cartoon All-Stars to the Rescue*, the current generation of children is becoming exposed to this kind of creative playfulness via the LEGO franchise of toys, video games, and movies. 2014's *The Lego Movie*, for example, featured its everyman protagonist interacting with characters as diverse as Batman, Gandalf, C-3PO, and Shaquille O'Neal. A 2015 video game called *LEGO Dimensions* takes this even further, with promotional materials focusing on the idea that the game allows players to immerse themselves in a mix-and-match experience of diverse characters and worlds from various media franchises: "For the first time ever characters from different universes join forces in worlds outside their own. A Dark Knight, a Wizard and a Master Builder traveling down the Yellow Brick Road are just the beginning." The game promises "An Extreme Cross-Over," where players can "Journey through worlds and team up with unlikely allies, because the only rule with LEGO Dimensions is that there are no rules." Of course, this isn't strictly true; as with all games, *LEGO Dimensions* relies upon its rules to make it fun.

The key to this, yet again, is fun. Retroactive continuity provides a way of engaging with fictional histories that can be entertaining and enjoyable, whether that is through the creation of satire or the development of literary detective games. People engage in this metatextual play because they enjoy it, whether that joy comes from working together or simply from immersing themselves individually in scholarship, lore, and complex charts. Though some may choose to pathologize these "fanboys" for being too obsessed with what is "just a piece of fiction," these are actually passionate, intelligent people who are having fun, and who understand the importance that fiction has to reality. They know how integral continuity is to the human mind and respect that sometimes knowledge is only gleaned retroactively.

As these "fanboys" become, more and more, the general public, repercussions can be seen and felt in the real world. In moving from relatively denigrated "cult" media to the most popular of television shows and film franchises, and even bringing those franchises together into a mega-franchise, retconning has turned into a widespread narrative trope that allows for creators to rewrite the historical narrative of a fictional world. Today, this has come to influence how audiences accept unstable memory and unstable historical narratives—unstable *history*—both on the Internet and in the real world.

CITATION NEEDED
Wikipedia and the Mutability of the Past

On May 27, 2011, Representative Anthony D. Weiner, a Democratic congressman from New York, sent a sexually suggestive photograph of himself in underwear to a young woman via the social media site Twitter. Meant as a private message, he accidentally posted it publicly, before quickly deleting it. The next day, however, conservative blogger Andrew Breitbart published the photograph on his website, having been alerted to it by a quick-moving Twitter follower of Representative Weiner. Beleaguered by the press, Weiner at first maintained that his computer had been hacked and that he had never met the woman it was sent to, but after Breitbart posted additional photos and e-mails the congressman was forced to come clean and admit that he had sent the initial photograph, along with other lewd photos and messages to women he had met on the Internet ("Milestones: Anthony D. Weiner").

Weiner was not the first public figure, nor would he be the last, to learn that the Internet is equal parts permanent and permeable. Though he was able to quickly delete his accidental public posting, a brief moment is all that the collective minds and fingers of Internet users require to permanently capture any image, message, text, video, or other media posted online. Weiner may have been able to erase his tracks on his own Twitter page, but he would prove unable to escape from the past no matter how much he altered his own social media web pages. As digital media scholar Paul Levinson notes in regards to Weiner, "nothing that happens via new new new media [Levinson's preferred term for social media] stays in the new new media system in which it happens . . . because the deeper reality is that whatever happens online is intrinsically and pervasively connected to all other media and therefore all people in the world" (36). Weiner might have tried to alter the tracings of his own online history, but that history was already irrevocably recorded elsewhere.

Another politician learned the ways in which history is simultaneously mutable and immutable on the Internet when, at around the same time as Weiner's scandal, former Alaskan governor (and former Republican vice presidential candidate) Sarah Palin found herself the center of an Internet battle regarding American historical icon Paul Revere. After being asked by a reporter what she had seen on a trip to Boston, Ms. Palin stated:

> We saw where Paul Revere hung out as a teenager, which was something new to learn. And you know, he warned the British that they weren't going to be taking away our arms, by ringing those bells and making sure, as he is riding his horse through town, to send those warning shots and bells, that we were going to be secure and we were going to be free. (quoted in Block)

Pundits and analysts—particularly liberals who were opposed to Palin's views and her close association with the conservative Fox News network—were quick to point out that Revere had actually rode carefully and quietly through the Boston area, warning colonists as to the arrival of British troops without alerting either Loyalists or the British themselves. In response, Palin's supporters visited the Wikipedia page for Paul Revere, editing it so that it related her statements, rather than the research of credited historians, as the truth. Palin encouraged these changes by doubling down on her inaccuracy, claiming, "I didn't mess up. I answered candidly and I know my American history. Part of his ride was to warn the British that we're already there" (quoted in Block). Other Wikipedia editors, however, motivated either by politics or by a desire to keep to the website's policy of a verifiable, neutral point of view, worked to revert those changes as soon as they were made. Eventually, moderators stepped in and locked the page, preventing it from being freely edited by anonymous, unregistered users, as is the typical Wikipedia editing policy. The discussion about Palin's comments moved from the Paul Revere Wikipedia page itself to its "Talk" page, where users are able to discuss and argue over a particular page's content in order to come to a collaborative decision about what should be reflected on the page. A Wikipedia spokesperson told news organizations that locking the page would provide a "cooling-off period" where discussion could dominate rather than edits (quoted in Weiner).

In response to the controversy over the Paul Revere page, one Wikipedia editor/contributor told the Associated Press, "When an item is in the news, it brings in the masses" (Associated Press).[1] These "masses," both in support of and in opposition to Palin, turned Wikipedia into a battleground over the interpretation of history, quibbling on such matters as what "warning" meant or who was "British" in the years leading up to the American Revolution. Clearly this was a contemporary political battle disguised as a conversation about history, but it provides a clear example of how those two topics—history and politics—are continually comingled on the Internet. As a website that is, as we shall see, dedicated to a stringently neutral point of view, Wikipedia strives to extricate those tangled threads, providing cited, sourced, factually based information, along with multiple interpretations, in order to provide a well-rounded primer on a particular person, event, topic, and so forth. However, as the Palin/Revere matter shows, when a particular historical issue becomes newsworthy, its Wikipedia page can quickly become a site of contestation, calling that neutrality into question. Wikipedia users must then rely on the ethos of the website's editors and moderators to maintain a neutral point of view in the face of an influx of partisan stakeholders. As such, Wikipedia stringently maintains the history of all of its pages, such that editors, moderators, and readers/researchers alike can pour through the entire line of changes going back to the inception of a particular page. Although the page itself may simply show the most recent (hopefully cooperatively-arrived-at) version, Wikipedia's support pages continually maintain traces of the site's history, and thus (in the case of pages like Paul Revere's) of its history of history.

As the above examples display, the Internet is as impermanent as it is implacable. Just as an old website or message board posting may disappear at any time without warning, thanks to some unannounced administrative decision by a site owner or through the random failure of a backup server, those same bits of older data and writing could reappear just as suddenly thanks to clever digital manipulation. Anything that is ever said or written online is fodder for future debate in the digital era, particularly in the case of public figures; nothing disappears forever. Similarly, the average American is more aware than ever that what appears online—increasingly the primary source of information for many people—can swiftly and easily be edited to reflect an updated version of "the truth" on a moment-to-moment basis. As our culture becomes more and more media savvy and Internet adept, we have come to increasingly understand that what we read on our computers, tablets, phones, watches, and so forth only reflects a current version of online "reality," one which is the culmination of multiple edits, rewrites, and, yes, retcons.

Nowhere is this awareness more pushed to the fore than in the case of Wikipedia, the world's largest open-source encyclopedia. As any beleaguered high school or college teacher can attest, today's students rely upon Wikipedia for the vast majority of their information. The reliance—some may say over-reliance—upon Wikipedia has created a national conversation, both in the academy and among various online and print media outlets, about what represents reliable information in an era where Internet sources are wholly ephemeral. The notion that online history is ever changeable has important resonances with historical revisionism, and thus with retroactive continuity.

The instability of information on the Internet, and the ever-changing fluidity with which digital data must be assessed and analyzed, is a crucial component of how thoughts and opinions are formulated in America today, and the prominence of retconning in American entertainment has helped to lay the groundwork for the acceptance of this sort of instability. The growing importance and acceptance of retroactive continuity in today's popular media better prepares audiences to face a society that is more and more defined by the hyperlink than the footnote.

This chapter will use Wikipedia as a case study through which to explore how historical revisionism has become an increasingly accepted practice in today's world, one that has transcended the halls of academia to become an important part of general cultural memory. Though this exploration, we will see how the understanding of a more fluid past resonates with the kinds of popular entertainment that have come to dominate the American mediascape, and how the two are intrinsically related. To get to this point, though, we must first understand Wikipedia's origins, functions, and policies.

Wikipedia: What It Is and How It Came to Be

Today, Wikipedia is one of the top-ten most visited websites in the world, a feat made all the more remarkable by the fact that it is a nonprofit enterprise surrounded in the top ten by massive, multi-billion-dollar companies like Google and Facebook. The site is particularly popular among high school and college students engaged in research and other learning activities. A 2010 study, in fact, found that over half of all college students frequently utilize Wikipedia for class-related work and research, and the site's popularity has only grown since then (Head and Eisenberg). Though many teachers, professors, and other academics may decry students' reliance on an open-sourced encyclopedia that can be edited by absolutely anybody with a computer and Internet access, this has clearly not hindered those students from using the site anyway. It is safe to say that, today, Wikipedia is used by a significant percentage of Americans as an information source; as Wikipedia historian Andrew Lih notes, "There are still enormous questions about the reliability of Wikipedia, though empirical use by millions of people suggests that the site is consistently helpful and, more often than not, accurate" (10). Not bad for a website that was originally a byproduct of a different project entirely.

Wikipedia arose out of a project created by the mid-1990s dot-com startup Bomis, Inc., cofounded by Internet entrepreneurs Jimmy Wales and Tim Shell. Bomis began as a Yahoo-style Internet directory, before expanding into other projects. One such project, an open source, collaborative encyclopedia, was started in 2000, spurred on by a third partner, Larry Sanger, a PhD student in philosophy (Sanger would obtain his doctorate within the year). Sanger and Wales worked closely together on developing this project, which they called Nupedia. Since Bomis was a commercial entity, their initial goal was to create a site that could generate advertising revenue; however, the project proved to be too time-consuming, and not interesting, engaging, or fun enough, to attract the volunteer contributors required of such a wide-scale open-sourced endeavor. Wales and Sanger, however, came upon a new collaborative type of software, called WikiWikiWeb, created by developer Ward Cunningham. The "wiki" software allowed for more efficient and enjoyable collaboration between contributors, and was originally attached to Nupedia as a way to perfect articles before adding them to the growing encyclopedia. When the Nupedia advisory board complained about just how open and anonymous the wiki was, it spun off into its own separate project, launched on January 15, 2001, as Wikipedia.com. In its first month, Wikipedia developed more articles than Nupedia had in the entire previous year. As Sanger noted at the time, "Wikipedia has definitely taken [on] a life of its own; new people are arriving every day and the project seems to be getting only more popular. Long live Wikipedia!" (quoted in Lih 67).

Though Wikipedia was up and running by early 2001, it would face multiple crises in the ensuing years, leading to conflict between users, contributors, and administrators.[2] What these controversies ultimately led to was the development of the three keystone policies by which Wikipedia has been guided ever since.

Wikipolicy

As Wikipedia contributors Phoebe Ayers, Charles Matthews, and Ben Yates explain, in their "user's manual" *How Wikipedia Works*, "Three policies are so central to Wikipedia's workings that the encyclopedia would be unrecognizable (or nonexistent) without them. These core policies are Verifiability (V), No Original Research (NOR), and Neutral Point of View (NPOV). In broad strokes, they form the framework in which content is created and edited on a daily basis with no top-down editorial control" (12). This is not hyperbole; Wikipedia's development, and its current success, is reliant upon the fact that those three policies mean the site's pages will continually be updated and improved according to a set of universal standards that require a certain amount of authority, reliability, and nonpartisanship.

Without those values, Wikipedia would run the risk of becoming an entirely opinion-based receptacle of extremist viewpoints. Instead, the policies have allowed for the site to become increasingly reliable as pages are added, debated, and cleaned up over the years. This has in turn led to sustained conversation on the site and within academia regarding who has "authority" over the creation of knowledge and the narrativization of history, a topic that has been going on for decades (if not centuries) in the liberal arts academy. English professor and Wikipedia supporter Thomas Leitch claims that "The value system Wikipedia shares with other wikis is not a challenge to liberal education but its logical extension into cyberspace, because Wikipedia does not resolve these paradoxes of authority in liberal education but faithfully replicates them" (23). Leitch further notes that the kinds of "authority" he is discussing "are not transcendent or timeless but temporal, rationally grounded, historically situated, and subject to change. This definition may seem narrow, but it is shared by both the academy and the Web" (13). Leitch's definition of authority is one that Wikipedia itself enables through its three core policies.

The first of these policies, Verifiability, "means that you should always be able to verify that the content of a Wikipedia article is factual, using reliable outside sources that are cited within the article" (Ayers et al., 13). In practice, this means that the ideal Wikipedia article is copiously cited, with every single major statement attributed to an outside source that a reader can consult with (and, by extension, can themselves judge the authenticity and authority of). Wikipedia is not meant to be an authority in and of itself, but rather a compendium of links to other sources that may or may not be considered authoritative; in some cases, questioning the authority of these sources is a part of the Wikipedia page itself. A statement that isn't sourced is considered suspect on Wikipedia and, if not outright deleted, is marked with the clear statement, "citation needed." Ayers, Matthews, and Yates even indicate that, "If a topic has never been discussed by any reliable, third-party sources, the Verifiability policy dictates that Wikipedia should not have an article about that topic. Writing the article should be put off until better sources have been published outside Wikipedia" (13).

This feeds into the next major policy, that of No Original Research. Wikipedia is not intended to be a place where researchers can post their work, but rather where others can make reference to that work, once it is published. Though theoretically this is simply a restatement of the Verifiability policy, in practice, "The initial motivation for the No Original Research policy was to prevent people with unconventional personal theories from using Wikipedia to draw attention to their ideas. These days, No Original Research is consistently used against the inclusion of material that is in no sense crackpot but is simply too novel for Wikipedia" (Ayers et al., 15). Furthermore, No Original Research also implies that "editors should not be tempted to provide historical interpretations or draw conclusions, even if they seem self-evident, without citing supporting outside sources giving the same interpretations" (Ayers et al., 15). Thus, facts and opinions alike need to be copiously sourced and cited in order to hold up to Wikipedia's standards, an attempt to separate the site from the multitude of personalized, opinionated blogs and "news" sources that populate the Internet.

The standard that both Verifiability and No Original Research attempt to create is the ultimate goal of any Wikipedia page—achieving a "Neutral Point of View." In an article with a Neutral Point of View,

> all points of view about a particular topic should be fairly represented. NPOV is one of the oldest, most respected, and most central policies on Wikipedia. A neutral article makes no case and concentrates on informing the reader by providing a good survey of its topic. It is fair-minded and accurate and deals with controversial matters by reporting the main points where there is disagreement. (Ayers et al., 16)

An article with a Neutral Point of View is ultimately one that is written by committee, representing all the various viewpoints of an issue, no matter how contentious they may be. This is intended to create the following effect, as described by Ayers, Matthews, and Yates: "An article on a contentious topic, such as a historical event that is seen differently by various groups, should not reveal where the article author stands on the matter. In almost all cases, such an article will have been worked over by a group of editors, and their opinions should not come through" (16). Andrew Lih also points to the central importance of this policy:

> Most important, the only way to assemble the "sum of all human knowledge," as a collaborative endeavor from many individuals, was to have neutrality as the core editorial policy. Wikipedia founder Jimmy Wales refers to having a "neutral point of view" (NPOV) as the community's only "nonnegotiable" policy, which "attempts to present ideas and facts in such a fashion that both supporters and opponents can agree" (10).

NPOV is thus what allows Wikipedia to function as a site with any amount of authority (even if said authority is frequently questioned by historians, researchers, and teachers), and it provides the tent pole around which the rest of the policies coalesce.

As Nathanial Tkacz notes, however, these policies do not inherently mean that Wikipedia arrives at some kind of "truth," bur rather that it arrives at a defined, agreed-upon version of what "neutral" and "verified" means:

> Together, these three core content policies sit atop a whole body of related policies, guidelines, and essays, which all work to define the contours of the project: the precise rules of a statement's formation and the threshold of statement inclusion; the arrangement and relation between statements; and what constitutes the "source" world beyond the encyclopedia formation and how to approach it. While outside battles for truth are explicitly rejected—"The threshold for inclusion in Wikipedia is *verifiability, not truth*"—Wikipedia nonetheless has a whole body of forceful statements whose function is to establish the truth of any particular statement; a truth of what is neutral, (non-)original, published, reliable, attributable, and verifiable. (110)

This particular vision of what represents accuracy and verifiability comes from a very specific place—the Objectivist ethos of Wikipedia's founders.

Jimmy Wales, Tim Shell, and Larry Sanger all initially met one another through philosophy e-mail lists, where they were attracted to the Objectivist views of writer/philosopher Ayn Rand. Rand's philosophy centers on the idea of gaining objective knowledge of reality (which exists independent of human consciousness) through sense perception and measurement. Furthermore, Objectivism relies on a foundational belief in the sovereignty of the self and of each individual's pursuit of happiness; thus, the respect and maintenance of each person's individual rights is the most important aspect of any social or governmental institution. According to Andrew Lih, this shared philosophy, "inspired faith in the idea of measurement by the masses creating an online reference work" (32). Lih further explains that Wales, Shell, and Sanger

> were attracted to objectivism for a reason. The objectivist stance is that there is a reality of objects and facts independent of the individual mind. By extension, a body of knowledge could be assembled that was considered representative of a single reality. Put simply, objectivity relates to what is true, rather than ruling whether something is true or false. And their encyclopedia could detail what is true in the world without judgments.... They saw the Nupedia project as turning objectivist theory into practice; the theory would be the guiding principle to pull it together. (36–37)

It is this faith in objective reality that allowed Nupedia, and later Wikipedia, to develop around the core concept that there *is* some kind of verifiable truth at which an article can arrive. By maintaining a neutral point of view, one negotiated by multiple individuals representing various sides, Wikipedia's founders believed they *could* arrive at "the truth" and provide a sense of authority about that truth. This process, Wales would note, was inherently social in nature, and could be applied socially beyond Wikipedia itself: "It's all about dialogue, it's all about conversation, it's all about humans making decisions. So that's extremely important. Let's take these ideals of Wikipedia and bring them out to lots and lots of people in lots and lots of areas far beyond simply encyclopedias" (xviii).

The Objectivist philosophy thus still informs Wikipedia to this day, and is the foundation for much of the collaborative work presented on the site as "the truth." However, the process of arriving at that "truth" is a long and arduous one, and as a part of its ethos of freedom and openness Wikipedia stringently maintains the entire record of that negotiation.

A Hyperlink to the Past

According to Wikipedia, "In computing, a hyperlink is a reference to data that the reader can directly follow either by clicking or by hovering. A hyperlink points to a whole document or to a specific element within a document"

("Hyperlink"). Hyperlinks are a crucial part of Wikipedia, and are increasingly important to *any* article or document posted on the Internet. Hyperlinks allow for a reader to easily follow a piece of information (a definition, a source, a citation, etc.) with the literal click of a button. For many articles, hyperlinks serve as footnotes, providing a connection between the text and the sources that the text is pulling from.[3]

This shift from a culture of information reliant upon footnotes to one reliant upon hyperlinks is important, for it points to an acceptance of the mutability of that information. Paul Levinson notes how this mutability fundamentally changes the medium of the written word:

> Writing used to be the archetypically immutable medium. . . . The printing press heightened this immutability. . . . Once published, a book or newspaper article was beyond being changed by the author, except via means of a new edition of a book . . . or an editor willing to publish an amending note by the reporter in the newspaper, neither of which were likely. . . . In the last two decades of the 1900s, word processing for the first time in history gave writers the capacity to change their written words with no tell-tale evidence of the original. . . . Blogging made the publication as easy to alter as the initial writing. . . . But what about the capacity of any blogger to easily change the material wording and meaning of a blog post after it has been published? (88–89)

In Levinson's estimation, what prevents such a circumstance—one that can be either completely innocent and innocuous or potentially nefarious, attempting to control the free flow of information—is the audience of readers:

> On the one hand, changing a text already extensively commented on can certainly generate confusion. . . . On the other hand, the greater the number of people who have read and commented on a text, the more difficult for the author to surreptitiously alter the text and pretend the altered text was in the blog post all along. The audience for the initial text thus serves as protection against the changing of the text for purposes of deception . . . The social group as a guarantor of truth or, at the very least, accuracy, is a check-and-balance that works to the benefit of all new media and their users. (89)

The veracity of information online is thus reliant upon a vigilant readership, one that has had to train itself, as a group, to vocally note when such information has been altered.

In part as a result of this social dynamic, in online journalism hyperlinks have essentially replaced footnotes. However, there remains one important difference between the two formats: whereas footnotes are a part of an article that can only be changed by the author or editors of that article, hyperlinks are also reliant upon the pages that they link *to*. Should that linked page change its URL, the hyperlink will be broken and nonfunctional. Perhaps even more problematic, that page might change its content, such that the hyperlink no longer actually provides a legitimate source for the article. Hyperlinks are thus malleable and fluctuating, reliant upon writers and editors on both sides of the link. This is a very different relationship to information than the traditional footnote, which is embodied as a part of a piece of text, one reliant only upon the author/editor of that text (and one that, in traditional media, is physically unchangeable once an article goes to print).

Citizens of the digital era, however, are growing savvy as to how this process works. For instance, although Anthony Weiner was able to quickly remove his inappropriate photo from Twitter, a follower saved the image before Weiner had a chance to take it down. Thus, despite the link to the photo no longer existing, the photo itself was saved for posterity. Users of the Internet are aware of its constant state of flux, and recognize that the history of a particular web page has become almost as important as what is currently visible there.[4]

Wikipedia has approached this reality of the web in an interesting way; the site archives and makes accessible a full account of every minor change and edit made to every single Wikipedia page. As Andrew Lih explains,

> The Wikipedia project is radically different from other writing methods because it is open. It strives for transparency, to allow inspection for everything within the community. Each article has a complete chronological log of every change ever made, back to its point of creation. The actions of each user (anonymous ones too) are meticulously recorded and tracked in the system and can be observed by anyone else. . . . Wikipedia can allow anyone to edit because any action can be easily undone by anyone else in the community. Only in the digital realm is it easier to repair things than to do harm. (5–6)

Through these logs of all changes, Wikipedia approaches transparency, enabling users to see how a page has evolved, and indeed how it continues to evolve. As Paul Levinson explains, this "hypertransparency of editing history" often "puts even the most diligent vandal at a disadvantage" (73).

The policy also allows the site to remain open sourced, even as it grows ever bigger and more popular. Because moderators can simply roll back a change—especially one that is transparent vandalism of a page—contributions can continue ad infinitum, with no risk of a more "true" (that is, verifiable, sourced, and neutral) version being permanently overwritten. This transparent history also allows users and moderators to negotiate through controversial topics and subjects, especially those that devolve into so-called edit wars, where two or more users fight back and forth over a series of changes to a page. In addition, certain policies have been implemented—such as temporarily locking a page to provide a cool-down period, as was the case with the Paul Revere page after Sarah Palin's comments—that provide further opportunity for conversation and negotiation on a page's "Talk" section (where discussions about edits are held) before changes are implemented on the main page. Through these negotiations, as is the case with the edit history itself, Wikipedia strives to maintain its goals of transparency and mutual consideration of what represents "verification" and "neutrality."

None of this, however, should be meant to imply that Wikipedia has by any means achieved some kind of utopian, idyllic position as a wholly open, welcoming, and stringently neutral arbiter of "truth." Over time, as with any system or structure of rules, Wikipedia's complicated methodology has made it less welcome to new contributors, and even openly hostile to newcomers who propose changes to what they view as outdated policies (see Halfaker et al., 664–68). Contributors tend to be overwhelmingly male (as much as 90 percent in some estimates), leading to sexist and misogynist decisions, such as having a separate page for "Female American Novelists" while leaving the "American Novelists" page as a list of only male writers (Sargent and Brady). This becomes especially troubling as Wikipedia's popularity and usage increases, potentially culturally reifying its current white, Western, male-dominated perspective. Even Wikipedia's cofounder Jimmy Wales is aware of this problem, admitting that "the biggest issue is editor diversity" (quoted in Simonite). Wales's hopes for improvement, though, lie in updating and improving Wikipedia's openness, so as to make it more welcoming to new contributors of diverse backgrounds. Once attracted to the site, these new editors will be able to contend with what is already present, as well as the history of what led up to that present condition, thanks to the long history of logged edits and changes, which provide the foundation upon which Wikipedia's success or failure ultimately rests.

This history of recorded, transparent change on each and every Wikipedia page is a cornerstone of the way the site works. Embedded in the literal code of Wikipedia is the fact that any piece of information, whether about a historical or contemporary person, topic, or idea, requires debate and change in order to arrive at a consensus. The editing history of a Wikipedia page is thus the digital embodiment of the process of historical revision at work, laid bare and made clear for any visitor to see. It contains permanent traces of the "retcons" made to Wikipedia, and thus to the retroactive continuity of the historical narrative itself.

Retconning History

As the above explanation of Wikipedia's editing process shows, though history *on* Wikipedia may constantly be in flux, the history *of* Wikipedia permanently reflects those changes. A particular Wikipedia page may change multiple times a day, or even several times an hour, but those changes are as ephemeral as the ones that came before them. In many ways, this reflects the ongoing cultural discussion regarding historical revisionism, particularly as it applies to what we teach in classrooms.

As Wikipedia grows ever more popular, it comes to play a larger role in American education as well. High school and college teachers are well versed in explaining to students how Wikipedia is a valid place to begin their research, but—because of its transient open-source nature—not a valid source to cite in and of itself. This is reflected in Wikipedia's own policies, which recognizes its articles as tertiary sources of information. Since no original research is allowed, and citation is constantly needed, a well-written Wikipedia article points a researcher in the direction of the primary and secondary sources through which they can find fuller explanations and arguments about a given topic. Citizens of the digital age are thus made increasingly aware of the fact that history, on Wikipedia (and, by extension, on much of the Internet in general), is not an ossified body of fact, but rather a constantly evolving set of interpretations of the past.[5]

"History," here, refers to the academic discipline, but it equally applies to the history of postings, sites, and edits made by various editors, bloggers, politicians, and other public stakeholders. On the Internet, the past is ever malleable, consisting of posts, deletions, and permanent captures of those deletions. This notion of an alterable and debatable past, which has become such an important part of the digital age, is reliant upon a culture that has been prepared for such views by decades of retconning in the world of popular entertainment. The places in which we spend our leisure time have a real and measurable impact upon our daily lives. As the understanding of the past as a site of contestation and ongoing change permeates our popular entertainment franchises, it leads to our culture having a deeper sense of how that same struggle applies to real-world history and historiography, a sensibility that has found its ultimate realization in Wikipedia.

Thanks to Wikipedia, and to the many other websites like it, citizens of the digital age have come to realize that "historical revisionism" is not merely a political appropriation of the past, but is in fact the very form that the discipline of history takes in the current day. Authority is no longer viewed as something provided mysteriously from on high, but rather as an ongoing development that must be continually questioned. As Thomas Leitch notes,

> Using Wikipedia in any capacity—consulting it, contributing to it, editing it, teaching with it—encourages trust-and-verify attitudes that are more likely to produce both a more critical tropism toward conscientious verification and a more mature brand of trust. Experienced users of Wikipedia can develop the ability to weigh competing claims by discounting them according to the authority of their sources, none of which could ever be absolute. (107)

The historical narrative is ever in flux as these claims are weighed and as further questions are brought to the fore and satisfactorily answered (or not). Just like in our fictional universes, our historical reality does not continually stay the same. To quote Leitch once more, "Playing with culture makes it more transparent and subject to revision, whether the players are editing Wikipedia, questioning the foundations of liberal education, or participating in their own governance" (132). Our own, real-world continuity is constantly retroactively changing, and the fact that increasingly we accept this as the way of the world (and of the past) goes to show just how well our media and escapist entertainments have prepared us for this important moment.

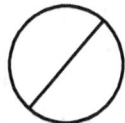

CONCLUSION:
PLAYING THE RETCON GAME

The website TV Tropes is a wiki dedicated to cataloging various tropes of fiction (not just those, as the name might imply, used by television series). The site defines these "tropes" as "devices and contentions that a writer can reasonably rely on as being present in the audience members' minds and expectations" ("Home Page"). That TV Tropes has chosen to catalog retcons, then, shows just how far the trope has come. It is no longer a desperation technique of cult media, used to enforce conformity on disparate texts, but has evolved into a well-known trope that can be found in all forms of media.

On TV Tropes, however, the contributors and editors don't merely catalogue the implementation of certain tropes in fiction, but also how they may appear or apply to the real world. On the site's page for "Retcon," the "Real Life" subheading provides over fifteen examples of how retroactive continuity has played out in real-world history. Of these examples, ten reference politically motivated retcons made by powerful/fascist regimes. Josef Stalin, for example, is listed as "constantly re-writing the history of the Communist revolution and the early USSR to take credit for opponents' accomplishments or to ghost them out entirely, even when the resulting narrative made no sense." Similarly, retconning is noted as "common practice in North Korea, especially with the details of the lives of Kim Il Sung and Kim Jong Il and of The Korean War." These descriptions are not too different from how the same page describes George Orwell's *1984*: "*1984* is hugely based off this trope. Big Brother can rewrite history at will, and the masses have to eat it up. Retconning is done at the Ministry of Truth, the protagonist's main place of work, and mainly consists of editing out people who fell from Big Brother's favor and were 'vaporized.'"

For many of the TV Tropes contributors, retconning can be a frightening prospect. Their examples link retroactive continuity to real-life political rewriting of history for extremist purposes. In this case, retconning is equated to the most biased, personal agenda-driven kind of historical revisionism: changing the past so as to represent the interests of the parties currently in power. In a certain sense, this is also what fictional retconning does. It overlooks the original intentions of a text in order to sublimate it to the narrative contingencies of the present creators, so as to forward their own agendas in their current creations.

However, as we have seen, this is typically not done out of disrespect for the past, but rather out of a love for past works, a desire to play with them, and a drive to modernize, update, and incorporate them into new works. For creators and fans who enjoy retcon games, retroactive continuity is not something nefarious, but rather celebratory. It involves interacting with the past and casting fictional history in a new light that—in a best-case scenario— reveals how important that history is to the present.

Retconning in the real world need be no more sinister than that, either. While conservative, traditionalist sources and agencies may decry "historical revisionism" as a politically biased rewriting of the past, in actuality it is merely the discipline of history at work. Far from being a Big Brother-like erasure of repressed groups, in our society today it is used to bring attention *to* those groups and their struggles, much as Roy Thomas did in his 1980s *All-Star Squadron* stories. A key part of the process of historiography is recontextualizing the past in order to create new understandings of what that past may have actually been like for various groups of people. To step away from the long-standing Cold War narrative of American Exceptionalism, for example, is not indicative of a "politically correct" attack upon American values. Rather, it is a questioning of just *whose* America, and *whose* values, have been valorized in the first place. Holding a nation responsible for its past misdeeds is not something intended to break that country down, but rather a way of *strengthening* it, to make sure it is more ethical going forward into the future. *This* is what our society uses historical revisionism for, as the "real-life" version of retroactive continuity. We are a culture of information exchange, not a totalitarian state, and that exchange only serves to illuminate the past rather than cast it into shadow. Shedding light on the stories of underprivileged, underrepresented Americans is not a means of undercutting the importance of the heterosexual white men who have been canonized as "Founding Fathers," but rather a way of understanding that everybody's story, everybody's life, matters. Their stories deserve to be told and represented in our official, national historical narrative, even if those stories are only added retroactively.

In this book I have endeavored to provide a history of how retroactive continuity has developed, emerged, and flourished as a narrative trope utilized by a wide variety of media franchises. This has been done with the fervent belief that the stories that we tell ourselves as a society matter, that they mean something important, and that they are not merely fictional "escapes" from the problems of the real world. Rather, they provide an ancillary reality where we can learn valuable lessons to take back with us into our everyday lives. Thus, it is meaningful that retconning has become an active and ubiquitous part of our stories. The fact that retroactive continuity is used to provide a sense of consistency in our fictional worlds, and to craft narrative throughlines that provide us with a sense of comfort and completeness, shows just how much our society craves narratives. We constantly take a "chronicle," in Hayden White's sense, and turn it into a narrative, a story. Sometimes we even do this by putting together the chronicle of other stories into one larger, expansive metanarrative, like the metanarrative of the American experience itself.

This is something we do with our fictional stories, but it is also increasingly a part of how we tell our own stories, both personal and societal. If we understand that the fictional past is an unstable ground on which to stand, one that may be reused and recycled and reimagined in order to create new narratives, then we have a foundation from which to understand how this process functions in reality and in historiography. Because our fictions have paved the way, as a society we have come to understand that the past is *not* a rigid, stagnant, solid mass that we can merely memorize and accept, but rather a continuously changing scroll of data and story that must be constantly recontextualized in order to be understood and meaningfully utilized in the present. History changes from a footnote to a hyperlink, an impermanent citation that we recognize can—and should—change along with the altering conditions of our lives today. As we move toward the future, the past must be reunderstood in order to make it meaningful to the present. The continuity of our world is always ever retroactive, and must not be assumed. History, and our understanding of it, turns out to be the biggest retcon game of all.

NOTES

Chapter 1

1. See chapter 3 for full details on *All-Star Squadron* and the origin of the phrase "retroactive continuity."

2. Though there may be some remaining isolated oral cultures in the world today, in general it is more appropriate to speak of them in the past tense.

3. All Bible citations come from the New Revised Standard Version Holy Bible (Nashville: Thomas Nelson Publishers, 1989).

4. Of course, in oral epics, as previously stated, there is no "original text," merely previous performances.

5. In selecting these three authors, I am in no small part influenced by Michael Saler's excellent work, *As If: Modern Enchantment and the Literary Prehistory of Virtual Reality*. Saler looks to Conan Doyle, Tolkien, and Lovecraft as exemplars of creators who fleshed out what he calls "virtual reality" characters; that is, characters and worldscapes so rich that they provide their own alternate fictional reality in which readers can immerse themselves. This is the same concept as what I call imaginary worlds and/or world-building. Saler goes to great pains to convincingly argue for these writers as creating the first and most potent virtual realities of the late 1800s and early 1900s, due to a "re-enchantment" of the

Western world during that time. As such, the works of these three authors will provide the richest ground from which to mine those realities, those imaginary worlds, for examples of early retroactive continuity.

6. More accurately, Bilbo has found the ring already and kept it in his pocket, but Gollum is very willing to hand it over upon losing the riddle game to Bilbo.

7. See chapter 5 for much more on these sorts of continuity games and their relation to retconning.

Chapter 2

1. British comic book writer Pat Mills and artist Kevin O'Neill, in their superhero parody comic, Marshal Law, point out the irony of how ineffective the heroes were in the context of World War II. In one story, the protagonist, a "hero hunter," notes of a Justice Society parodic stand-in that "They were a bunch of Don Quixotes tilting at windmills! For all their boasting, they did nothing about the real villains of the war." When one of the heroes notes, "We were always capturing mad scientists," Law responds, "Except the Japanese scientists whose medical experiments on G.I. prisoners were too useful to the allies . . . or our own mad scientists who dropped atom bombs after the war." He counters the argument that "Most of our work was on the home-front—dealing with saboteurs and fifth columnists," with the question, "Why didn't you go after the famous American corporations who traded with the enemy and who were never brought to . . . justice?" See Pat Mills, writer, Kevin O'Neill, artist, et al., *Marshal Law: Blood, Sweat, and Fears* (Milwaukie, OR: Dark Horse Comics, 1993).

2. For more information on this era, see Pierre Comtois's excellent, if somewhat hyperbolic, *Marvel Comics in the 1960s: An Issue by Issue Field Guide to a Pop Culture Phenomenon* (Raleigh, NC: TwoMorrows Publishing, 2009).

3. This refers only to DC Comics' main Batman continuity. In alternate universe stories set in a vaguely defined future, such as Frank Miller's *The Dark Knight Returns* series or the animated *Batman Beyond* television show, Bruce Wayne does age, sometimes to the point of being unable to physically serve as Batman any longer.

4. A counterexample of a less conservative take on World War II history would be writer/director Quentin Tarantino's historically revisionist movie *Inglourious Basterds*, in which the film's heroes execute Adolf Hitler in a French movie theater and end World War II early. See *Inglourious Basterds*, directed by Quentin Tarantino (2009: Universal Pictures).

5. For example, in Alan Moore and Dave Gibbons's much-heralded miniseries *Watchmen*, the appearance of just one superhuman so completely alters history that Richard Nixon is still president in the 1980s, electric cars are a readily available commercial product, and the Cold War comes precariously close to erupting into nuclear Armageddon.

6. See John Bodnar, *The "Good War" in American Memory* (Baltimore: Johns Hopkins University Press, 2010), 14.

7. This included those heroes whom DC had not actually published during the 1940s, but were published by other comic book companies whose characters DC had later purchased.

8. For much more on the cultural demonization of the Japanese during World War II, see John W. Dower, *War without Mercy: Race and Power in the Pacific War* (New York: Pantheon, 1986).

9. For more about "historical narrativization," particularly as utilized by theorist Hayden White, see the next chapter.

10. One white member of the crowd, once the hypnotic spell has worn off, sees Amazing Man fighting Real American and proclaims, "What do you expect? They're all animals, aren't they?"

11. All-Star Squadron would never come to deal explicitly with the larger-scale Detroit race riot of June 1943 because the book was canceled before Thomas was able to reach that point in the historical timeline.

12. Given that the entirety of Earth 2's continuity was wiped out in 1985 by DC's massive crossover series Crisis on Infinite Earths, Thomas elected to create a different title focused on newly created, younger heroes who "took the place" of Earth 2 versions of Superman, Batman, Wonder Woman, and so forth, who "no longer existed." For more on this rewriting of continuity in the wake of *Crisis on Infinite Earths*, see the next chapter.

Chapter 3

1. Though DC Comics was the first comic book publisher to reach this anniversary, technically the corporate entity itself was not quite that old. Rather, according to Shirrel Rhoads, "in 1935, Major Malcolm Wheeler-Nicholson's National Allied Publications came out with *New Fun: The Big Comic Magazine* #1—the first time original characters and stories had appeared in a comic book format" (12). This is the anniversary that DC Comics celebrated in 1985, despite the fact that "In 1937, Major Wheeler-Nicholson found himself financially overextended with his printer. In order to continue publishing, he had little choice to take Harry Donenfeld on as a partner. Detective Comics, Inc., was formed early that year, with Wheeler-Nicholson and Donenfeld's business manager, Jack S. Liebowitz, listed as owners. The new company's first production, *Detective Comics* #1 (March 1937) was the first true DC comic book" (Rhoades 15).

2. Technically, Marvel Comics' twelve-issue *Secret Wars* story was published prior to *Crisis on Infinite Earths*. However, as a potentially apocryphal story (perpetuated by DC Comics itself) has it, Marvel Comics' editor-in-chief Jim Shooter caught wind of DC's plans and rushed production of *Secret Wars* in order to tie in with a toy line of Marvel characters. Whether or not this is true, *Secret Wars*, though a sales success, was a critical failure, and did not have the same long-reaching effects as *Crisis*, either industrially or narratively. Nevertheless, DC was aware of the sales impact that *Secret Wars* had, and planned *Crisis* accordingly. See, for example, a memo from Marv Wolfman to all DC editors: "One thing we've learned from SECRET WARS is that the main book feeds all the others. Sales went up on all the titles connected to that catastrophe and I'm sure they will with this one, too [that doesn't sound right, does it?]" (quoted in *Crisis Compendium* 19). For the purposes of this chapter, I will be taking this story at face value, and, given that the planning of *Crisis* preceded *Secret Wars* (public mentions of *Crisis*, in its early stages, date back to at least 1982), continue to refer to *Crisis* as the "first" major company-wide crossover, as that is largely the legacy it has achieved in hindsight.

3. White describes the chronicle as follows: "The chronicle . . . often seems to wish to tell a story, aspire to narrativity, but typically fails to achieve it. More specifically, the chronicle usually is marked by a failure to achieve narrative closure. It does not so much conclude as simply terminate. It starts out to tell a story but breaks off in media res, in

the chronicler's own present; it leaves things unresolved, or rather, it leaves them unresolved in a storylike way" (1987, 5). On page 42 of the same text, he goes on to explain, "A chronicle, however, is not a narrative, even if it contains the same set of facts as its informational content, because a narrative discourse performs differently from a chronicle. Chronology is no doubt a code shared by both chronicle and narrative, but narrative utilizes other codes as well and produces a meaning quite different from that of the chronicle."

4. Cornell is talking about the long-running Doctor Who franchise here, but he has also written for both Marvel and DC Comics, and his comments can easily apply to both of those fictional universes as well as the world of Doctor Who.

5. Until Crisis's official sequel, *Infinite Crisis*, and its follow-up 52, discussed in more detail below.

6. Other examples of such self-criticism of superhero comics from the same era include the "deconstructionist" texts *The Dark Knight Returns* and *Watchmen*, both of which dealt with teasing apart the tropes of the superhero genre. *Crisis*, on the contrary, reveled in those tropes, taking them to absurdist heights, and thus reflected a different sort of criticism/awareness than these more pessimistic, if more critically acclaimed, deconstructionist works.

7. In the interest of full disclosure, the fan mentioned in the article who recognized Jimenez ("Hey, are you Phil Jimenez? *Infinite Crisis* looks amazing.") was actually me.

Chapter 4

1. "Returned" might be a better verb here, given that movie serials from the 1920s and 1930s were episodic in nature.

2. This has led to the amusing "Tommy Westphall Universe Hypothesis," which will be examined in greater depth in the next chapter.

3. This version was eventually adapted as a comic book miniseries called *Buffy: The Origin*, which Whedon has referred to as more or less canonical, taking the place of the film itself in the story world of the TV series of *Buffy* (and its spin-off show *Angel*).

4. I am here referring to Joss Whedon as something of an auteur, which is not strictly true. Multiple writers, producers, and performers contributed to the narrative of *Buffy, the Vampire Slayer* over its seven-season run. As the showrunner for the first five years, however, Whedon was the final authority on all decisions about *Buffy* and any storytelling related to the show; in the final two years he was less directly involved on a day-to-day basis but still maintained final oversight. Thus, it is not wholly inappropriate to attribute narrative choices in *Buffy* to Whedon.

Chapter 5

1. This was published through Wildstorm Comics, which was a part of Image Comics when Moore signed on board, but was later purchased by DC Comics and run as its own label.

2. The most blatant exception to this comes when voice actors for particular characters have passed away, and the producers have thus retired those characters (generally through having them die on the series). It is telling that when other changes have been made in order to create a slightly more realistic timeline, such as the 2008 episode "'That '90s Show"

which retconned Homer and his wife Marge's history such that they now met in the 1990s rather than the previously established 1970s, fans have reacted unfavorably.

3. See the next chapter on how retconning has become a part of reality in a different, more serious way.

Chapter 6

1. A similar influx of "mass edits" could be seen when late-night talk-show host and comedian Stephen Colbert urged his viewers to edit the Wikipedia page on elephants in order to state that the number of elephants in the world had tripled in the last six months. Although Wikipedia administrators were able to quickly negate the vandalism and lock down the page, Colbert's joke about the subject was telling: "Together we can create a reality that we all agree on—the reality we just agreed on." See Lih, 201–2.

2. See Lih for a full accounting of these crises in Wikipedia's development.

3. Wikipedia itself, however, is a bit more complex in its use of footnoting. Hyperlinks within an article will lead a viewer to the bottom of the page, where specific footnotes are listed under a "References" heading, often with separate hyperlinks to the individual sources.

4. Note, for example, the popularity of "The Wayback Machine," a digital archive of the Internet created and administered by a nonprofit organization known as the Internet Archive. Similar to Wikipedia, the Internet Archive is focused on universal access to knowledge; in this case, access to past iterations of websites on the Internet, and to an understanding of how those sites have changed over time. See http://archive.org/web/ and https://archive.org/.

5. This relates to Hayden White's differentiation between the "chronicle" and the "narrative" of history, as previously described in chapter 3.

WORKS CITED

Allie, Scott. "Introduction." In *Buffy the Vampire Slayer: Omnibus Volume 1*, edited by Scott Allie. Milwaukie, OR: Dark Horse Books, 2007.

———. "Introduction." In *Buffy the Vampire Slayer: Omnibus Volume 6*, edited by Scott Allie. Milwaukie, OR: Dark Horse Books, 2009.

"Amazing Readers." *Amazing Heroes* 91, March 15, 1986.

The Associated Press. "Wikipedia Locks Revere Page after Palin Remarks." *CBS News*, June 7, 2011. Accessed March 10, 2016. http://www.cbsnews.com/news/wikipedia-locks-revere-page-after-palin-remarks/#ixzz1obUBnGFb.

Ayers, Phoebe, Charles Matthews, and Ben Yates. *How Wikipedia Works*. San Francisco: No Starch Press, 2008.

Bails, Jerry. Untitled letter. *All-Star Comics* 58, DC Comics, January/February 1976.

Belinkie, Matthew. "The Shocking Complexity of the Saw Movies." Overthinking It, October 26, 2010. Accessed March 10, 2016. https://www.overthinkingit.com/2010/10/26/saw-movies/.

Bernstein, Sharo. "That's Not All, Folks—Cartoons Join Drug War." *Los Angeles Times*, April 20, 1990. Accessed March 10, 2016. http://articles.latimes.com/1990-04-20/entertainment/ca-1433_1_drug-abuse.

"Biographies: Geoff Johns." In *Blackest Night*, edited by Sean Mackiewicz. New York: DC Comics, 2010.

Works Cited

Block, Melissa, host, with Robert Allison. "How Accurate Were Palin's Paul Revere Comments?" *NPR*, June 8, 2011. Accessed March 10, 2016. http://www.npr.org/2011/06/06/137011636/how-accurate-were-palins-comments-on-paul-revere.

Bodnar, John. *The "Good War" in American Memory*. Baltimore: Johns Hopkins University Press, 2010.

Buchanan, A. Russell. *Black Americans in World War II*. Santa Barbara, CA: Clio Books, 1977.

Byrne, John. "Bullets, Bracelets and Byrne." In *Wonder Woman: Second Genesis*. New York: DC Comics, 1997.

Carlyle, Thomas. *On Heroes, Hero-Worship, and the Heroic in History*. Berkeley: University of California Press, 1993.

Casey, Todd, and Mike Cotton. "Coast to Coast." *Wizard*, January 2006.

Cole, Sean. "Sherlock Holmes Fans Play 'Great Game.'" *NPR*, December 1, 2005. Accessed March 10, 2016. http://www.npr.org/templates/story/story.php?storyId=5035037.

Comtois, Pierre. *Marvel Comics in the 1960s: An Issue by Issue Field Guide to a Pop Culture Phenomenon*. Raleigh: NC: TwoMorrows Publishing, 2009.

Conan Doyle, Sir Arthur. "The Adventure of the Empty House." In *The Annotated Sherlock Holmes: Volume II*, edited by William S. Baring-Gould. New York: Clarkson N. Potter, 1967.

———. "The Final Problem." In *The Annotated Sherlock Holmes: Volume II*, edited by William S. Baring-Gould. New York: Clarkson N. Potter, 1967.

Coogan, Peter M. "From Love to Money: The First Decade of Comics Fandom." *International Journal of Comic Art* 12, no. 1 (Spring 2010).

———. "Wold-Newtonry: Theory and Methodology for the Literary Archeology of the Wold Newton Universe." In *Myths for the Modern Age: Philip José Farmer's Wold Newton Universe*, edited by Win Scott Eckert. Austin, TX: MonkeyBrain Books, 2005.

Cornell, Paul. "Canonicity in Doctor Who." *PaulCornell.com*, February 10, 2007. Accessed February 1, 2012. http://www.paulcornell.com/2007/02/canonicity-in-doctor-who.html.

Cornell, Paul, and Kate Orman. "Two Interviews about *Doctor Who*." In *Third Person: Authoring and Exploring Vast Narratives*, edited by Pat Harrigan and Noah Wardrip-Fruin. Cambridge, MA: MIT Press, 2009.

Crisis on Infinite Earths: The Compendium. New York: DC Comics, 2005.

Cronin, Brian. "Comic Book Urban Legends Revealed #272." *Comic Book Resources*, August 5, 2010. Accessed July 1, 2012. http://www.americanquarterly.org/submit/guidelines.html.

Day, David. *Tolkien's Ring*. London: Pavilion Books, 2011.

DiDio, Dan. Introduction to *Infinite Crisis Omnibus*, edited by Peter Hamboussi. New York: DC Comics, 2012.

DiDio, Dan, and Jim Lee. "Welcome to the New 52!" *DC Comics: The New 52*. DC Comics, July 2011.

Dower, John W. *War without Mercy: Race and Power in the Pacific War*. New York: Pantheon, 1986.

Eckert, Chris. "Five Years Later: The Oral History of Countdown to Final Crisis." *Funnybook Babylon*, May 10, 2012. Accessed July 2, 2012. http://funnybookbabylon.com/2012/05/10/five-years-later-the-oral-history-of-countdown-to-final-crisis/.

Eckert, Win Scott. *Crossovers 1: A Secret Chronology of the World (Dawn of Time-1939)*. Encino, CA: Black Coat Press, 2010.

———. "Introduction." In *Myths for the Modern Age: Philip José Farmer's Wold Newton Universe*, edited by Win Scott Eckert. Austin, TX: MonkeyBrain Books, 2005.

Eco, Umberto. "The Myth of Superman." In *Arguing Comics: Literary Masters on a Popular Medium*, edited by Jeet Heer and Kent Worcester. Jackson: University Press of Mississippi, 2004.

Ellis, Warren. *From the Desk of Warren Ellis*. Urbana, IL: Avatar Press, 2002.

Farmer, Philip José. *Tarzan Alive: A Definitive Biography of Lord Greystroke*. Lincoln: University of Nebraska Press, 2006.

Fassbender, Tom, and Jim Pascoe, writers, Cliff Richards, penciller, et al. "False Memories." In *Buffy the Vampire Slayer: Omnibus Volume 6*, edited by Scott Allie. Milwaukie, OR: Dark Horse Books, 2009.

Foley, John Miles. "The Impossibility of Canon." In *Teaching Oral Traditions*, edited by John Miles Foley. New York: Modern Language Association, 1998.

Foner, Eric. "Introduction to the First Edition." In *The New American History: Revised and Expanded Edition*, edited by Eric Foner. Philadelphia: Temple University Press, 1997.

Fox, Gardner, writer, Carmine Infantino, penciller, and Julius Schwartz, editor, et al. "Flash of Two Worlds." *Flash* 123. Reprinted in *Crisis on Multiple Earths: The Team-Ups*, edited by Robert Greenberger. New York: DC Comics, 2005.

Fox, Gardner, writer, and various artists. "The Justice Society Joins the War on Japan." *All-Star Comics* 11, June–July 1942. Reprinted in *All-Star Comics Archives Volume 3*, edited by Bob Kahan. New York: DC Comics, 1997.

Frisch, Marc-Oliver. "The 'New 52' and DC Comics Month-to-Month Sales: The Long View," *Comics Debris*, June 4, 2012. Accessed July 3, 2012. http://comiksdebris.blogspot.com/2012/06/new-52-and-dc-comics-month-to-month.html.

Goldstein, Hilary. "*Crisis on Infinite Earths*: The Absolute Edition Review." *IGN*, January 6, 2006. Accessed January 31, 2012. http://comics.ign.com/articles/679/679514p1.html.

Gordon, Ian. *Comic Strips and Consumer Culture, 1890–1945*. Washington: Smithsonian Institution Press, 1998.

Gould, Kevin. "Considering the Alternative: The Theories of Aging in Comic Books." *Amazing Heroes*, February 1, 1988.

Grandinettie, Fred. Editorial cartoon in "Amazing Readers." *Amazing Heroes* 91, March 15, 1986.

Greenberger, Robert. "Crisis at 30: Looking Back at the Most Influential Crossover in Comics History." *Back Issue* 82, August 2015.

Grossman, James R. "The New History Wars." *New York Times*, September 1, 2014. Accessed March 10, 2016. http://www.nytimes.com/2014/09/02/opinion/the-new-history-wars.html?_r=0.

Halfaker, Aaron, R. Stuart Geiger, Jonathan T. Morgan, and John Riedl. "The Rise and Decline of an Open Collaboration System: How Wikipedia's Reaction to Popularity Is Causing Its Decline." *American Behavioral Scientist* 57, no. 5 (May 2013).

Hayward, Jennifer. *Consuming Pleasures: Active Audiences and Serial Fictions from Dickens to Soap Opera*. Lexington: University Press of Kentucky, 1997.

Head, Alison J., and Michael B. Eisenberg. "How Today's College Students Use *Wikipedia* for Course-Related Research." *First Monday* 15, no. 3 (2010). Accessed March 10, 2016. http://journals.uic.edu/ojs/index.php/fm/article/view/2830/2476.

Hechtlinger, Adelaide, and Wilbur Cross. *The Complete Book of Paper Antiques*. New York: Coward, McCann & Geoghegan, 1972.

Hills, Matt. "Defining Cult TV: Texts, Inter-texts and Fan Audiences." In *The Television Studies Reader*, edited by Robert C. Allen and Annette Hill. London: Routledge, 2004.

"Home Page." *TVTropes.com*. Accessed March 10, 2016. http://tvtropes.org/.

Hutcheon, Linda. *A Theory of Parody: The Teachings of Twentieth-Century Art Forms*. Urbana: University of Illinois Press, 2000.

"Hyperlink." *Wikipedia*. Accessed March 10, 2016. https://en.wikipedia.org/wiki/Hyperlink.

"Infinite Discussions." In *Infinite Crisis*, edited by Anton Kawasaki. New York: DC Comics, 2006.

Itzkoff, Dave. "Heroes Take Flight, Again." *New York Times*, August 30, 2011.

Jenkins, Henry. *Textual Poachers: Television Fans and Participatory Culture*. New York: Routledge, 1992.

Johns, Geoff, Grant Morrison, Greg Rucka, and Mark Waid, writers, Keith Geffen, art breakdowns, et al. "A Year in the Life." 52 52, DC Comics, June 2008.

Johnston, Rich. "Tuesday Comics Reviews: Stormwatch, Batgirl, Batwing, Animal Man, Detective Comics, Action Comics, Men of War, Swamp Thing, JLI, Green Arrow, OMAC, Hawk & Dove, Static Shock." *Bleeding Cool*, September 6, 2011. Accessed January 9, 2013. http://www.bleedingcool.com/2011/09/06/tuesday-comics-reviews-stormwatch-batgirl-batwing-animal-man-detective-comics-action-comics-men-of-war-swamp-thing-jli-green-arrow-omac-hawk-dove-static-shock/.

Jones, R. A. "Crisis in Review." *Amazing Heroes* 91, March 15, 1986.

Jones, Stephen, and Kim Newman, eds. *Horror: The 100 Best Books*. New York: Carroll and Graff Publishers, 1998.

Klock, Geoff. *How to Read Superhero Comics and Why*. New York: Continuum, 2002.

Kruse, Kevin M., and Stephen Tuck. "Introduction: The Second World War and the Civil Rights Movement." In *Fog of War: The Second World War and the Civil Rights Movement*. Oxford: Oxford University Press, 2012.

Lachmann, Renate. "Mnemonic and Intertextual Aspects of Literature." In *A Companion to Cultural Memory Studies*, edited by Astrid Erill and Ansgar Nunning. Germany: De Gruyter, 2010.

"Lego Dimensions." *Lego*. Accessed March 10, 2016. http://www.lego.com/en-us/dimensions.

Leitch, Thomas. *Wikipedia U: Knowledge, Authority, and Liberal Education in the Digital Age*. Baltimore: Johns Hopkins University Press, 2014.

Leith, Sam. "One of These Comic Heroes Really Is Dead." *Telegraph*, March 12, 2007.

Lepore, Jill. *The Name of War: King Philip's War and the Origins of American Identity*. New York: Vintage Books, 1998.

Levine, Lawrence W. *Highbrow/Lowbrow: The Emergence of Cultural Hierarchy in America*. Cambridge, MA: Harvard University Press, 1988.

Levinson, Paul. *New New Media*, 2nd ed. Boston: Pearson, 2013.

Levitz, Paul, writer, Joe Staton, artist, et al. "The Defeat of the Justice Society." *Adventure Comics* 466, DC Comics, November/December 1979.

Levitz, Paul, writer, Joe Staton and Bob Layton, artists, et al. "The Untold Origin of the Justice Society." *DC Comics Special* 29, DC Comics, August/September 1977.

Lewis, A. David. "The Secret, Untold Relationship of Biblical Midrash and Comic Book Retcon." *International Journal of Comic Art* 4, no. 2 (Fall 2002).

Lih, Andrew. *The Wikipedia Revolution: How a Bunch of Nobodies Created the World's Greatest Encyclopedia*. New York: Hyperion, 2009.

Lord, Albert B. *The Singer of Tales*, 2nd ed. Cambridge, MA: Harvard University Press, 2000.

Macneal, Caitlin. "RNC Condemns AP Exam's 'Radically Revisionist View' of U.S. History." *Talking Points Memo*, August 13, 2014. Accessed March 10, 2016. http://talkingpointsmemo.com/livewire/rnc-ap-exam-revisionist-history.

Martin, Keith. "A New Sith or Revenge of the Hope: Reconsidering *Star Wars IV* in the Light of I–III." *Loose Connections*. LiveJournal, January 3, 2011. Accessed March 10, 2016. http://km-515.1ivejournal.com/746.html.

McMillan, Graeme. "*Final Crisis* Is Frustrating, Flawed and Arguably Worth It All." *io9*, June 10, 2009. Accessed January 9, 2013. http://io9.com/5284580/final-crisis-is-frustrating-flawed-and-arguably-worth-it-all.

Melrose, Kevin. "DC Comics Dominates October Sales." *Comic Book Resources*, November 4, 2011. Accessed July 3, 2012. http://www.comicbookresources.com/?page=article&id=35298.

Meltzer, Brad. "Brad Meltzer and Rags Morales Dissect *Identity Crisis*." In *Identity Crisis*, edited by Robert Greenberger. New York: DC Comics, 2005.

"Milestones: Anthony D. Weiner." *New York Times*, June 11, 2011. Accessed March 10, 2016. http://www.nytimes.com/2011/06/11/nyregion/20110611anthony_weiner_timeline.html.

Mills, Pat, writer, and Kevin O'Neill, artist, et al. *Marshall Law: Blood, Sweat, and Fears*. Milwaukie, OR: Dark Horse Comics, 1993.

Mitchell, Kurt. "A Capsule History of Earth-Two." In *The All-Star Comics Companion: Volume 3*, edited by Roy Thomas. Raleigh, NC: TwoMorrows Publishing, 2008.

Moore, Alan. Introduction to *A Blazing World: The Unofficial Companion to the League of Extraordinary Gentlemen Volume Two*, by Jess Nevins. Austin, TX: MonkeyBrain Books, 2004.

Moore, Alan, writer, Gene Ha and Zander Cannon, artists, et al. "Court on the Street," *Top 10* 12, DC Comics/Wildstorm Comics, October, 2001.

Moore, Alan, writer, Jim Baikie, artist, et al. "The Origin of the First American." *Tomorrow Stories* 9, DC Comics/Wildstorm Comics, December 2000.

Moore, Alan, writer, Joe Bennett, artist, et al. "The Supreme Story of the Year Part 1: The Double Exposure Doom!" *Supreme* 41, Image Comics, August 1996.

Morrison, Grant. *Supergods*. New York: Spiegel & Grau, 2011.

Morrison, Grant, writer, Doug Mahnke, artist, et al. "New Heaven, New Earth." *Final Crisis* 7, DC Comics, March 2009.

Murdough, Adam C. "Worlds Will Live, Worlds Will Die: Myth, Metatext, Continuity and Cataclysm in DC Comics' *Crisis on Infinite Earths*." Master's thesis, Bowling Green State University, August 2006.

Ndalianis, Angela. *Neo-Baroque Aesthetics and Contemporary Entertainment*. Cambridge, MA: MIT Press, 2005.

Nevins, Jess. *Heroes and Monsters: The Unofficial Companion to the League of Extraordinary Gentlemen*. Austin, TX: MonkeyBrain Books, 2003.

New Revised Standard Version Holy Bible. Nashville: Thomas Nelson Publishers, 1989.

Newman, Kim. "Anno Dracula: The Background." *The Kim Newman Website*. Accessed March 10, 2016. http://johnnyalucard.com/non-fiction/articles/anno-dracula-background/.

Okubo, Miné. *Citizen 13660*. Seattle: University of Washington Press, 1983.

Ong, Walter. *Orality and Literacy*. London: Routledge, 2002.

O'Neill, Patrick Daniel. "*Spotlight*: Crisis on Infinite Earths." *David Anthony Kraft's Comics Interview* 26, 1985.

Orwell, George. *1984*. New York: Signet Classics, 1950.
Parkin, Lance. "Truths Universally Acknowledged: How the 'Rules' of *Doctor Who* Affect the Writing." In *Third Person: Authoring and Exploring Vast Narratives*, edited by Pat Harrigan and Noah Wardrip-Fruin. Cambridge, MA: MIT Press, 2009.
Proctor, William. "Ctl-Alt-Delete: Retcon, Relaunch, or Reboot?" *Sequart*, February 8, 2013. Accessed June 22, 2014. http://sequart.org/magazine/18508/ctl-alt-delete-retcon-relaunch-or-reboot/.
Reece. "The Berenstain Bears: We Are Living in Our Own Parallel Universe." *The Wood between Worlds*, August 23, 2012. Accessed March 10, 2016. http://woodbetweenworlds.blogspot.com/2012/08/the-berenstein-bears-we-are-living-in.html.
Renaud, Jeffrey. "Grant Morrison's Multiversity." *Comic Book Resources*, May 6, 2009. Accessed March 10, 2016. http://comicbookresources.com/?page=article&id=21104.
"Retcon." *TVTropes.com*. Accessed March 10, 2016. http://tvtropes.org/pmwiki/pmwiki.php/Main/Retcon.
"Retcon / Real Life." *TVTropes.com*. Accessed March 10, 2016. http://tvtropes.org/pmwiki/pmwiki.php/Retcon/RealLife.
"Review: Final Crisis collected hardcover/paperback (DC Comics)." *Collected Edition*, August 3, 2009. Accessed January 9, 2013. http://collectededitions.blogspot.com/2009/08/review-final-crisis-collected.html.
Rhoades, Shirrell. *A Complete History of American Comic Books*. New York: Peter Lang, 2008.
Roberts, Jeffrey. "Stalin, the Pact with Nazi Germany, and the Origins of Postwar Soviet Diplomatic Historiography." *Journal of Cold War Studies* 4, no. 4 (Fall 2002).
Robinson, James. Letters column. *Starman* #3, DC Comics, January 1995.
Rosenbaum, Richard. "Rewriting the Future: Retroactive Continuity as Marketing." *Overthinking It*, July 29, 2014. Accessed March 10, 2016. https://www.overthinkingit.com/2014/07/29/rewriting-future-retroactive-continuity-marketing/.
Saler, Michael. *As If: Modern Enchantment and the Literary Prehistory of Virtual Reality*. Oxford: Oxford University Press, 2012.
Sargent, J. F., and Abigail Brady. "Wikipedia Hates Women: 4 Dark Sides of the Site We All Use." *Cracked*, August 15, 2015. Accessed March 10, 2016. http://www.cracked.com/personal-experiences-1738-wikipedias-war-women-4-weird-realities-inside.html.
Savage, William W., Jr. *Commies, Cowboys, and Jungle Queens: Comic Books and America, 1945–1954*. Middletown, CT: Wesleyan University Press, 1990.
Siede, Caroline. "How You Spell 'The Berenstain Bears' Could Be Proof of Parallel Universe." *The A.V. Club*, August 10, 2015. Accessed March 10, 2016. http://www.avclub.com/article/how-you-spell-berenstain-bears-could-be-proof-para-223615.
Siegel, Harry. "Marv Wolfman on What's Got to Die for a New DC World to Live." *The Village Voice Blog*, August 31, 2011. Accessed September 22, 2011. http://blogs.villagevoice.com/runninscared/2011/08/marv_wolfman.php.
Siegel, Jerry, writer, and Joe Shuster, artist. "How Superman Would End the War Drawn Especially for Look." *Look*, February 27, 1940.
Simonite, Tom. "The Decline of Wikipedia." *MIT Technology Review*, October 22, 2013. Accessed March 10, 2016. http://www.technologyreview.com/featuredstory/520446/the-decline-of-wikipedia/.
The Simpsons. "The Principal and the Pauper." Directed by Steven Dean Moore. Fox Broadcasting Company: originally broadcast September 28, 1997.

Smith, Philip, and Michael Goodrum. "'We have experienced a tragedy which words cannot properly describe': Representations of Trauma in Post-9/11 Superhero Comics." *Literature Compass* 8, no. 8 (2011).

Thomas, Roy. "All-Star Comments." *All-Star Squadron* #6, DC Comics, February 1982.

———. "All-Star Comments." *All-Star Squadron* #7, DC Comics, March 1982.

———. "All-Star Comments." *All-Star Squadron* #14, DC Comics, October 1982.

———. "All-Star Comments." *All-Star Squadron* #18, DC Comics, February 1983.

———. "All-Star Comments." *All-Star Squadron* #34, DC Comics, June 1984.

———. "All the Stars There Are in (Super-hero) Heaven!" *Alter Ego* 3, no. 14 (April 2002).

———. "An Open Letter to the Readers of All-Star Squadron #1." *All-Star Squadron* 1, DC Comics, September 1981.

———. "Another Agonizingly Personal Recollection." *Giant-Size Invaders* 1, Marvel Comics, June 1975.

———. "'Hail, Hail, the Gang's All Here!'—Part I: The All-Winners Squad." *Alter Ego* 1, no. 2 (Summer 1961).

———. "The Justice Society (and Friends) in the 1980s." In *The All-Star Companion*, edited by Roy Thomas. Raleigh, NC: TwoMorrows Publishing, 2000.

———. "Meanwhile . . . : Spotlight On . . . All-Star Squadron." Various DC Comics, September 1984.

———. "'This Means War!': A Personal and Historical Note." In *All-Star Comics Archives Volume 3*, edited by Bob Kahan. New York: DC Comics, 1997.

Thomas, Roy, and Dann Thomas, writers, Brian Murray, artist, et al. "A Gathering of Heroes!" *Young All-Stars* 3, DC Comics, July 1987.

Thomas, Roy, and Dann Thomas, writers, Brian Murray and Howard Simpson, artists, et al. "California, Here We Come . . ." *Young All-Stars* 4, DC Comics, September 1987.

———. "Hollywood Knights (1942 Model)." *Young All-Stars* 5, DC Comics, October 1987.

Thomas, Roy, and Kurt Mitchell. "*All-Star Squadron* Issue by Issue." In *All-Star Companion: Volume 2*, edited by Roy Thomas. Raleigh, NC: TwoMorrows Publishing, 2006.

———. "*The Young All-Stars* Issue by Issue." In *All-Star Companion: Volume 3*, edited by Roy Thomas. Raleigh, NC: TwoMorrows Publishing, 2008.

Thomas, Roy, writer, Adrian Gonzales, artist, et al. "Carnage for Christmas!" *All-Star Squadron* 7, DC Comics, March 1982.

Thomas, Roy, writer, Frank Robbins, penciller, et al. "The Coming of the Invaders!" *Giant-Size Invaders* 1, Marvel Comics, June 1975.

Thomas, Roy, writer, Rich Buckler, artist, et al. "The All-Star Squadron." *Justice League of America* 193, DC Comics, August 1981.

———. "Day of the Dragon King." *All-Star Squadron* 4, DC Comics, December 1981.

———. "The World on Fire!" *All-Star Squadron* 1, DC Comics, September 1981.

Thomas, Roy, writer, Richard Howell, artist, et al. "The Rise and Fall of the Phantom Empire!" *All-Star Squadron* 40, DC Comics, December 1984.

Thomas, Roy, writer, Rick Hoberg, artist, et al. "Detroit Is Dynamite!" *All-Star Squadron* 38, DC Comics, October 1984.

———. "Nobody Gets Out of Paradise Valley Alive!" *All-Star Squadron* 39, DC Comics, November 1984.

Tkacz, Nathaniel. *Wikipedia and the Politics of Openness*. Chicago: University of Chicago Press, 2015.

Tolkien, J. R. R. *The Hobbit*. New York: Galantine Books, 1966.

———. *The Letters of J. R. R. Tolkien*, edited by Humphrey Carpenter. Boston: Houghton Mifflin Company, 1995.

———. *The Lord of the Rings, Volume I: The Fellowship of the Ring*. New York: Galantine Books, 1975.

"The Top 500 Sites in the World." *Alexa Internet, Inc.* Accessed March 10, 2016. http://www.alexa.com/topsites.

Toplin, Robert Brent. *History by Hollywood*, 2nd ed. Urbana: University of Illinois Press, 2009.

Truitt, Brian. "DC Comics Unleashes a New Universe of Superhero Titles." *USA Today*, May 31, 2011.

Tucker, Aviezer. "Historiographic Revisionism and Revisionism: The Evidential Difference." In *Past in the Making: Historical Revisionism in Central Europe after 1989*. Budapest: Central European University Press, 2008.

Waid, Mark. "Beginnings and Endings." *Amazing Heroes* 66, March 1, 1985.

———. "Editorial." *Amazing Heroes* 91, March 15, 1986.

Wales, Jimmy. Foreword to *The Wikipedia Revolution: How a Bunch of Nobodies Created the World's Greatest Encyclopedia*, by Andrew Lih. New York: Hyperion, 2009.

Wandtke, Terence R. *The Meaning of Superhero Comic Books*. Jefferson, NC: McFarland & Company, 2012.

Ward, Chris. "Crisis Almighty." *Wizard*, November 2005.

———. "Crisis Confidential." *Wizard*, May 2005.

Weiner, Rachel. "Fight Brews over Sarah Palin on Paul Revere Wikipedia Page." *Washington Post*, June 6, 2016. Accessed March 10, 2016. https://www.washingtonpost.com/blogs/the-fix/post/sarah-palin-fans-fight-over-paul-revere-wikipedia-page/2011/06/06/AGxtzHKH_blog.html.

White, Hayden. *The Content of the Form: Narrative Discourse and Historical Representation*. Baltimore: Johns Hopkins University Press, 1987.

———. "The Historical Text as Literary Artifact." In *The Writing of History*, edited by Robert H. Canary and Henry Kozicki. Madison: University of Wisconsin Press, 1978.

———. *Tropics of Discourse: Essays in Cultural Criticism*. Baltimore: Johns Hopkins University Press, 1978.

Wildman, Robin, ed. *Showcase Presents: All-Star Comics Volume One*. New York: DC Comics, 2011.

Willingham, Bill, writer, Mark Buckingham, artist, et al. "Kill Your Darlings." *The Literals* 3, DC Comics, June 2009.

Wolf, Mark J. P. *Building Imaginary Worlds: The Theory and History of Subcreation*. New York: Routledge, 2012.

Wolfman, Marv. "Crisis Mail." *Crisis on Infinite Earths* 4, DC Comics, July 1985.

Wolfman, Marv, writer/editor, and George Perez, penciller. *Crisis on Infinite Earths: The Absolute Edition*. New York: DC Comics, 2005.

Wolfman, Marv, writer, and George Perez, penciller. *History of the DC Universe*. New York: DC Comics, 2002.

Wolk, Douglas. *Reading Comics: How Graphic Novels Work and What They Mean*. Cambridge, MA: Da Capo Press, 2007.

Wright, Bradford. *Comic Book Nation: The Transformation of Youth Culture in America*. Baltimore: Johns Hopkins University Press, 2003.

INDEX

Abrams, J. J., 113, 115–16
Allie, Scott, 118–19
All-Star Comics, 12, 37–38, 44, 48
"All-Star Comments," 53–57
All-Star Squadron, 9, 12, 15, 35, 48–69, 163n1
All Winner Comics, 39
Alter Ego, 39
Amazing Heroes, 84–85
Amazing Man, 60, 64, 165n10
American Exceptionalism, 11, 34
America's Best Comics, 129–30
Anno Dracula, 140–41
Anti-Monitor, The, 78–79, 86
AP US History, 5
Armstrong, Lance, 24
Ayers, Phoebe, 150–52

Baikie, Jim, 129
Bails, Jerry, 39, 44

Batman, 6, 10–11, 41, 51, 73, 78–80, 84, 90, 92–93, 95, 98, 100, 143, 164n3, 165n12
Batman Beyond, 164n3
Berenstain Bears, The, 132
Bible, 16, 19–23, 163n1
Black Americans in World War II, 62
Bloom, Harold, 97
Brothers in Arms, 63
Buffy the Vampire Slayer, 9–10, 116–20, 166n3, 166n4
Burroughs, Edgar Rice, 25, 136–37
Byrne, John, 46, 117

Cartoon All-Stars to the Rescue, 136, 143
Cervantes, Miguel de, 133–34
"Chronicle," 75–76, 81, 85–89, 161, 165n12, 167n5
Churchill, Winston, 43, 52–53, 56–59
Citizen 13660, 66–67

177

Index

Colbert, Stephen, 5, 167n1
Community, 132
Continuity, conservatism of, 39–43, 46, 49–50, 52, 90
Coogan, Peter, 34, 138–39
Cornell, Paul, 80, 166n4
Countdown, 99–100
Crisis on Infinite Earths, 12, 71–92, 95–98, 101, 103, 105, 108, 129, 139, 165n12
Crossovers: A Secret Chronology of the World, 140
"Crossover Universe, The," 140
Cthulu Mythos, 31–32
"Cult TV," 107–8, 112, 116
Cultural history, 57–59

Dallas, 111
Dark Horse Comics, 117–19
Dark Knight Returns, The, 164n3, 166n6
DC Comics, 9, 12, 33–38, 44–69, 71–105, 139, 164n3, 164n7, 165n12, 165n1, 165n2, 166n4, 166n1
DC Comics Special, 45–47
DC Countdown, 95
Derleth, August, 32
Detroit Race Riot, 60–64, 165n11
DiDio, Dan, 83, 91–96, 99–100, 103
Doc Savage: His Apocalyptic Life, 137, 140
Doctorow, E. L., 134
Doctor Who, 40, 112, 132, 166n4
Don Quixote, 133–34
Doublethink, 4–5
"Double V" campaign, 62
Doyle, Sir Arthur Conan, 16, 25–27, 29–31, 134–35, 163n5

Eckert, Win Scott, 137–38, 140–41
Eco, Umberto, 40–41
Elementary, 135
Ellis, Warren, 68
"Emplotment," 75–76
Event, The, 120

Fables, 130, 143
Farmer, Philip José, 136–41
Fforde, Jasper, 143

52, 98–99, 101–2, 166n5
Final Crisis, 99–102, 104
Flash Forward, 120
"Flash of Two Worlds," 76
Flashpoint, 103
Foley, John Miles, 19
Foner, Eric, 58, 60
Fox, Gardner, 37–38

Game of Thrones, 9
General Hospital, 110–11
Gibbons, Dave, 164n5
Giordano, Dick, 74, 85–86
"Great Men" theory, 52–53, 58–59
Grimm, 143
Grossman, John, 11

Harbinger, 67–68
Harry Potter, 10
Hayward, Jennifer, 109–11
Heroes, 120
Hills, Matt, 112, 116
Historical revisionism, 3, 5–6, 12–13, 23, 34–35, 53, 69, 148, 157, 160–61
Historiography, 12, 34–35, 57–58, 62, 67, 73, 75–76, 157, 160–61
History of the DC Universe, 87–90
Hitler, Adolf, 35–36, 45–46, 51–52, 61, 164n4
Hobbit, The, 28–31
Holocaust Denial, 11, 35
Howard, Robert E., 25
How Wikipedia Works, 150–52
Hutcheon, Linda, 127–28
Hyperlink, 8–10, 15, 148, 153–55, 161

Identity Crisis, 92–98
I Love Lucy, 143
Infinite Crisis, 95–98, 101–2, 166n5, 166n7
Inglourious Basterds, 164n4
Invaders, 38–39, 42–43

Japanese internment camps, 60, 64–67
Jenkins, Henry, 113–14
Jimenez, Phil, 96, 166n7
Johns, Geoff, 95–98, 103

Justice League, 92–95, 98, 100, 141
Justice Society of America, 12, 37–38, 43–69

Kim Il Sung, 160
Kim Jong Il, 160
King, Stephen, 132–33
Kingdom Hearts, 143
Klinger, Leslie, 135
Klingons, 115
Kruse, Kevin M., 62–63

Lachmann, Renate, 72
League of Extraordinary Gentlemen, The, 141–43
Lee, Stan, 33, 39, 41, 109
LEGO Dimensions, 143
Lego Movie, The, 143
Leitch, Thomas, 150, 158
Lepore, Jill, 59
Levine, Lawrence, 127
Levinson, Paul, 154–55
Levitz, Paul, 44–49, 67–68, 79
Lewis, A. David, 22
Lih, Andrew, 149, 152–53, 155, 167n2
Look magazine, 36–37
Lord, Albert, 18–19, 25
Lord of the Rings, The, 10, 28–31
Lost, 9–10, 120–22, 124
Lovecraft, H. P., 16, 25, 31–32, 163n5
Lucas, George, 122–23

Mad Men, 121
Marshal Law, 164n1
Marvel Comics, 9, 33–34, 38–44, 46, 50, 79–80, 84, 88, 90–91, 93, 104, 108–9, 117, 164n2, 165n2, 165n4, 166n4
Marvel Cinematic Universe, 10, 108
Matthews, Charles, 150–52
McCarthy, Joseph, 47–48
McCauley, Johnston, 25
McMillan, Graeme, 101
Meltzer, Brad, 92–93
Middle-earth, 28–31
Midrash, 21–23
Misery, 132–33

Monitor, 74, 78, 86–87
Moore, Alan, 128–30, 141–42, 164n5
Morrison, Grant, 98–102, 104–5
Mr. Holmes, 135
Multiverse, 76–80, 86, 97–98, 101–5, 143
Multiversity, 104

Nevins, Jess, 142
New 52, The, 103–5
New Deal, 45, 47–48, 51
"New history," 57–59
Newman, Kim, 32, 140–41
1984, 4–5, 160
9/11. *See* September 11, 2001
Nolan, Christopher, 6

Objectivism, 152–53
Okubo, Miné, 66–67
Once Upon a Time, 130
O'Neill, Kevin, 141–42, 164n1
One Life to Live, 111
Ong, Walter, 16–18
Oral cultures, 16–19, 42
Orman, Kate, 40
Orwell, George, 4–5, 11, 13, 160

Palin, Sarah, 146–47, 156
Pearl Harbor bombing, 37–38, 46, 49–51, 56, 59, 64
Penny Dreadful, 143
Pentimento, 24
Perez, George, 72, 76, 83, 86–89
Proctor, William, 7

Rand, Ayn, 152–53
Reagan, Ronald, 51, 57, 69
Real American, 60–61, 63, 165n10
Reboot/rebooting, 7, 21, 79, 82–83, 98, 103, 113, 116,
Retcon (fictional drug), 132
Retroactive continuity, definition of, 6–12
Revere, Paul, 146–47, 156
Robinson, James, 68
Roddenberry, Gene, 112
Roosevelt, Franklin Delano, 46–53, 56–59, 61, 64–66

Saler, Michael, 9, 25, 29 31–32, 163n5
Sanderson, Peter, 85–87
Sanger, Larry, 149, 152–53
Saw, 124
Secret Wars, 165n2
September 11, 2001, 12, 91, 93–95, 102–3
Shell, Tim, 149, 152–53
Sherlock, 135
Sherlock Holmes, 25–27, 134–37
Sherlockian Great Game, 134–40
Shuster, Joe, 37
Siegel, Jerry, 36–37
Simpsons, The, 128, 130–32, 166n2 (Chapter 5)
Soap operas, 10, 13, 42, 91, 107–12, 133
Stalin, Joseph, 23–24, 36, 159–60
Starman, 68
Star Trek, 108, 112–16
Star Wars, 108, 122–24
St. Elsewhere, 111, 143
Superman, 35–38, 40–41, 46, 49, 51–52, 73, 78–79, 83, 89–90, 97–98, 100, 102–3, 128, 165n12
Supreme, 128–29

Tarantino, Quentin, 164n4
Tarzan, 25, 136–37, 140–41
Tarzan Alive, 136, 140
Thomas, Roy, 9, 12, 33–35, 38–39, 42–45, 48–69, 90, 97, 115, 160, 165n12
Tojo, Emperor, 51–52
Tolkien, J. R. R., 16, 25, 28–32, 163n5
Tommy Westphall Universe, 143, 166n2
Tomorrow Stories, 129
Top 10, 129–30
Torchwood, 132
Tsunami, 64–66, 90
Tuskegee Airmen, The, 63
TV tropes, 7–8, 159–60

University of Pennsylvania, 24

Wales, Jimmy, 149, 152–53, 156
Walking Dead, The, 9
Watchmen, 128, 164n5, 166n6
"Wayback Machine, The," 167n4

Wein, Len, 72–75, 80, 83, 85–86, 89
Weiner, Anthony D., 145–46, 155
Whedon, Joss, 116–20, 166n3, 166n4
Wheeler-Nicholson, Major Malcolm, 165n1
White, Hayden, 73, 75–77, 81, 85, 88–89, 161, 165n12, 167n5
Wikipedia, 8, 10, 13, 135, 145–58, 167n1, 167n2, 167n3, 167n4; and neutral point of view, 146–47, 150–51; and no original research, 150–51, 155–57; and verifiability, 146–47, 150–53, 155–56
Wold Newtonry, 136–40
Wolf, Mark J. P., 28–29, 31, 143
Wolfman, Marv, 72–89, 103, 139, 165n2
Wonder Woman, 52, 73, 79, 90, 98, 165n12
World War II, 34–69, 164n4, 164n6, 164n8
World-building, 8–10, 16, 25, 28, 120, 163n5

X-Files, The, 9, 119

Yates, Ben, 150–52
Young All-Stars, 57, 64–67, 90

www.ingramcontent.com/pod-product-compliance
Lightning Source LLC
Chambersburg PA
CBHW070316240426
43661CB00057B/2662